Gilliard Novels *minotaur*

The Telegraph

1

marilyn Robinson?

General Knowledge CROSSWORDS

grandstand

Boswell

City of Lies

Tehran

The Telegraph 1

General Knowledge CROSSWORDS

60
testing puzzles from the pages of your favourite paper

hamlyn

An Hachette UK Company
www.hachette.co.uk

First published in Great Britain in 2012 by
Hamlyn, an imprint of Octopus Publishing Group Ltd
Carmelite House, 50 Victoria Embankment
London EC4Y 0DZ
www.octopusbooks.co.uk

ISBN 978-0-600-62497-4

A CIP catalogue record for this book is available from the British
Library.

Printed and bound in Great Britain
14

Produced for Octopus Publishing Group by Crosswords Ltd

PUZZLES

The Telegraph

1

Across

1   English actress who was married to John Le Mesurier, remembered for her roles in the *Carry On* series (7)

5   Game of chance said to have originated in 16th-century Italy (5)

8   In piquet, the act of winning the game before one's opponent scores 100 (7)

12 1990 film by *Jacob's Ladder* and *Deep Impact* screenwriter Bruce Joel Rubin, starring Patrick Swayze and Demi Moore (5)

13 Italian operatic tenor who was known as the "King of the High Cs" (9)

14 Endangered tree-dwelling lemur native to Madagascar which is one of the largest of its species still in existence (5)

15 County on the Irish Sea with the administrative centre Preston (10)

16 Amino acid found in vegetables (10)

18 French Impressionist artist whose notable works include *Luncheon of the Boating Party* and *Dance at Le Moulin de la Galette* (6)

20 Style of music with a syncopated melody such as the cakewalk, usually accompanied by a piano (7)

22 Presiding bishop of the Scottish Episcopal Church; also the brand name of a type of portable stove used by campers (6)

26 Silicate mineral occurring in hexagonal crystals; varieties of which include aquamarine and emerald (5)

27 ___ *to Lady*; reality television series that features teachers Rosemary Shrager and Gill Harbord (7)

29 Plane figure with 10 angles and 10 sides of equal length (7)

31 Crumbly biscuit traditionally baked in the form of petticoat tails (10)

32 Constellation containing the star Procyon, said to represent one of the dogs following Orion the hunter (5,5)

35 City and industrial port in California, located on San Francisco Bay (7)

37 In North African cuisine, a variety of sauce made with piri piri chilli peppers, assorted spices, garlic and olive oil (7)

38 Hawaiian acknowledgement which may be used to say either hello or goodbye (5)

39 Flowering plant with jagged leaves covered in trichomes (6)

41 Russian dancer noted for her role in the ballet *The Dying Swan*, choreographed by Mikhail Fokine (7)

43 Member of a light-infantry corps in the French army with a distinctive uniform including baggy trousers (6)

47 The study of the statistics of human populations (10)
49 Denoting frequencies below the usual audible limit (10)
52 Exercise designed to strengthen the leg muscles based on repeatedly assuming a crouching position (5)
53 Branch of geology concerned with the scientific study of rocks (9)
54 Swedish physiologist and pharmacologist who was co-awarded the 1970 Nobel Prize in Medicine for his work on neurotransmitters (5)
55 The main protagonist in the *Pirates of the Caribbean* film series, played by Johnny Depp (7)
56 Film-maker, writer and director of *Blue Velvet* and *Wild at Heart* (5)
57 Description of an inactive volcano which is considered unlikely to erupt again (7)

Down

1 Name of any one of the large veins in the neck responsible for transporting blood from the head to the heart (7)
2 Old English coin that was worth five shillings, originally minted in gold (5)
3 Electromagnetic radiation with a wavelength shorter than visible light but longer than X-rays (11)
4 Ancient Greek lyric poet (6)
5 German state famous for beer (7)
6 The common name of the Roman emperor Lucius Domitius Ahenobarbus, infamous for cruelty, vice and a fire which destroyed much of Rome (4)
7 English clergyman who fabricated the King Charles II conspiracy known as the Popish Plot (5)
8 Relating to the nose or the parts of the brain concerned with olfaction (6)
9 1980 children's television series presented by Brian Cant in a fictional junk store (4-1-4)
10 Chemical element occurring in zinc ores, atomic number 48 (7)
11 "Whence is that knocking? How is't with me, when every ___ appals me? What hands are here? Ha - they pluck out mine eyes." *Macbeth*: Act II, Scene 2 (5)
17 An organised political community under one government (5)
19 County east of The Wash (7)
21 The female followers of Bacchus (7)
23 Spanish or Portuguese punch (7)

1

24 Sauce to accompany fettuccine pasta, made with Parmigiano-Reggiano cheese, cream and garlic (7)

25 The most senior commander of a naval fleet (7)

26 Instrument used to depict the grandfather in Sergei Prokofiev's *Peter and the Wolf* (7)

28 Former monetary unit of Greece (7)

30 Flat-bottomed Venetian boat (7)

33 The common name of the Eurasian plant with clusters of fragrant creamy-white flowers, *Filipendula ulmaria* (11)

34 Planktonic crustaceans eaten in large numbers by baleen whales and other large mammals (5)

36 Semi-aquatic reptile with an armoured body, saved from extinction in recent years (9)

40 Japanese dish of seafood or strips of vegetables coated in batter and fried (7)

42 Post-Impressionist painter noted for his expressive use of colour (3,4)

44 Passage selected from a book (7)

45 Name of the actress who co-starred in six films with Clark Gable (6)

46 Diamond pattern derived from the tartan of Clan Campbell (6)

47 Tarot suit, also called coins (5)

48 The 8th codeword of the Nato phonetic alphabet (5)

50 Synthetic polymer invented at the DuPont research facility in 1935 (5)

51 Television series starring Michael Elphick which ran from 1986-95 (4)

Armadillo

35 Alone with a smile, union ... ... to ... (11)
36 ... hardly clever ... same ... ...

37 ... on a ... ... with a difficult to ... ...
38 ... ... in the ... ... machine
    ... (11) ...

39 ... on an ... ...
    ... plane ... to travel ... like the ... ... the ...
    ... ... regular ... ...

2

Across

1 Creator of the characters Lord Emsworth and Empress of Blandings, considered to be one of the greatest comic authors of the 20th century (9)

6 Quantity of paper equal to 1/20 of a ream, or 25 sheets (5)

9 English architecture and landscape painter who designed the stained-glass windows in Coventry and Llandaff cathedrals (5)

12 Port city in western Turkey located on an inlet of the Aegean Sea, formerly called Smyrna (5)

13 Large three-headed muscle responsible for straightening and flexing the human elbow joint (7)

14 National emblem of Scotland (7)

15 Liverpudlian entrepreneur who managed The Beatles (7)

16 Russian empress prior to 1917 (7)

17 Tall, cylindrical cap with a peak and a feather plume which formed part of the military uniform of the Hungarian hussars in the 18th century (5)

18 English poet who wrote: "The wind was a torrent of darkness among the gusty trees, The moon was a ghostly galleon tossed upon cloudy seas..." (5)

19 Variety of pasta similar to spaghetti but thinner; also strands of chocolate used to decorate cakes and truffles (10)

22 A set of switches or sockets; also an organised group of labourers working together (4)

25 English term for a small but hardy breed of chicken that originated in the Tuscan city Livorno (7)

28 The floating leaf of the ornamental aquatic plant Nymphaeaceae (4,3)

30 A group or gathering of 13 witches (5)

31 Peninsula in Canada which separates the Bay of Fundy from the Gulf of St Lawrence (4,6)

33 A bakery which specialises in French cakes and confections (10)

36 __ sinister; heraldic charge once used to indicate an illegitimate birth in a family (5)

37 Shakespearean tragedy with the line: "O, beware, my lord, of jealousy; It is the green-eyed monster which doth mock "The meat it feeds on; that cuckold lives in bliss..." (7)

38 The official residence or offices of an ambassador (7)

40 US musician and composer who released the single *Piano Man* in 1973, considered to be his signature song (4)

41 Instrument for measuring the specific gravity or density of liquids (10)
44 Set of clothing worn for hunting on horseback or riding sidesaddle (5)
47 In snooker and billiards, a stroke made with an inclined cue so as to achieve a sharp swerve to the ball (5)
49 The lower part in a duet (7)
51 Small Greek café or restaurant, typically serving salads, breads, appetisers and meze (7)
53 Radioactive chemical element, atomic number 92, used as a fuel in nuclear reactors (7)
54 Legendary knight of the Round Table who fell in love with his uncle's bride, Iseult, after accidentally consuming a love potion (7)
55 Gold medallist and world record- breaker at the 1936 Berlin Olympics whose success as a black contender outraged Hitler (5)
56 Tree in the birch family which bears catkins and cones (5)
57 Small anvil used by blacksmiths and tinsmiths (5)
58 Botanical condition characterised by foliage producing insufficient amounts of green pigment (9)

Down

1 British author born in Bombay who wrote *The Once and Future King* tetralogy (5)
2 US boxer nicknamed the "Manassa Mauler" who held the world heavyweight title from 1919-26 (7)
3 One of Bianca's suitors in *The Taming of the Shrew* who is thwarted by Lucentio and ends up marrying a widow (9)
4 British actor and dramatist of Russian descent who starred in *Spartacus* and *Death on the Nile* (7)
5 Pen name of the writer whose first published novel was *Adam Bede* (5)
6 Mexican dish of a tortilla filled with cheese, meat or vegetables with spices, grilled or fried (10)
7 "Our chief want is someone who will __ us to be what we know we could be." Ralph Waldo Emerson (7)
8 In cricket, a run scored from a bye, leg bye, no-ball or a wide (5)
9 With allusion to administering the last rites, a blunt tool for quickly killing a caught fish (6)

2

10 Variety of Middle-Eastern bread (5)
11 Harmonium-like instrument (4,5)
18 Australian painter noted for his series of depictions of Ned Kelly (5)
20 Explorer who introduced tobacco and potatoes to England, later beheaded in a public execution in 1618 (7)
21 One of a band of protesters during the Industrial Revolution (7)
23 2006 novel by Daniel Handler (7)
24 Fifth book of the New Testament (4)
26 A French folk dance popular in the 18th century (7)
27 Practice of coining new words (7)
29 Heavy double-breasted jacket formerly worn by sailors (3,4)
32 In mathematics, one of the six trigonometrical functions of an angle (4)
34 Country which is currently the scene of angry protests against President Hosni Mubarak (5)
35 Variety of mandarin orange (10)
36 The capital city of Burundi (9)
39 1990 album by Pet Shop Boys (9)
42 Variety of unsalted Italian cheese (7)
43 Compound essential for vision and growth, also called vitamin A (7)
45 Author of A Clockwork Orange (7)
46 Unit of weight used to indicate the fineness or thickness of hosiery (6)
48 The grassy surface of the ground (5)
49 Ancient Roman bronze coin equal to half an as (5)
50 Device for measuring spirits (5)
52 Either of two points on the orbit of a planet of greatest or least distance from the central body (5)

The Telegraph

3

Across

1 Poet Laureate and OM who was married to Sylvia Plath; his notable collections include *The Hawk in the Rain* and *Birthday Letters* (6)

4 Scottish statesman who served as prime minister from 1852-55 (8)

9 Medieval musical instrument played like a violin, typically with three strings (5)

13 "Wit without discretion is a __ in the hand of a fool." Spanish proverb (5)

14 According to the New Testament, each of the 12 chief disciples chosen by Jesus Christ, including Andrew, Batholomew and Judas (7)

15 Sporting event held annually on the River Thames since 1839 (7)

16 *The __*; classic piano rag written by "king of ragtime" Scott Joplin in 1902 (11)

17 Fast-paced team sport played with sticks and a puck; the official national winter sport of Canada (3,6)

18 Greek dramatist who wrote *The Oresteia* trilogy; considered to be the father of tragedy (9)

20 From the French literally meaning "lightning", a choux pastry confection resembling an elongated profiterole (6)

21 English playwright who penned the controversial work *Saved,* set in 1960s London (4)

24 Middle-Eastern country on the Mediterranean Sea, capital city Beirut (7)

26 Edge section of an aeroplane wing which controls lateral motion during a roll (7)

28 English novelist who wrote about the characters Pop, Ma and Mariette Larkin in a series of five books (5)

29 Substance present in milk, eggs and leafy green vegetables, essential for metabolic energy production, more commonly called vitamin B2 (10)

31 Rank of non-commissioned officer in the British artillery, equivalent to corporal (10)

35 From the Latin literally meaning "millstone", a tooth at the rear of a mammal's mouth for grinding food (5)

36 Duct for conveying water; also a protective case for electrical wiring (7)

37 Decorative handicraft performed with yarns and a single hook (7)

39 The __ Worthies; term for the group of heroes including Alexander the Great, Godfrey of Bouillon, Julius Caesar and King Arthur (4)

40 German-born British composer noted for his oratorio *Messiah* and collection of orchestral movements *Water Music* (6)
42 Bramble fruit with the cultivars heritage, regency and royalty (9)
45 Natural rocky fragment that has fallen to Earth from outer space, typically at speeds of around 11km per second (9)
47 Latinised name of a French astrologer whose predictions in rhyming quatrains continue to be the subject of controversy (11)
50 Agave-based Mexican spirit (7)
51 Section of an equine mammal's leg between the pastern and the cannon bone (7)
52 Musical note with a time value equal to two crotchets or half a semibreve (5)
53 The female of the ruff; also a chief magistrate of a district or town in Anglo-Saxon England (5)
54 "__: doing the same thing over and over again and expecting different results." Albert Einstein (8)
55 The capital and second largest city in Turkey, formerly called Angora (6)

Down

1 German-born Swiss novelist who was awarded the Nobel Prize in Literature for "inspired writings of classical humanitarian ideals" (5)
2 Section of the human larynx which affects voice modulation and pronunciation (7)
3 Any of a group of opiate-like substances produced by the brain and nervous system which function as neurotransmitters (9)
5 Scottish aviator who, in 1919 with John Alcock, made the first successful non-stop transatlantic flight (5)
6 A short instrumental prelude or refrain in a vocal work (10)
7 Hebrew prophet and son of Buzi in the Old Testament (7)
8 __ *Wood*; 1965 song by The Beatles on their album *Rubber Soul* (9)
9 Any one of the sections of a county outside the capital (6)
10 Traditional Javanese method of creating decorative designs on cloth (5)
11 Mythological ship-devouring sea monster or whirlpool opposite Scylla (9)
12 1942 Warner Bros movie based on the play *Everybody Comes to Rick's* (10)
18 Austrian psychotherapist noted for individual psychology (5)

19 Species of pinniped (3,4)
22 The largest living bird in existence (7)
23 Lift for towing skiers uphill (1-3)
25 Ancient city in Mesopotamia (7)
27 One of the 12 animals of the Chinese zodiac (7)
30 Republican who became president of the US in the wake of the Watergate scandal (4)
32 Swimming style based on an upside-down front crawl (10)
33 Water vole character in Kenneth Grahame's *The Wind in the Willows* (5)
34 Canadian city on Lake Ontario (10)
35 Instrument for measuring the pressure of fluids (9)
36 Traditional noisy mock serenade to newly-married couples (9)
38 Independent official appointed to investigate a complaint made against a government department (9)
41 French army officer falsely accused of treason, whose trial caused a major political crisis in France (7)
43 Country with the capital Bucharest (7)
44 The ___; English band who released *Every Breath You Take* in 1983 (6)
46 Hat traditionally worn by a chef (5)
48 English conservationist who was one of the founders of the World Wide Fund for Nature (5)
49 Brazilian dance of African origin (5)

global   Dytress   hungry
molar   meteorite
       raspberry   Lebanon's
Sascatuwh   croquet

4

Across

11 Bafta-winning 2010 historical film starring Colin Firth and Helena Bonham Carter (3,5,6)

12 A place where bees and their hives are kept (6)

13 Large species of bird with a cooing call, shy but conspicuous because of its clattering wings during flight (4,6)

14 Historical term for an authoritative letter from a monarch or a pope (5)

15 The imperial ruling dynasty of China from 618-907, regarded as a period of great wealth and the golden age of Chinese art and poetry (4)

16 Area in the heart of the New York theatre district, nicknamed the "Crossroads of the World" (5,6)

19 A type of ornamental branched candlestick or chandelier, often with a mirror (9)

23 International decimalised system of weights and measurements first proposed by Gabriel Mouton in 1670 (6)

25 Any of the 12 peers and warriors of Charlemagne's court (7)

26 A branch of the Afro-Asiatic language such as Hausa (6)

27 According to Scandinavian mythology, the resting place of the souls of heroes killed in battle, ruled by Odin for eternity (8)

29 Genus of flowering perennial plant with brightly coloured flowers made from sepals instead of petals (7)

31 Variety of pasta in the form of grains of rice or barley, used in Greek cuisine and to thicken soups (4)

32 SI unit of electromotive force, named after the Italian physicist who invented the battery (4)

34 A type of juggling game also known as "the devil on two sticks" (7)

35 Branch of biology concerned with the scientific study of the structure and function of plant and animal cells (8)

37 Nickname of Peregrin Took in Tolkien's *The Lord of the Rings* (6)

38 Monetary unit in several countries until the introduction of the euro that was equal to 1/100 of a franc (7)

40 Bite-size pastry or piece of toast with a savoury topping, served with drinks (6)

42 Conservative Prime Minister and statesman who said: "If you're going through hell, keep going." (9)

44 Rhetorical device of breaking off in the middle of a speech or sentence (11)

47 Small flag flown by a ship to indicate its nationality (4)

50 Small set of steps allowing human access over a rural fence (5)
51 Last book of the New Testament, also known as the Apocalypse of John (10)
54 Orchestral piece by Ravel to which Jane Torvill and Christopher Dean figure-skated their way to Olympic gold victory in 1984 (6)
55 Country in Oceania which is the site of the second largest island on earth (5,3,6)

Down

1 Chemical element in the form of a pale yellowish-green toxic gas, atomic number 17 (8)
2 Acronym of the Russian name of the secret police in the former USSR, also called the People's Commissariat for Internal Affairs (1,1,1,1)
3 Banded form of metamorphic rock, typically composed of feldspar, quartz and mica (6)
4 *The Lake __ of Innisfree*; poem by William Butler Yeats which begins: "I will arise and go now, and go to Innisfree, And a small cabin build there, of clay and wattles made." (4)
5 In architecture, the almost triangular space between the curve of an arch (8)
6 City in the East Midlands located on the banks of the River Derwent (5)
7 The 20th Prime Minister of Canada (8)
8 The chief ore of lead (6)
9 Unit of measure for shellfish (4)
10 English architect who redesigned St Paul's Cathedral following the Great Fire of London in 1666 (4)
17 *Planet __*; 2006 nature documentary series that was narrated by Sir David Attenborough (5)
18 The fourth largest city of Sweden and the oldest in northern Europe (7)
20 Constellation in the northern sky said to represent the dragon killed by Cadmus (5)
21 City in east central Germany once famous for its trade fairs (7)
22 Musical terminology indicating a piece must be performed slowly (6)
24 A greyish-green pottery glaze (7)
26 Sedimentary rock composed of fragments of older rocks (7)

28 French dramatist noted for his play *Antigone,* inspired by Greek mythology (7)

29 English author who wrote *Religio Medici*, first published in 1643 (6)

30 The most dense section of the head of a comet (7)

33 Hoofed mammal with a flexible proboscis, closely related to horses (5)

36 Spear-like weapon designed to be used during mounted combat (5)

38 The mythological Greek muse of epic poetry (8)

39 Former UK paper size measuring 30 × 22 inches (8)

41 *The __;* 1960s British television series starring Patrick McGoohan as the character Number Six (8)

43 US screenwriter and actor who directed the films *The Maltese Falcon* and *The African Queen* (6)

45 The science or study of birds' eggs; also the hobby of collecting them (6)

46 From the Italian literally meaning "time", musical direction indicating the speed at which a passage of music is or should be played (5)

48 One thousand million years (4)

49 Structure extending along the base of a ship from stem to stern (4)

52 "Alas, that love, whose __ is muffled still, Should, without eyes, see pathways to his will! Where shall we dine? O me! What fray was here?" *Romeo and Juliet:* Act I, Scene 1 (4)

53 In cricket, the end of the batting order using the weakest batsman (4)

square

Candelabra

4

agon
ozo
derby bulle.
sesura
Jack
MacMillan
Milton
pausa
Milton
Browne
N_A
cesura
Penntig

5

Across

11 Scottish crime novelist who wrote the series of 17 *Inspector Rebus* detective books (6)

12 2010 psychological thriller movie starring Natalie Portman as ballerina character Nina Sayers (5,4)

13 Description of a horse with either a bay, strawberry or blueish-coloured coat, inter-sprinkled with white or grey hairs (4)

14 The group of five bones of the human hand between the fingers and the wrist (10)

15 Device used to automatically regulate the temperature of a heating or cooling system (10)

16 Clothes made in standard sizes as opposed to being bespoke or tailor-made; translated in French as prêt-à-porter (5-2-4)

19 Dish typically consisting of meat, potatoes, vegetables, herbs and stock, slow-cooked in a vessel with the same name (9)

23 Short course offering instruction in a particular field or activity such as horse riding or tennis (6)

25 One of the oldest native breeds of British sheep (7)

26 Largest country in central Europe (6)

27 The married name of the daughter of Lord Byron who is considered to be one of the world's first computer programmers (8)

29 From the French literally meaning "velvety", a variety of white sauce made from roux and a meat-based stock (7)

31 Section of a hen's egg which is suspended in the albumen (4)

32 An artificial wall or embankment used in warfare as defence against tanks (4)

34 In heraldry, the relative status of a younger branch of a family (7)

35 The centre of the target board in archery, darts and shooting (5-3)

37 Historically, the informal term for the pre-decimal sixpence coin (6)

38 Musical instrument which is pitched an octave higher than an ordinary flute (7)

40 British television game show that was aired from 1988-97, originally hosted by Bruce Forsyth (3,3)

42 The lowest female singing voice (9)

44 *To Kill a __*; Pulitzer Prize-winning classic novel written by Harper Lee (11)

47 English city on the River Stour, largely associated with 24 down (10)

50 Christian celebration lasting 50 days, ending on Whitsunday (10)
53 Unit length equal to 0.3048m (4)
54 Constellation in the northern hemisphere with the Latin name Ursa Major (5,4)
55 Item of Roman armour in the form of a corslet or cuirass of leather (6)

Down

1 "Hope is like a ___, trembling from its birth, Love is like a rose, the joy of all the earth, Faith is like a lily, lifted high and white, Love is like a lovely rose, the world's delight." Christina Rossetti (8)
2 Large predatory gull-like sea bird which often pursues other birds to steal their catches (4)
3 According to law, a person who has not attained legal majority (6)
4 Abbreviated measure of volume used in cookery equal to 15ml (1,1,1,1)
5 Character in the *Merry Wives of Windsor* who says: "Good worts! good cabbage. Slender, I broke your head: what matter have you against me?" (8)
6 Edible cartilaginous marine fish in the ray family (5)
7 Variety of twice-baked melba toast-like sweetened bread made with eggs, sometimes given to teething children (8)
8 According to Jungian psychology, the masculine part of a woman's inner personality (6)
9 2001 biographical film starring Kate Winslet and Judi Dench about the life of the author who wrote *A Severed Head, The Black Prince* and *The Sea, the Sea* (4)
10 The basic monetary unit of Bangladesh, subdivided into 100 poisha (4)
17 English actor, director and screenwriter who starred in the television series *The Jewel in the Crown* as Sgt. Guy Perron (5)
18 Area of central London, site of Covent Garden, Mayfair, Soho and Westminster (4,3)
20 A sequence of shots in tennis (5)
21 US astronomer, physicist and aviation pioneer who invented the bolometer in 1878 (7)
22 A strike of the ball before it reaches the ground in football (6)
24 English author and poet whose 14th-century magnum opus describes a pilgrimage to 47 across (7)
26 Singer known as "the King" (7)

5

28 Aromatic culinary herb related to marjoram, used to enhance the flavour of lamb, tomato and pizza dishes (7)

29 City in northern Italy and capital of the region Veneto, situated on a lagoon of the Adriatic Sea (6)

30 In bridge, a technique deployed in a Vienna coup (7)

33 French artist who was the founder of the Impressionists, noted for his "en plein air" works such as the *Water Lilies* series of paintings (5)

36 A young unfledged pigeon and the meat of which as food (5)

38 From the French literally meaning "pot on the fire", a traditional soup or stew-like dish made from beef and vegetables (3-2-3)

39 Instrument for measuring the distance travelled by a wheeled vehicle (8)

41 Mythological wife of Orpheus (8)

43 The Latin name for the charioteer constellation, said to represent a man holding a whip (6)

45 Section of a hypodermic syringe (6)

46 English architect who designed Fonthill Abbey in Wiltshire (5)

48 Former English county that was abolished in 1996 (4)

49 Yugoslav revolutionary born Josip Broz who served as prime minister from 1945–53 and president from 1953–80 (4)

51 Mineral similar to carnelian (4)

52 __ Boy; character in the sketch show *Harry Enfield and Chums* (4)

5

avon
cont
Yard
Penelope
easter   Perseus

Across

11 Opéra comique by Bizet with the arias *Habanera* and *Toreador Song*, recently produced by the Royal Opera House in 3-D (6)

12 The first film of Oliver Stone's Vietnam War trilogy, followed by *Born on the Fourth of July* and *Heaven & Earth* (7)

13 Common name for any of various species of short-billed wading birds in the Charadriidae family, which includes dotterels and lapwings (6)

14 Fossilised cephalopod with a spiral-shaped shell resembling a nautilus, common from around 65 million to 400 million years ago (8)

15 Former rugby union player who replaced Brian Ashton as the England team manager in 2008 (7)

16 English equestrian and 2004 Olympic silver medallist for team eventing who has also won Badminton Horse Trials on two occasions (4)

17 British actor born in Swaziland who starred in the film *Withnail and I*, based on the life of Bruce Robinson (5)

19 The brainless character in L. Frank Baum's children's novel *The Wonderful Wizard of Oz* (9)

22 Liquor made from meat, fish or bones boiled with herbs, vegetables and wine, used as the basis for soups and sauces (5)

26 Woodwind instrument originally invented by Johann Christoph Denner, based on an improved version of the chalumeau (8)

27 Computer keyboard key typically between Caps lock and Ctrl (5)

28 English novelist who wrote: "The family of Dashwood had long been settled in Sussex. Their estate was large, and their residence was at Norland Park..." (6)

30 The study of the history and origins of proper names (10)

33 Regimental headquarters where military recruits are assembled and trained (5)

34 Form of precipitation typically produced by nimbus clouds (4)

35 A symmetrical three-dimensional solid or hollow shape which is contained by six equal squares, also called a regular hexahedron (4)

36 Crow-like bird which is bigger than a buzzard; seven of which preside over the Tower of London (5)

38 "Nephew, what means this __ discourse, This peroration with such circumstance? For France, 'tis ours; and we will keep it still." *King Henry VI, Part II*: Act I, Scene 1 (10)

39 Word linking comedy and irony (6)
40 Picturesque alpine province and popular ski resort in western Austria (5)
41 Precious gem, such as a diamond, cut in a long rectangular shape (8)
43 Informal cricketing term for an innings made by an individual batsman (5)
45 In geometry, a plane figure with 12 angles and sides (9)
46 Headdress worn by a bishop (5)
49 A row of stables with living quarters above (4)
51 Silvery-white metallic element, atomic number 3, used in the treatment of bipolar disorder (7)
54 Republic in the Pacific Ocean which includes the Gilbert, Banaba, Line and Phoenix Islands (8)
56 Chemical element named after the smallest of the five identified dwarf planets (6)
57 Culinary herb which is related to carrot, dill and fennel (7)
58 *The Color* __; Pulitzer Prize-winning novel by Alice Walker (6)

Down

1 Estate and castle in Royal Deeside, described by Queen Victoria as her "dear paradise in the Highlands" (8)
2 Section of a shield, a bivalve shell, a toadstool or a mushroom (4)
3 Common name of a member of the taxonomic class of creatures Gastropoda (5)
4 In boxing, a blow delivered to the opponent's chin at close range (8)
5 In the Islamic faith, the annual pilgrimage to Mecca (4)
6 German financier who founded a banking house in Frankfurt in the 18th century (10)
7 Insects with more than 10,000 known species, which can carry three times their own weight (4)
8 Section of the human body typically containing over 100 joints, 120 muscles and 220 ligaments (5)
9 Pendant for a small photograph (6)
10 A streak of different colour in stone, cheese, marble or wood (4)
18 German city where Nazi war criminals were tried by International Military Tribunal for war crimes and crimes against humanity (9)
20 Wars of the __; the series of civil wars for the throne of England between 1455 and 1487 (5)

6

21 Cephalopod mollusc with four pairs of arms (7)
23 Breed of sheep originally from a range of hills with the same name (7)
24 The capital city of 40 across (9)
25 Container holding a spool of photographic film for a camera (9)
29 Vast plain in Tanzania which hosts the largest mammal migration in the world (9)
31 Subatomic particle with a slightly larger mass than that of a proton (7)
32 From the Latin literally meaning "within glass", a biological procedure performed in a test tube or Petri dish (2,5)
37 Alternative term for an axon (5,5)
38 Lively Bohemian dance (5)
41 One of the boroughs of New York (8)
42 Valve for controlling the supply of fuel or power to an engine (8)
44 Main protein in milk and cheese (6)
47 An artificial channel for water (5)
48 Black silk fabric formerly used for mourning dress (5)
50 Conservative politician who served as Prime Minister from 1955-57 (4)
52 In India, a grove or plantation, especially of mangoes (4)
53 Philosopher and proponent of utilitarianism who wrote *On Liberty* (4)
55 Winner of a prize for Welsh verse at an Eisteddfod festival (4)

Across

1 British film actor who starred in *Schindler's List*, *The English Patient*, *Red Dragon* and *The Reader* (7)

5 The common name of the charitable organisation identified by its oak leaf and acorn logo (8,5)

12 English astronomer who calculated the position of a supposed planet beyond Uranus which later led to the discovery of Neptune (5)

13 French term literally meaning "free verse" (4,5)

14 Canadian folk singer-songwriter, poet and novelist who wrote *Let Us Compare Mythologies* and *The Spice-Box of Earth* (5)

15 City in Central Alberta; also the common name of the large land mammal *Cervus elaphus* (3,4)

16 "Be not __ of going slowly; be only __ of standing still." Chinese proverb (6)

17 From the Spanish literally meaning "saw", a long jagged mountain chain (6)

18 A type of clamp-like device secured over the fingerboard of a fretted musical instrument to raise the pitch of the strings (4)

20 Culinary herb grown for its seed-like fruits, used dried in breads (7)

22 Fish-eating bird of prey, in decline due to illegal killing (6)

27 Italian composer who wrote the 1835 tragedy *Lucia di Lammermoor* and the 1843 opera buffa *Don Pasquale* (9)

28 The sixth novel in the *Rutshire Chronicles* series by Jilly Cooper (5)

29 Scottish physician who discovered and identified carbon dioxide, latent heat and specific heat (5)

30 A highly flammable petroleum-based jelly, used in flame-throwers and incendiary bombs (6)

31 Personification of Shakespeare's character Katherina Minola (5)

33 The only chess piece permitted to "jump over" the standard pieces (6)

36 The Roman god of love, said to wound victims with his bow and quiver of arrows (5)

37 The girth of a Western saddle (5)

39 Species of duck inhabiting fast-flowing streams around the Arctic and North Pacific, named after a Commedia dell'arte character (9)

40 US Nobel Prize-winning playwright who disowned his daughter Oona for marrying Charlie Chaplin (1'5)

42 An infringement of rules in rugby characterised by a player moving the ball forward with the hand or arm (5-2)

44 Construction toy invented by carpenter Ole Kirk Christiansen (4)

47 According to Greek mythology, the wife of Priam and mother of Cassandra, Hector, Paris and Troilus (6)

49 Members of the only living species in the *Homo* genus (6)

51 Cathedral city in England, founded by the Romans as Lindum Colonia (7)

54 Labour statesman who, following a landslide victory in 1997, became the youngest prime minister since the 2nd Earl of Liverpool in 1812 (5)

55 Common name for the talus (5,4)

56 Flowing from the Swiss Alps to the North Sea coast, one of the longest rivers in Europe (5)

57 The third-brightest star in the night sky, also known as Rigil Kentaurus (5,8)

58 The SI unit of conductance, equal to the reciprocal of one ohm (7)

Down

1 The killing of one's brother (10)

2 Largest of the African antelopes (5)

3 The president of Egypt who nationalised the Suez Canal, waging war with Britain, France and Israel (6)

4 The longest river in Great Britain (6)

5 Small constellation between Scorpius and Centaurus, said to represent a rule (5)

6 The winged sandals worn by the Roman god Mercury (7)

7 A musical accompaniment of integral importance which should not be omitted in performance (9)

8 Penalty __; rectangular section of a football pitch in front of each goal (4)

9 The art of organising armed forces prior to engaging in conflict with an enemy (7)

10 Courtroom official responsible for swearing in jurors and witnesses and generally keeping order (5)

11 Located between Tanzania and the Congo, the second-largest freshwater lake in the world by volume (10)

19 Name of a dance studio in Covent Garden which was the location of a recent docusoap starring founder Debbie Moore and Louie Spence (9)

21 The first sign of the zodiac (5)

23 1989 action movie starring Patrick Swayze as a professional bar bouncer (4,5)

24 English comedian whose stand-up performances include *Dress to Kill* and *Stripped* (6)

25 Internal human organ which links the oesophagus to the small intestine (7)

26 Scottish sailor whose experiences as a castaway for four years inspired Daniel Defoe's novel *Robinson Crusoe* (7)

28 According to the Old Testament, the wife of Abraham and mother of Isaac (5)

29 Danish novelist who wrote *Seven Gothic Tales* and *Out of Africa* (6)

32 Speedy blue-coloured fish known as an ono in Hawaii (5)

34 An extreme fear of heights (10)

35 *Close ___ of the Third Kind*; 1977 sci-fi movie by Steven Spielberg (10)

38 Island south of Cape Cod (9)

41 A republic in West Africa (7)

43 The French word for hat (7)

45 Hand tool for bending wire and gripping small objects (6)

46 A small dish served between the main courses of a formal dinner (6)

48 A heap of root vegetables protected by a layer of earth or straw (5)

50 A traditional Japanese screen or sliding door (5)

52 Dish consisting of a slice of veal or beef rolled round a savoury stuffing (5)

53 A hardy and highly nutritious variety of cabbage (4)

Red deer
udder?
childrens
Trust

Helena
Hecuba RHINE
ONE
Cul
tracea
Tahitian
bucco
55 horse shoe
Severn
pliers
osprey
entree
O'Neill
far Kale
Limassole
Dun-u

Across

1   Market town in Wiltshire on the River Kennet, near Stonehenge, Silbury Hill and West Kennet Long Barrow (11)

7   Odourless form of suffocating gas typically consisting of carbon dioxide, found in poorly ventilated or disused coalmines (9)

12 Large type of sailing ship such as the Golden Hind, in which Sir Francis Drake circumnavigated the globe between 1577 and 1580 (7)

13 Common name for the plant in the olive family with highly fragrant, typically pale purple-coloured flowers, *Syringa* (5)

14 General name for a weapon designed to temporarily immobilise an attacker by means of electric shock (4,3)

15 Trademark name of a brand of sticking plasters for general first aid (11)

16 The common name of the Central Criminal Court in London; the present building of which stands on the site of Newgate Prison (3,6)

17 The largest city in Turkey and third-largest in the world; historically known as Byzantium and later Constantinople (8)

19 __ the Younger; Roman statesman, Stoic philosopher and dramatist who was ordered to kill himself by his tutee, Nero (6)

21 A score of two strokes under par for a hole in golf (5)

24 English metaphysical poet whose works *To His Coy Mistress* and *The Garden* were published posthumously (7)

27 Former Conservative MP and Chief Secretary to the Treasury from 1994-95 who was jailed for perjury in 1999 (6)

29 One of a number of German prisoner-of-war camps that were used for non-commissioned officers during the Second World War (6)

32 Small, gregarious Australian parakeet typically with green, yellow or blue plumage, popular as a pet (10)

33 1923 collection of poetry written in prose by Lebanese artist and philosopher Khalil Gibran (3,7)

35 Soft skin covering a deer's antlers (6)

36 Nocturnal fox with large pointed ears found in the Sahara Desert which is smallest species of canid in the world (6)

37 Large town in the south-west of England noted for the "Magic Roundabout", listed as one of the "scariest junctions in Britain" (7)

40 Finno-__; group of languages including Estonian, Finnish and Hungarian/Magyar (5)

42 ___ VIII; blood protein essential for clotting; a deficiency of which results in the genetic disorder haemophilia (6)

44 1925 pop standard by Irving Berlin, covered by artists including Ella Fitzgerald, Frank Sinatra and Billie Holiday (8)

47 Principal church of a diocese (9)

49 Italian political philosopher who said: "Before all else, be armed", "Never was anything great achieved without danger" and "It is better to be feared than loved, if you cannot be both." (11)

52 Of igneous rock, to be forced into an existing formation (7)

53 English physician and lexicographer noted for his *Thesaurus of English Words and Phrases* (5)

54 "You shall set in it four rows of stones. A row of ___, topaz, and carbuncle shall be the first row..." *Exodus*, 28:17, Revised Standard Version (7)

55 A method of painting in grey monochrome (9)

56 The science of flight (11)

Down

1 Chemical element which burns with a brilliant white flame, atomic number 12 (9)

2 The manufacturer of the three-wheeled yellow van driven by Trotters Independent Traders owners Del Boy and Rodney (7)

3 River in Greater London which is a tributary of the Thames (5)

4 In cricket, the bowler's approach before delivering the ball (3-2)

5 In computing, to transmit data from one system to a larger one (6)

6 English composer noted for his orchestral suite *The Planets* (5)

7 Severe system of winds rotating spirally inwards towards a centre of low barometric pressure (7)

8 Glass bottle-like volcanic rock formed by the rapid solidification of lava with minimal crystal growth (8)

9 "Those who trust us ___ us." T. S. Eliot (7)

10 Star in the constellation Perseus, also known as the Demon Star (5)

11 Unit of mass equal to 24 grains or 1/20 of a troy ounce (11)

18 The first prime minister of Tanzania and later its first president (7)

20 English painter of nudes (4)

22 The son of Sir Lancelot (7)

The Telegraph

8

23 Mexican dish of highly-seasoned meat and maize dough, steamed or baked in corn husks (6)
25 The ___; an enemy of Batman (7)
26 Cut of meat taken from the lower section of an animal's back (4)
28 The science of moral principles (6)
30 Radioactive mineral commonly found in the chemical element, atomic number 90 (7)
31 Egyptian god depicted as a bull (4)
32 The act or hobby of encamping in makeshift tents or shelters (11)
34 Ornamental box worn suspended from an obi as part of traditional Japanese dress (4)
38 Genus containing daffodils (9)
39 British author who wrote the novels *After You'd Gone*, *My Lover's Lover* and *The Hand That First Held Mine* (1'7)
41 A pause or natural breathing space near the middle of a line (7)
43 A unit of food energy (7)
45 Italian composer who wrote the opera semiseria *La sonnambula* (7)
46 Sea duck related to swans and geese, Latin name *Melanitta nigra* (6)
48 Musical term meaning "with all voices or instruments together" (5)
49 Substance from which lava and other igneous rock is formed on cooling (5)
50 Norwegian dramatist who wrote *Peer Gynt* and *A Doll's House* (5)
51 A concept theorised by 49 across (5)

8

schoner

cesura

toHo   Mossilunia

Across

1 English civil engineer known as the "Father of Railways" who built the famous Rocket steam locomotive with his son Robert (10)

6 ___ Championship; the annual international rugby union competition contested by England, France, Ireland, Italy, Scotland and Wales (3,7)

13 Driving manoeuvre performed to reverse the direction of travel (1-4)

14 An afternoon performance of a play, concert or movie (7)

15 Portrait painter noted for works including *Lady Godiva, Lilith* and *Guinevere's Maying* (7)

16 According to Greek myth, Titaness and sea goddess who was the daughter of Uranus and Gaia (6)

17 Bird species in the Corvidae family which includes jackdaws, jays, magpies, rooks and ravens (4)

18 2007 movie starring James McAvoy and Keira Knightley, based on a 2001 novel by Ian McEwan (9)

20 Large, lofty nest of an eagle (5)

21 Solid geometrical figure bounded by many plane faces, typically more than six (10)

24 Golf or tennis tournament characterised by being free from restrictions on who may compete (4)

27 English dramatist who wrote the 1956 play *Look Back in Anger* (7)

29 Unitary authority bounded by Leicestershire, Lincolnshire, Cambridgeshire and Northamptonshire (7)

31 President of Argentina who married the actress and politician known as Evita (5)

32 The leader of the Soviet Union who denounced Stalin and presided over the Cuban Missile Crisis (10)

35 Television sports show broadcast between 1958 and 2007, first presented by Peter Dimmock (10)

38 Epithet for Apollo (5)

39 US actor and comedian who starred in the movies *When Harry Met Sally...* and *City Slickers* (7)

40 Traditional form of Japanese therapy based on applying pressure to specific points of the body (7)

42 The outer peel of a citrus fruit (4)

43 The fourth-largest island in the world by area (10)

45 Style of upper storey bay window projecting from a wall, typically supported by brackets or corbels (5)

48 *An__ Calls*; play written by English dramatist J. B. Priestley (9)

51 Social groups of cetaceans such as dolphins, porpoises or whales (4)

53 "Sweet rose, fair flower, untimely pluck'd, soon vaded, Pluck'd in the bud, and vaded in the spring! Bright orient pearl, alack, too timely __!" *The Passionate Pilgrim*, X, Shakespeare (6)

55 Toxic plant genus containing the "queen of poisons" (7)

56 Italian dish of boiled cornmeal served as an accompaniment to other foods (7)

57 To cook with dry heat, especially meat or vegetables (5)

58 A common name of the flowering plant *Leucanthemum vulgare*, also called marguerite (5,5)

59 Thoroughfare where horses and their riders have right of way (6,4)

Down

1 Lightweight projectile used in badminton and battledore (11)

2 Imaginary circle around Earth dividing the northern and southern hemispheres (7)

3 A common name of a rainforest-dwelling mammal which robs the nests of wild bees, more correctly called a kinkajou (5,4)

4 *Comfortably __*; song by Pink Floyd on their 1979 album *The Wall* (4)

5 The smallest of all marine mammals in existence; males of which are called meowters and the females, queens (5)

7 Island country in the North Atlantic Ocean, site of the peak Hvannadalshnjúkur and the largest glacier in Europe, Vatnajökull (7)

8 Tortilla chip typically served with a topping of melted cheese, salsa and pickled jalapeño peppers (5)

9 Hungarian-born US physicist known as "the father of the hydrogen bomb" (6)

10 An architectural arch, pointed or in the Gothic style (5)

11 Compound present in blood platelets acting as a neurotransmitter, referred to as the "happiness hormone" (9)

12 A fairy tale collected by the Brothers Grimm (4,5)

19 Foil-like fencing sword (4)

22 In English law, the term for the offence of theft until 1968 (7)

23 Linguist who designed the system of Basic English with I. A. Richards (5)

25 From the French literally meaning "perfect", a type of frozen dessert containing whipped cream and fruit (7)
26 A work of musical composition (4)
28 British spy for MI5 while ostensibly employed by the BBC (7)
30 Synthetic textile fibre made from various polymers (7)
33 In maths, a function of an angle (4)
34 Substance made from roasted and ground cacao beans (5)
36 Skipping game played with a pair of long ropes (6,5)
37 A type of unofficial ballot with non-binding results (5,4)
38 Of instruments in the violin family, to be played by plucking the strings (9)
40 A brownish-red-coloured mineral similar to carnelian (4)
41 The __; nickname of the New York Yankees baseman Lou Gehrig (4,5)
44 One of the three Fates (7)
46 The US "Hoosier" state (7)
47 Country on the Caribbean coast of Central America, formerly called British Honduras (6)
49 A type of quick bread confection, sweetened or unsweetened, traditionally served in a cream tea (5)
50 The eighth letter of the Greek alphabet (5)
52 The standard monetary unit in various countries including Algeria, Bahrain, Jordan and Iraq (5)
54 Unit of measurement for equines, equal to four inches or 10.2 centimetres (4)

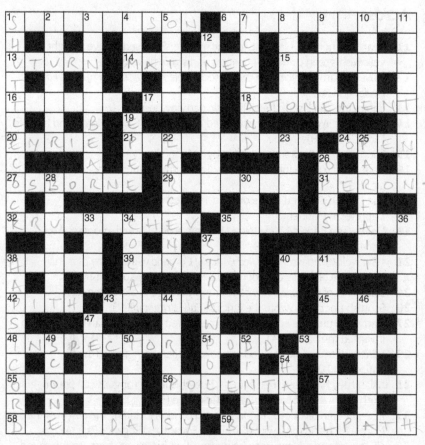

9

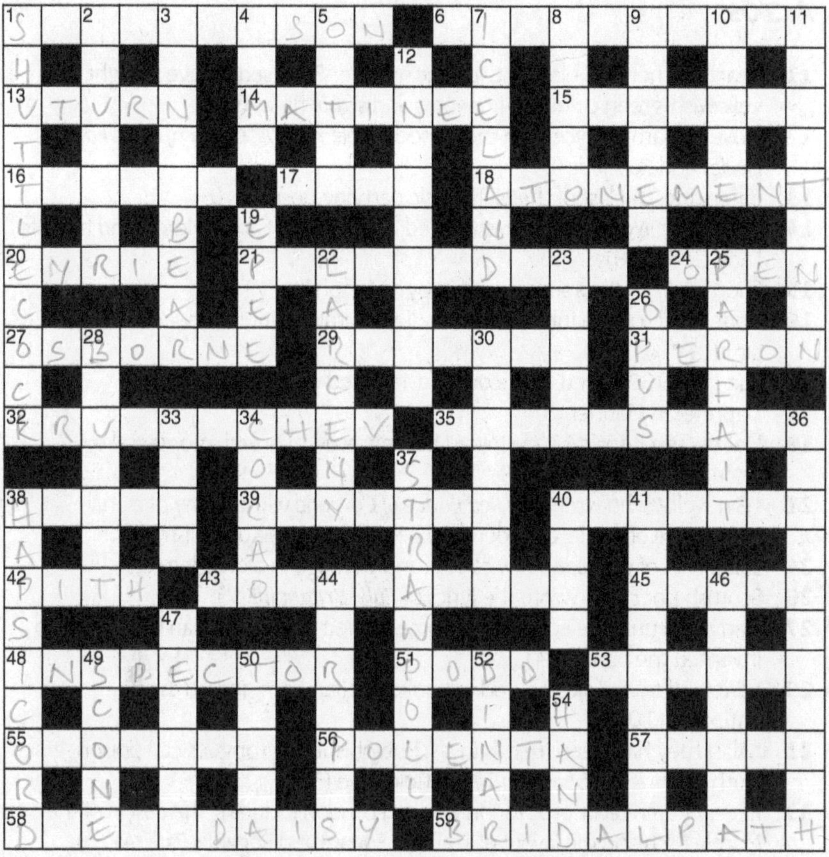

10

Across

11 Reactive chemical element, atomic number 56, used to give a bright yellowish-green colour to fireworks and signal flares (6)

12 Novel by James Joyce with the episodes *Telemachus*, *Calypso*, *Lotus Eaters*, *Hades* and *Penelope* (7)

13 In fencing, the last of the eight basic parrying positions (6)

14 City in the West Midlands associated with Leofric, Earl of Mercia and his wife Lady Godiva (8)

15 Sport, skill, art or practice studied by a toxophilite (7)

16 Codeword used in international radio communication between Juliet and Lima (4)

17 *The __*; 1963 Alfred Hitchcock movie based on a novelette by Daphne du Maurier (5)

19 Hot dessert consisting of stewed fruit encased in bread, sponge cake, biscuits or breadcrumbs (9)

21 US novelist who wrote *The Red Badge of Courage* without any personal experience of battle; considered to be a masterpiece of realism (5)

24 Salad dish of shredded raw carrots and cabbage in a dressing (8)

26 Scottish poet who wrote the lyrics of *Rule, Britannia!* (7)

27 Derived SI unit of electromotive force named after the Italian physicist who invented the battery (4)

29 Variety of thinly-sliced cured uncooked Italian ham, served as an antipasto (10)

31 "Alas! they had been friends in __; But whispering tongues can poison truth..." *Christabel*, Samuel Taylor Coleridge (5)

33 Regency architect noted for his works in London including the design of the Marble Arch and the layout of Trafalgar Square and Regent's Park (4)

34 US lawyer and adventurer who wrote about his voyage from Boston round Cape Horn to California in his memoir *Two Years Before the Mast* (4)

35 SI unit of magnetic flux density (5)

37 Latin phrase literally meaning "scraped tablet", John Locke's theory which postulates that the human mind is free from innate ideas at birth (6,4)

38 Box-like device from which playing cards are dealt in casinos (4)

39 David Bowie song on his 1980 album *Scary Monsters (and Super Creeps)* (7)

41 The killing of a king (8)

43 Collective noun for a group of apes or chimpanzees (5)

46 Control panel situated in front of the driver of a car or pilot of a plane (9)

48 German physicist who invented the first electromagnetic telegraph with Carl Friedrich Gauss (5)

51 South African Archbishop and Nobel Peace Prize-winner who was a leading voice in the struggle against apartheid (4)

52 Mythological Greek hero who decapitated the Gorgon Medusa and rescued Andromeda from a sea monster (7)

54 Typographical symbol typically in the form of a five-pointed star (8)

56 US newspaper publisher and magnate who was the inspiration for the protagonist in Orson Welles's 1941 film *Citizen Kane* (6)

57 Team sport nicknamed the "gentleman's game" (7)

58 Island in the Caribbean Sea with the largest town Scarborough (6)

Down

1 The colour of the horses Trigger and Mister Ed (8)

2 English lyricist who wrote *Joseph and the Amazing Technicolor Dreamcoat* and *Jesus Christ Superstar* with Andrew Lloyd Webber (4)

3 Lead singer of The Cure (5)

4 An Aboriginal bush hut (6)

5 Constellation containing the bright star Vega, said to represent a musical instrument invented by Hermes (4)

6 The science of the mind (10)

7 Heat-resistant silicate mineral used extensively as a building material between the 1950s and 1980s (8)

8 The capital city of Japan, formerly called Edo (5)

9 Irish novelist and personal assistant of Sir Henry Irving, noted for his character depicted by Béla Lugosi in a 1931 film (6)

10 English writer whose posthumously-published diary describes historical events including the Great Fire of London (6)

18 __ Nine; space station in the *Star Trek* universe (4,5)

20 Imitative of a design, fashion or style from the recent past (5)

22 In law, a person who brings a case against another in court (9)

23 A collection of published poems or songs chosen by the compiler (9)

25 Victorian painter and sculptor noted for his Symbolist oil painting *Hope* (5)

27 Either of the two pumping chambers of the heart (9)

28 In jousting, the palisades which enclosed a tournament area (5)

30 Freshwater fish related to carp and minnows (5)

32 Natural brown clay pigment, darker than ochre (5)

36 Branch of mathematics concerned with numerical calculations (10)

37 Ballroom dance that originated in Buenos Aires (5)

40 A symbol of Ireland (8)

42 From the French literally meaning "training", the highly-skilled equestrian discipline referred to as "horse ballet" (8)

44 According to the Book of Genesis, Hebrew patriarch who was the eldest son of Jacob and Leah (6)

45 Term for the complete body of work of an author, composer or painter (6)

47 Commercial district of Venice, site of the Grand Canal (6)

49 US swimmer who won seven gold medals at the Munich Olympic Games in 1972, nicknamed "Mark the Shark" (5)

50 "Something is rotten in the ___ of Denmark." *Hamlet*: Act I, Scene 4 (5)

53 Pen name of the short story writer Hector Hugh Munro (4)

55 The traditional gift for a 40th wedding anniversary (4)

10

Tutu   ouevre
     Saki   Milton
              tabula rosa
   Wren   oevre   K
   ynth

Across

1 Edible bivalve mollusc which swims by rapidly opening and closing its fan-shaped shell (7)

5 According to Greek myth, the nymph who was transformed into a laurel tree to save her from the amorous pursuit of Apollo (6)

8 *The __*; one of the paintings by Edvard Munch that were stolen from Oslo's Munch Museum in 2004 and recovered two years later (6)

12 Four-time Pulitzer Prize-winning US poet noted for his depictions of rural life in New England (5)

13 Country on the Horn of Africa, ruled by Emperor Haile Selassie from 1930-74 (8)

14 Book of the New Testament between *Acts* and *Corinthians* (6)

16 A type of toothed wheel used to engrave rows of perforations on sheets of postage stamps (8)

17 Musical term indicating a passage must be performed in a smooth flowing manner without breaks (6)

18 A division of a bulb of garlic or shallot; also an old English measure of weight for cheese and wool (5)

19 Khaki-coloured cloth used to make trousers and military uniforms (5)

21 Branch of medicine concerned with the scientific study of drugs (12)

27 Basic monetary unit of Egypt, equal to 100 qirsh (5)

28 Located between Auvergne, Centre, Champagne-Ardenne and Rhône-Alpes, one of the 22 regions of France (8)

29 Deer-like water buffalo native to the Indonesian island of Sulawesi (4)

33 The colloquial term for artificial respiration (4,2,4)

34 Game played in a walled court, similar to squash but using the hand to strike the ball instead of a racket (5,5)

36 A bowling technique in cricket (4)

37 Knighted horseman who was champion jockey 26 times, best remembered for winning the 1953 Epsom Derby on Pinza (8)

38 Egyptian sun god depicted as a falcon-headed man (5)

41 With allusion to a hero of the Trojan War, a metaphor for a seemingly small but potentially fatal weakness (8,4)

42 From the Italian literally meaning "quill", a variety of pasta in the form of short tubes (5)

46 "__ is not only better than war, but infinitely more arduous." George Bernard Shaw (5)

48 US cavalry general who led his men to their deaths at a disastrous clash with the Sioux at the Battle of Little Bighorn (6)

50 The second-brightest star in the constellation Leo, approximately 36 light years from Earth (8)

53 Pen name of the Irish novelist who wrote *At Swim-Two-Birds* and *The Third Policeman* (1'5)

54 Carbonated beverage invented by US pharmacist John Pemberton (4-4)

55 Informal term for a person employed to run general errands on a film set (5)

56 Anglican theologian who was a founding member of the Oxford Movement and later converted to Roman Catholicism (6)

57 Latin epic poem by Virgil (6)

58 English naturalist who wrote the autobiographical trilogy comprising: *My Family and Other Animals*, *Birds, Beasts and Relatives* and *The Garden of the Gods* (7)

Down

1 An overland African expedition to observe wildlife (6)

2 The Greek god of the winds (6)

3 Hot beverage consisting of a shot of espresso blended with frothy steamed milk (5)

4 Situated on the River Ribble, the administrative centre of Lancashire which gained city status in 2002 (7)

5 English novelist and fighter pilot who wrote *The Witches*, *The Twits*, *The BFG* and 40 down (4)

6 Radioactive metal of the lanthanide series, atomic number 61 (10)

7 The basic monetary unit of Nigeria, equal to 100 kobo (5)

9 Breed of dog with a blue-black tongue; also a Chinese condiment similar to piccalilli (4,4)

10 The Muse of lyric love poetry, typically depicted playing a lyre (5)

11 Genre of novel or movie based on the unravelling of a puzzling crime (7)

15 Radio and television broadcaster who retired from his BBC Radio 2 breakfast show in 2009 (5)

20 English sea explorer who, in 1611, was set adrift by his own crew in an act of mutiny, never to be seen again (6)

22 Member of a strict Maoist youth movement in China during the Cultural Revolution (3,5)
23 Person or animal that eats food of both animal and vegetable origin (8)
24 Running shoes with metal points (6)
25 A person who repairs, makes and sells firearms (8)
26 The director and producer of silent films *The Birth of a Nation* and *Intolerance* (8)
28 Scottish-born US scientist who is credited with inventing the first practical telephone (4)
30 The birthplace of the patron saint of animals (6)
31 Wading bird worshipped by the ancient Egyptians (4)
32 __ hound; the breed of Frank Muir's fictional dog, What-a-Mess (6)
35 Rich and sweet tart-like dessert with a buttery biscuit base (10)
39 Substance obtained from a genus of succulent plant, said to have many medicinal properties (4,4)
40 *James and the Giant* __; children's novel by 5 down (5)
41 Wind instrument used for signalling in mountainous regions (7)
43 Traditional birthstone for May (7)
44 Sugar and butter confection (6)
45 French surgeon and Nobel laureate who developed techniques for suturing arteries and veins (6)
47 US economist noted for his work on social choice theory (5)
49 Shawl for formal occasions (5)
51 Composer of *Enigma Variations* (5)
52 1983 single by Spandau Ballet (4)

scallop preston   allegro

Grid answers (handwritten):

SCALLOP · DAPHNE · SCREAM
FROST · ETHIOPIA
RACHETTE · CLOVE
PHARMACOLOGY
BORDEAUX
KISSOFLIFE
SPIN · RICHARDS
ACHILLESHEEL · PENNE
PEACE · COCACOLA · GOFOR

v.
aloa Adams   Chester   Busset   Peace   Turnot
                                    Daphne   guard
Alphine   dinar
cloak   Codey Terry D
Derwent
            Assisi   veuvre et
                              tourne

Across

10 Variety of rich fruitcake with a lightly-toasted marzipan topping, traditionally eaten at Easter (6)

12 Tall upright pillar decorated with flowers and ribbons, erected for dancing around on the first day of the fifth month of each year (7)

13 Christian festival held on the Sunday after the first full moon following the spring equinox (6)

14 Corn goddess and mother of Persephone, queen of the underworld who personifies the return of spring (7)

15 Author who wrote the nonsense poems *The Hunting of the Snark* and *Jabberwocky* under the pen name Lewis Carroll (7)

16 African-American tennis player who was the first black male to win a major singles title (4)

17 Flower of the genus *Papaver* associated with 14 across, used as a symbol of remembrance since 1920 (5)

19 Any one of the three tendons at the back of the human thigh responsible for flexion of the knee and rotation of the lower leg (9)

21 English architect who redesigned the Houses of Parliament in the mid-19th century (5)

24 Red supergiant and second- brightest star in the constellation Orion (10)

26 An alloy of copper and zinc used as a substitute for gold leaf (5,5)

29 Hollow chocolate confections filled with treats, traditionally given as gifts on Easter Sunday (4)

31 English economist who was awarded the 1977 Nobel Memorial Prize in Economic Sciences (5)

32 Department of France in the Burgundy region, named after a river with the same name (5)

33 Paschal __; offspring of 25 down sacrificed and eaten at the Passover; an emblem of Christ (4)

34 In the Christian church, a period of 40 weekdays from Ash Wednesday to Holy Saturday devoted to fasting and abstinence (4)

35 Nickname of the retired basketball player Earvin Johnson who won a gold medal at the 1992 Barcelona Olympics with the "Dream Team" (5)

38 Name of the otter character created by the English naturalist and novelist Henry Williamson (5)

40 A single page in a book of postage stamps (4)

41 The scientific study of the natural history of trees (10)

42 From the Latin literally meaning "to the city and to the world", a papal address and blessing which takes place from St Peter's Basilica annually at Easter (4,2,4)

44 English television personality who presented *This is Your Life* and *Antiques Roadshow* (5)

47 Christian festival held on the seventh Sunday after Easter, also called Whitsunday; also the Jewish festival held on the fiftieth day after the Passover (9)

48 French phrase literally meaning "for or involving two people" (1,4)

51 Spanish Cubist painter and sculptor who was born Victoriano González Pérez (4)

52 Swimming stroke similar to front crawl but with scissor kicks (7)

54 SI derived unit of electric charge (7)

56 One of the six counties forming Northern Ireland (6)

57 Prime Minister of Canada awarded the 1957 Nobel Peace Prize for his part in ending the Suez Crisis (7)

58 Interstellar cloud of dust and gas (6)

Down

1 Meteorologist's diagram showing the relative frequency and strength of air currents at a particular location (4,4)

2 Dwarf planet discovered by Clyde Tombaugh in 1930 (5)

3 Period of seven weeks between the second day of Passover and 47 across (4)

4 English composer who was joint organist of the Chapel Royal with Thomas Tallis (4)

5 Religious holiday prior to Easter Sunday, observed to commemorate the crucifixion of Christ (4,6)

6 London district, site of the Royal Albert Hall and the Natural History Museum (10)

7 French novelist who wrote *Twenty Thousand Leagues under the Sea* and *Around the World in Eighty Days* (5)

8 The capital city of Eritrea (6)

9 1959 Academy Award-winning film based on a novel by Lew Wallace (3-3)

11 Game in which two players take turns to collect objects from a number of heaps whilst trying to avoid collecting the last remaining object (3)

18 Fastener also called a popper (5,4)
20 Island of the Lesser Antilles (5)
22 King of Mycenae who was murdered by his wife Clytemnestra and her lover Aegisthus (9)
23 *The Elves and the __*; a fairy tale collected by the Brothers Grimm (9)
25 A female sheep (3)
27 Quadric surface with plane sections all being ellipses or circles (9)
28 Capital and largest city of Jordan (5)
30 Freshwater diving duck which is unable to walk on dry land (5)
36 Series of spooky novels for children written by R. L. Stine (10)
37 Text written in cipher or code (10)
38 The 19th Greek letter (3)
39 A type of puzzle which uses pictures to represent words, names or parts of words (5)
43 Spring-flowering woodland plant also called wild hyacinth (8)
45 The first concerto of Vivaldi's *The Four Seasons* (6)
46 Germanic goddess associated with Easter (6)
49 Item studied and collected by a philatelist (5)
50 Easter __; imaginary creature said to deliver 29 across to children (5)
53 Structure such as a drey, nide, sett or vespiary (4)
54 Ancient town in Galilee where Christ is said to have performed his first miracle by changing water into wine (4)
55 Sovereign's __; part of the Crown Jewels (3)

Simnel

12

Palm Sunday.

Dodds

encryption cry

best Agamemnon

Verne

D'

Palendrom

13

Across

1 The Roman god of water and the sea with the Greek counterpart Poseidon (7)

5 Vast region of Russia extending between the Ural Mountains and the Pacific Ocean, once a traditional place of exile (7)

9 The first name of the group leader in William Golding's 1954 novel *Lord of the Flies* (5)

12 *A Fish Called __*; 1988 comedy film starring John Cleese, Jamie Lee Curtis and Michael Palin (5)

13 Musician's device that produces regular ticking sounds to indicate the exact tempo of a piece of music (9)

14 In astronomy, the point of a celestial sphere diametrically opposite to the zenith (5)

15 A past or present member of the school for boys founded by Henry VI around 600 years ago (7)

16 In cricket, a ball bowled so that it bounces on the popping crease, directly under the bat (6)

17 Plant in the Apiaceae family; a stalk of which was worn on the lapel of the fifth incarnation of the Doctor portrayed by Peter Davison (6)

18 Market town in Staffordshire on the River Churnet (4)

20 Small breed of dog typically produced by crossing a greyhound with a terrier or a spaniel (7)

22 Ancient Chinese martial art and system of armed or unarmed combat resembling karate (4,2)

27 The largest country in Central America, capital city Managua (9)

28 Chemical compound formed by condensing an alcohol with an acid while eliminating water (5)

29 Group of typically three or more notes sounded simultaneously as the basis of a harmony (5)

30 Political system or other power structure governed by a small number of people (9)

31 US aviator nicknamed "Slim" and "The Lone Eagle" who made the first solo transatlantic flight in a single-engined monoplane (9)

36 English name of the Italian explorer who sailed from Bristol in search of Asia but landed on the mainland of North America (5)

37 Small dwelling at the gates of a stately home, occupied by its gardener or caretaker (5)

39 City on the River Tyne with the Premier League football club nicknamed "The Magpies" (9)

40 US pop artist noted for his series of 32 *Campbell's Soup Cans* canvases (6)

42 Fish used in the dish kedgeree (7)

43 Monetary unit of the Philippines (4)

46 Middle Eastern country which lies on junction of three continents (6)

48 Circular pen for cattle or horses (6)

50 Italian dish of arborio rice cooked in broth until creamy, served with seafood and/or vegetables (7)

53 African mammal in the Equidae family, each individual having a unique pattern of stripes (5)

54 Alternative term for a garment bought "ready-to-wear" (3-3-3)

55 Mayonnaise-like Spanish sauce or dip flavoured with garlic (5)

56 Musical composition with a recurring principal theme, typically in the final movement of a sonata (5)

57 Greek mountain once believed to be the home of the 12 greater gods (7)

58 Three-pronged spear of 1 across (7)

Down

1 Island country, slightly bigger than Great Britain but with a population of around 4 million (3,7)

2 North American term for a piebald horse or pony (5)

3 The muse of astronomy (6)

4 King of England with the cognomen "Ironside" who was one of the sons of Æthelred the Unready (6)

5 Indonesian and Malaysian dish of pieces of marinated meat grilled or barbecued on skewers, served with a peanut-based spicy sauce (5)

6 A person who writes a written account of an individual's life (10)

7 Twenty-sixth president of the US who was awarded the 1906 Nobel Peace Prize for his part in ending the Russo-Japanese War (9)

8 Genus of trees and shrubs commonly called maple (4)

9 Form of French poetry with 10 or 13 lines based on two rhymes (7)

10 Vessel used to transport molten metal in a foundry (5)

11 Musical instrument with strings sounded by a turning wheel (5-5)

13

19 King Arthur's legendary sword (9)

21 Conservative politician who served as prime minister from 1970-74 (5)

23 A thin crepe-like material named after a French dressmaker (9)

24 "Tyger, tyger, burning __ In the forests of the night, What immortal hand or eye Could frame thy fearful symmetry?" William Blake (6)

25 Chinese-style appetiser of meat or chopped vegetables wrapped in a pancake and deep fried (3,4)

26 Small tool for boring holes (7)

29 Roman general who was murdered on the Ides of March in a conspiracy led by Brutus and Cassius (6)

32 Relating to or denoting a classical Greek order of architecture characterised by volutes on either side of the capital (5)

33 Franco-German theologian and philosopher who was awarded the 1952 Nobel Peace Prize (10)

34 The collective audience of a newspaper or magazine (10)

35 A person who studies prison management (10)

38 Predatory insect also called devil's darning needle (9)

41 Herb in the mint family (7)

44 English footballer who was the first player to make more than 100 appearances for his country (6)

45 Founder of the Ottoman Empire (5,1)

47 Batman's sidekick also known as "The Boy Wonder" (5)

49 Constellation between Centaurus and Scorpius depicting the wolf (5)

51 A choice cut of steak (1-4)

52 Han __; character in *Star Wars* with the wookiee companion Chewbacca (4)

Uranis Dali

13

Pinto Pinky

oligarch Toll brogue

readership Newcastle

Denge Tch Lyndburg

grossamer

Rabat

14

Across

1   Author born in The Hague who wrote the 2002 novel *The Crimson Petal and the White* (5)

4   Trick-taking card game for four players similar to ombre; also a square dance for four couples in five movements (9)

9   Spring-flowering plant in the lily family, extensively sold in the markets of Amsterdam (5)

12   Pseudonym of the French dramatist Jean-Baptiste Poquelin, who developed many of the stock characters for Commedia dell'arte (7)

13   Inconspicuous constellation in the southern hemisphere bordering Grus, Pavo, Sagittarius, Telescopium and Tucana (5)

14   The working area of a computer screen where the icons and windows are displayed (7)

15   Fictional land created by English novelist Anthony Hope in which his adventure stories *The Prisoner of Zenda* and *Rupert of Hentzau* are based (9)

16   Common name of a poisonous woodland plant in the spurge family, similar to Good King Henry (4,7)

17   Italian game similar to boules (5)

18   The capital and largest city of Rhode Island, founded in 1636 as a religious exile and haven from the Massachusetts Bay Colony (10)

19   Greek founder of the Stoic school of philosophy (4)

21   The US Hawkeye State (4)

23   Type of fibre obtained from the leaves of the abacá plant, used to make envelopes and paper (6,4)

27   Vice-admiral who helped defeat the Spanish Armada and, in his ship the *Golden Hind*, was the first Englishman to circumnavigate the globe (5)

29   Emperor who divided the Roman Empire between himself in the east and Maximian in the west (10)

31   Personification of a feminine ideal of the late 19th century, depicted by the illustrator of the novels in 15 across (6,4)

34   Protagonist in 1 across, played by actress Romola Garai in a recent television adaptation (5)

35   Another term for vermilion (7,3)

36   Small white patch on the muzzle of a horse or pony (4)

38   Large groups of kangaroos (4)

40 English name of the evergreen coniferous tree in the genus *Pseudotsuga*, cultivated for timber (7,3)

44 US businessman and food manufacturer who devised the "57 Varieties" slogan (5)

47 Arm of the Indian Ocean between India, Myanmar and Thailand (3,2,6)

48 Technical drawing instrument in the shape of a right-angled triangle (3,6)

51 In geology, the natural process of rock, soil or sediment being gradually worn down by water or wind (7)

52 The aft edge of a sail (5)

53 Rare chemical element, atomic number 75, named after one of the longest rivers in Europe (7)

54 Special edition of a newspaper (5)

55 Soldier of the 7th British Armoured Division who served in the North African campaign of 1940–43 and wore the jerboa insignia (6,3)

56 Variety of wheat used in health food products (5)

Down

1 The longest and largest bone of the human body (5)

2 A type of belt or holster for a sword, bugle or drum, worn over one shoulder and extending to the opposite hip (7)

3 English spelling of the German who is credited with the discovery of X-rays, for which he was awarded the first ever Nobel Prize in Physics (8)

4 Hand mill for grinding corn (5)

5 Musical terminology indicating a piece must be performed in a restless or spasmodic manner (7)

6 Species of migratory butterfly with a fondness for buddleia nectar (3,7)

7 Italian dish of meat or vegetables baked with a cheese sauce, layered between sheets of pasta (7)

8 Of a disease or condition, regularly found among a particular people or in a certain district (7)

9 In the Jewish calendar, the first month of the civil year and seventh of the ecclesiastical (6)

10 Leaf vegetable with the cultivars butterhead, cos and romaine (7)

11 1960 Paul Anka song that was revived by Donny Osmond in 1972 (5,4)

17 Scottish engineer who invented the first practical television (5)

18 Generic name for a synthetic material such as nylon or PVC (7)

14

20 According to Norse mythology, the chief god and creator, ruler of Aesir (4)

22 The __ Trousers; 1993 Aardman Animations production featuring Wallace and Gromit (5)

24 City on the Japanese island Kyushu, noted for a style of highly-decorative porcelain (5)

25 Size of typewriter letter allowing 12 letters to the inch (5)

26 French microbiologist who invented a system to partially sterilise foods (7)

28 1979 sci-fi horror movie directed by Ridley Scott (5)

30 "You can muffle the drum, and you can loosen the strings of the __, but who shall command the skylark not to sing?" Kahlil Gibran (4)

32 US actress and singer who starred in The Wedding Planner and Maid in Manhattan (5)

33 A type of variable bicycle gear (10)

34 Musical note with a time value equal to two minims or four crotchets (9)

37 Tudor mansion in Buckinghamshire which serves as the country residence of the Prime Minister (8)

39 The captain of Yorkshire County Cricket Club from 1971–78 (7)

41 A mythological sea nymph (7)

42 Protective eyewear for swimming (7)

43 World champion chess player from 1972-75 (7)

45 1971 song by John Lennon (7)

46 The second-largest continent (6)

49 Fortune-telling cards with the suits swords, cups, coins and wands (5)

50 Regional dialect for an ant (5)

14

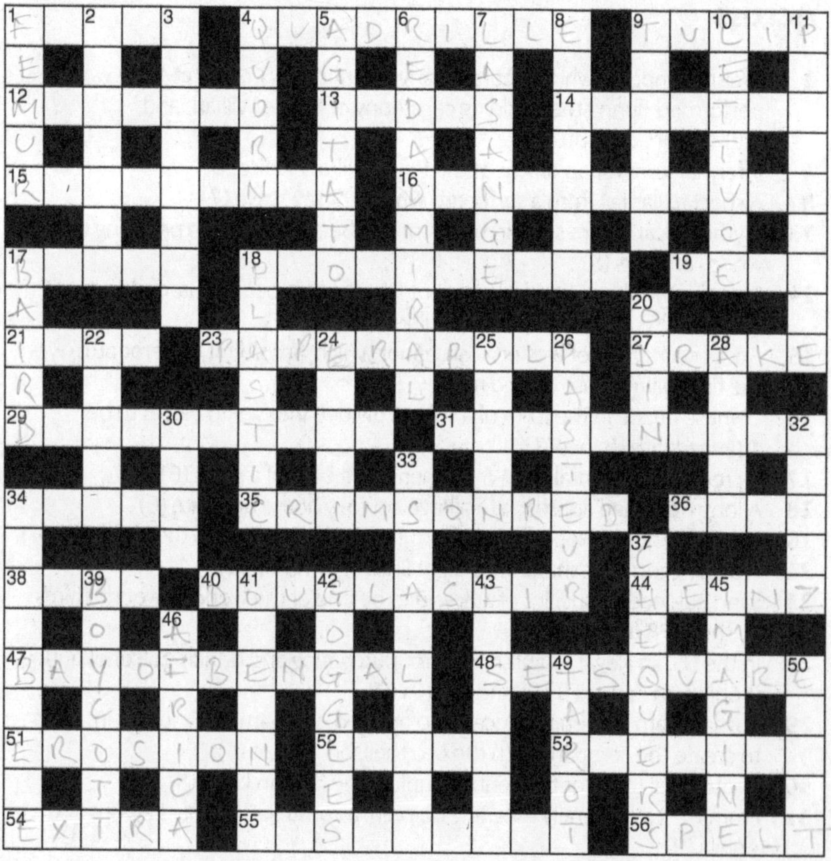

15

Across

1 Welsh composer whose choral arrangement of *Ubi Caritas et Amor* was performed during the wedding ceremony of Prince William and Catherine Middleton (6)

4 Informal term for an officer of the Royal Military Police (6)

8 A spectacular fall from a surfboard whilst riding a wave (7)

13 Mythological nature spirit in the form of a beautiful maiden presiding over woods or rivers (5)

14 Rare silvery-white chemical element, atomic number 46, named after an asteroid discovered by Heinrich Wilhelm Olbers (9)

15 Ancient kingdom of western Asia Minor which, according to Herodotus, was the first realm to use coined money (5)

16 Chinese puzzle in the form of a square divided into seven pieces to be arranged into shapes (7)

17 A creeping horizontal stem or runner at the base of a plant (6)

18 A long tree-lined approach to a large country house or estate (6)

19 River of central Europe flowing from the Czech Republic to the North Sea (4)

21 A plane geometric shape with eight lines of symmetry (7)

23 Sand eel-feeding species of auk said to be one of the world's favourite birds by the RSPB (6)

28 In the US, an illegal establishment for purchasing and drinking alcohol during Prohibition in the 1920s and 1930s (9)

29 Russian-born US film producer who merged with Samuel Goldwyn in 1924 to create the company with the Leo the Lion mascot (5)

30 Anatomical term for the central trunk of the human body (5)

31 From the Latin literally meaning dolphin, a constellation near Pegasus and Aquila (9)

32 Informal term for birdwatching (9)

38 Common name for any tree or shrub in the *Acer* genus; a leaf of which features on the national flag of Canada (5)

40 English town where the Derby and Oaks have been hosted annually since 1779/80 (5)

42 __ *Dogs*; 1992 Quentin Tarantino crime movie with the characters Mr Pink, Mr White and Mr Orange (9)

43 Europe's northernmost country (6)

44 Rich bread confection in the form of a small roll made with large quantities of butter and eggs (7)

45 __ David's; large breed of deer, formerly a native of China but now found only in captivity (4)

48 German social scientist and political philosopher who wrote *The Condition of the Working Class in England in 1844* (6)

50 Literary term for the west wind (6)

52 Optical phenomena caused by atmospheric conditions (7)

55 English journalist and television presenter who hosted *The Clothes Show* with designer Jeff Banks (5)

56 2004 comedy film starring Will Ferrell and Christina Applegate (9)

57 *The* __; 1947 novella by John Steinbeck based on the characters Kino, Juana and Coyotito (5)

58 Variety of rich and creamy white sauce served with chicken (7)

59 Sportswear company named after an antelope (6)

60 Third-largest moon of Neptune (6)

Down

1 The doctrine or belief in the existence of one god (10)

2 Largest and capital city of Jordan (5)

3 *The* __; 2001 psychological thriller starring Nicole Kidman (6)

5 Saxophonist associated with James Brown and Van Morrison, nicknamed "Pee Wee" (5)

6 Distinctive heraldic bearings of a person, family or country (4,2,4)

7 The study of language and its historical development (9)

8 Muggle-__; fictional monkey character in some of the children's stories written by Roald Dahl (4)

9 Track and field event contested at the Olympic Games since 1896 by men and 2000 by women (4,5)

10 Town in Utah settled by Mormons in the 1840s (5)

11 An organised association of employees formed to protect and further their common interests (5,5)

12 Another term for sea foam (5)

20 The common name for an apiarist or apiculturist (9)

22 Large semi-aquatic rodent also known as a swamp beaver (5)

24 Lively Provençal dance for dancers joined by hands in a long chain (9)

25   The captain of a curling team (4)

26   Name of the series of NASA space programmes designed to investigate Mars, Venus and Mercury in the 1960s and 1970s (7)

27   "Fie, foh, and fum, I smell the blood of a __ man." *King Lear*: Act III, Scene 4 (7)

33   English couturier noted for introducing the bustle (5)

34   Stringed instrument which is used as the corporate logo for Guinness stout (4)

35   Literary assistant who takes dictation or copies manuscripts (10)

36   Firearm with an unrifled barrel (10)

37   Dish consisting of a medley of tomatoes, kalamata olives, feta cheese, red onion and cucumber (5,5)

39   Ornamental shoulder piece on the coat or jacket of a military uniform (9)

41   *A __ Named Desire*; Pulitzer Prize-winning play by Tennessee Williams (9)

46   Botanical term for a catkin (5)

47   Variety of frothy-topped iced coffee drink, popular in Greece (6)

49   Small number of galaxies within close proximity of one other (5)

51   Codeword used in radio communication between Quebec and Sierra (5)

53   English amateur cricketer nicknamed "The Doctor" who scored 54,896 runs in his career (5)

54   1980 musical film with the characters Doris Finsecker, Coco Hernandez and Leroy Johnson (4)

15

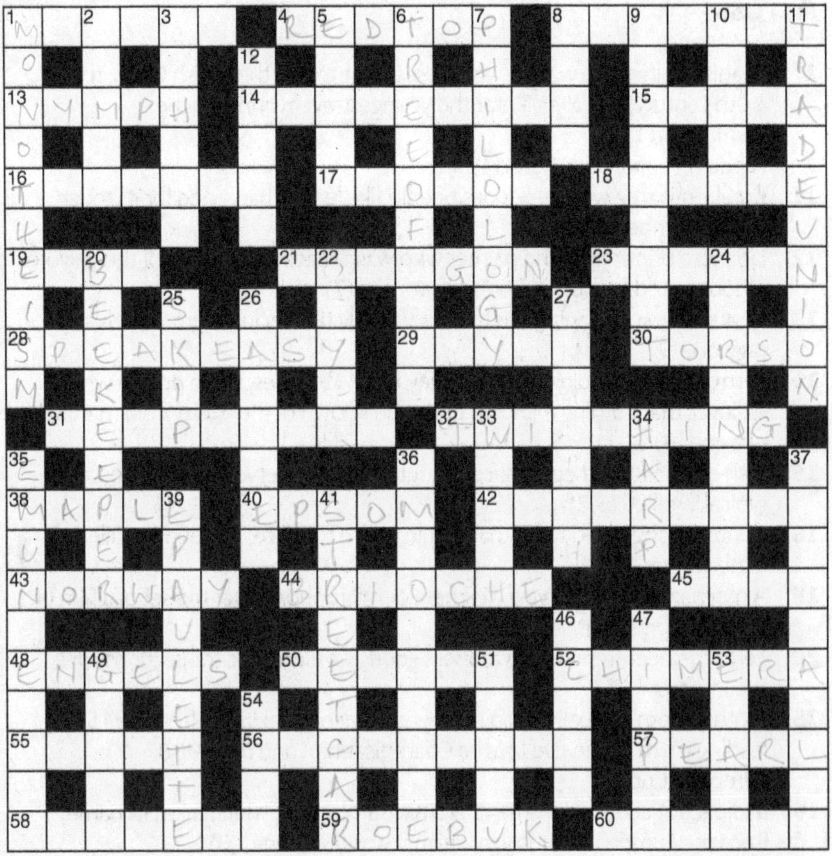

Across

1 Spanish golfer who was the youngest player to win the British Open in the 20th century, and a year later the youngest-ever winner of the US Masters (11)

7 Leader of a marching band (4,5)

11 Coniferous tree with deciduous needle-like leaves, harvested for its tough, durable timber (5)

12 Japanese printmaker and painter who was a leading exponent of the ukiyo-e school, noted for his depictions of women (7)

13 Genus of flowering plants in the daisy family that includes groundsels and ragworts (7)

14 Term coined by biologist T. H. Huxley in 1869 to describe a person who believes that nothing is known or can be known of the existence or nature of a god (8)

15 Dish of a savoury cheese sauce flavoured with ale served hot over toast, typically grilled (5,7)

16 Genus of long-tailed terrestrial reptile native to Africa, sometimes called a rainbow lizard (5)

18 A mechanical arm carrying a camera or microphone over the set of a film or television programme (4)

20 Term for an entrepreneur who sells goods via electronic transactions over the internet (1-6)

25 Scottish-born footballer who managed Manchester United from 1945-69, leading them to win five League Championships and the 1968 European Cup (5)

26 Radioactive chemical element, atomic number 87, which takes its name from the European country in which it was discovered (8)

27 Fish of Atlantic coastal waters commonly called a porgy (4)

31 ___ chicken; dish of poultry served in a mayonnaise-based sauce flavoured with curry powder, raisins and chopped apricots (10)

32 A stadium for horse and chariot racing in Ancient Greece and Rome (10)

34 Aromatic culinary herb with greyish-green velvety leaves, used in stuffing mixes for meat (4)

35 SI base unit of mass equal to approximately 2.205 lb (8)

36 Japanese dish of cold vinegared rice and raw seafood wrapped in nori, typically accompanied by wasabi or soy sauce (5)

39 Italian director and screenwriter whose major films include *La Strada* and *La Dolce Vita* (7)

40 Austrian chemist noted for his work on rare earth elements (4)

41 Monetary unit of Denmark and Norway, equal to 100 øre (5)

45 Ancient inscribed granite stela discovered near an arm of the Nile, that was used to decipher Egyptian hieroglyphs (7,5)

48 Orchestral prelude to an opera, oratorio or play (8)

51 Eastern European country with a blue and yellow national flag (7)

52 Small flute pitched an octave higher than the ordinary one (7)

53 Term for the two on playing cards or dice; also a throw of two at dice (5)

54 Nazi concentration camp that was near the Polish town Oswiecim, which claimed up to 1.5 million lives during the Second World War (9)

55 Country with the capital and largest city Riyadh (5,6)

Down

1 Narrative song or poem in short stanzas, often with unknown authorship (6)

2 Austrian zoologist who shared the 1973 Nobel Prize in Physiology or Medicine with Nikolaas Tinbergen and Karl von Frisch for discoveries in social behaviour patterns (6)

3 From the Greek meaning "character", the distinctive spirit of a culture or an era (5)

4 Soft metallic element of the lanthanide series, atomic number 69, used in portable X-ray devices (7)

5 Quantity of 500 sheets of paper (4)

6 1939 John Ford Western movie starring John Wayne as The Ringo Kid and Claire Trevor as Dallas (10)

7 The __; US rock band remembered for songs including *Light My Fire*, *Break on Through* and *People are Strange* (5)

8 Dutch painter who co-founded the De Stijl art movement (8)

9 Hebrew patriarch who tricked his brother Esau into selling him his birthright and wrestled with God (5)

10 Red-skinned cultivar of potato suitable for boiling, mashing, baking and steaming (7)

13 One of the Home Counties (6)

17 Country on the northern coast of South America (6)

16

19 Literally meaning "miller's wife", fish coated in flour and fried in butter, served with lemon juice and parsley (8)

21 Team sport played with long-handled netted sticks (8)

22 Primitive counting frame (6)

23 A type of bar used to separate panes of glass in cabinet-making (8)

24 Common name of the genus of shrubs *Chaenomeles* (8)

26 Term for each one of the goddesses Clotho, Lachesis and Atropos (4)

28 Abstract or summary of a speech (6)

29 Unsolicited email messages sent in bulk indiscriminately (4)

30 Inventor who said: "I haven't failed, I've found 10,000 ways that don't work" (6)

33 Polish astronomer who produced a workable model of the solar system in which the planets orbited in perfect circles around the sun (10)

37 Actress remembered for her role as Lola in *The Blue Angel* (8)

38 Roman procurator of Judaea who authorised the crucifixion of Jesus (6)

39 Roman goddess of good luck (7)

42 Meat-filled envelopes of pasta (7)

43 Residential district adjoining a city (6)

44 Tutor and adviser of Nero (6)

46 All __; liquorice confections formerly marketed with the catchphrase: "One too many and you might turn Bertie" (5)

47 Birthstone of November (5)

49 Charles __; *Brideshead* character (5)

50 Food made from soy bean curd (4)

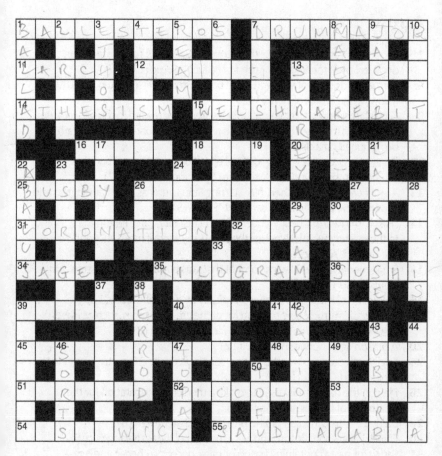

16

ream   Jacob

muse
R   Snake   Coronation
                                  resume
                            margin
        white   white
                                   uranium
                    Flavia
                              mae babes

Across

1   Speech therapist who successfully treated George VI for his stammer, depicted by actor Geoffrey Rush in *The King's Speech* (5)

4   Former gold coin that was worth one pound sterling, first minted in 1489 following the orders of Henry VII (9)

9   Greek fabulist and slave who, after being freed as a reward for his wit, took up residence in the court of King Croesus and was later condemned to death by being hurled off a cliff (5)

12 Relating to or denoting the geological epoch of the Tertiary period that extended from around 23.3 million to 5.3 million years ago (7)

13 *A __ at Oxford*; 1940 short film starring Stan Laurel as Lord Paddington and Oliver Hardy as his valet nicknamed "Fatty" (5)

14 "Heigh, my hearts! Cheerly, cheerly, my hearts! Yare, yare! Take in the ___. Tend to the master's whistle. Blow, till thou burst thy wind, if room enough!" *The Tempest*: Act I, Scene 1 (7)

15 Small medieval lute-like instrument that was popular with minstrels and troubadours (7)

16 Catalogue of musical recordings, typically by a specific artist (11)

17 Large-scale musical composition for orchestra and voices, such as Haydn's *The Creation* and *The Seasons,* and Handel's *Messiah* (8)

20 A person aged between 80-89 (12)

24 English athlete who was the first person to break the 18 metre barrier in the triple jump (7)

26 Plant in the daisy family used to make a medicinal preparation for the treatment of bruises and sprains (6)

28 Capital of the Canadian prairie province Saskatchewan (6)

30 French painter and theorist who was a member of the Les Nabis group (5)

31 Sauce for pasta containing bacon or ham, pecorino cheese and eggs, typically enriched with cream (9)

32 In Welsh literature, a group of three compositions, stories or sayings about related subjects (5)

33 1987 horror novel by Stephen King with the psychopathic character Annie Wilkes (6)

35 Piece of land where grapes or other crops are cultivated (6)

36 An uncooked fillet of pickled herring wrapped around slices of onion and gherkin (7)

39 Organic compound which, according to the Atkins Diet, must be eaten in small quantities (12)

41 English physician who was the first woman to gain both a medical qualification in Britain and a BMA membership (8)

44 Complex substance such as RNA and DNA, essential for life (7,4)

47 Taxonomic category ranking between domain and phylum (7)

50 Member of the oldest university in England and second-oldest surviving university in the world (7)

51 The final decision or judgment by an arbitrator (5)

52 Spanish artist noted for the oil paintings *Les Demoiselles d'Avignon*, *Guernica* and *The Weeping Woman* (7)

53 Long-legged fish-eating wading bird noted for sitting motionless for considerable amounts of time (5)

54 Wing-like structure mounted below the hull of a boat, used to raise it from the water as it increases in speed (9)

55 Russian revolutionary who served as the first premier of the Soviet Union (5)

Down

1 Variety of sedimentary rock mainly composed of calcium carbonate (9)

2 The US Peach State; also a country on the eastern shore of the Black Sea (7)

3 Equestrian competition whose three-day form consists of dressage, cross-country and showjumping (5)

4 Unit of volume equal to one cubic metre, used for timber (5)

5 Wild relative of the llama native to high grassland areas of the Andes (6)

6 A thick disc of beef, a slice of bread or one complete sandwich (5)

7 Artistic technique where paint or pigment is applied thickly to a surface to create a raised texture (7)

8 Chemical element which forms over 98 per cent of the atmosphere of Saturn's largest moon, Titan (8)

9 Artificial substance used as a sugar substitute which is around 200 times sweeter than sucrose (9)

10 Music teacher who founded the English Folk Dance Society in 1911 (5)

11 Classic children's novel written by Eleanor Hodgman Porter (9)

18 The violet-scented rootstock of *Iris germanica* and *Iris florentina*, used in perfumery (5)

19 Any one of a class of living creatures representing over 90 per cent of the life forms on earth (6)

21 Speech sound other than a vowel (9)

22 Second-densest of the elements (7)

23 Marshal of the RAF nicknamed "Bomber" who organised mass raids against German cities which resulted in large-scale civilian casualties (6)

25 Berkshire town near Eton (7)

27 French couturière noted for the "little black dress" (6)

29 US poet and novelist who wrote *All the King's Men*, for which he was awarded the 1947 Pulitzer Prize for Fiction (6)

32 Net-like textile used for veils (5)

33 Brand of various lines of personal computers designed and developed by Apple Inc. (9)

34 __ ridgeback; breed of dog originally developed to hunt lions (9)

37 *Commedia dell'arte* character (9)

38 Mythical Greek hero, son of Clio (8)

40 Cliff __; the stage name of the singer born Harry Rodger Peavoy Webb in 1940 (7)

42 Married name of Wallis Warfield before she married Edward VIII (7)

43 Brand of motorised sledge (3-3)

45 Collective group of singers (5)

46 Constellation said to represent the dragon killed by Hercules (5)

48 Site of the highest mountain on earth above sea level (5)

49 A type of transfer designed to be applied to porcelain or glass (5)

Event

mammoth
choir
ensemble

vinery
repertoise

18

Across

1   Johannesburg-born batsman who is the current captain of England's Test cricket team (7)
5   The most populous African country, capital city Abuja (7)
8   Common name of a shrub in the olive family bearing highly-fragrant flowers in spring, genus *Syringa* (5)
11 Giant Boeotian huntsman of Greek mythology who was slain by Artemis and placed in the sky as a constellation (5)
12 Rich cream-based soup or stew typically made with clams, corn, diced potatoes and onion (7)
14 System of rules governing language, consisting of syntax, morphology, phonology and semantics (7)
15 Major river which rises in Staffordshire and flows to the Ouse forming the Humber estuary (5)
16 A type of upper-storey bay window, typical in neo-Gothic architecture (5)
17 The scientific study of rocks (9)
18 Cuban president who survived 638 assassination attempts by the CIA (6)
19 Card game also known as blackjack or pontoon (6-3)
22 Single sheet of postage stamps (4)
26 Pen name of the English novelist born Mary Mackay who wrote *Thelma, Barabbas* and *The Sorrows of Satan* (7)
28 Small savoury pancake-like food cooked on a griddle, typically eaten toasted and buttered (7)
30 Czech novelist who wrote in German whose most notable works were published posthumously (5)
32 Member of vitamin B complex found in milk, leafy green vegetables and eggs, essential for promoting growth in children (10)
34 Parapet at the top of a castle (10)
36 Any one of a network of filaments responsible for transmitting electrochemical impulses to the brain and spinal cord (5)
37 Mythological musician and poet who could move inanimate objects by playing his lyre (7)
38 One of the largest river systems in South America, rising in Venezuela and flowing into the South Atlantic Ocean (7)
40 Semicircular or polygonal recess in a cathedral or church (4)
41 The capital city of Laos (9)

18

43 Common name of a flowering woodland plant in the mint family also called self-heal and lamb's ears (6)
47 Italian conductor of the New York Philharmonic Orchestra from 1926–36 who was later the music director of the NBC Symphony Orchestra (9)
50 Claw of a bird of prey (5)
52 Flowering plant in the genus *Primula* resembling a cross between a cowslip and a primrose (5)
54 Dutch humanist and theologian who wrote *The Praise of Folly* and *Handbook of a Christian Knight* (7)
55 Point at which a spacecraft in orbit is furthest from the moon (7)
56 Poet who wrote: "Season of mists and mellow fruitfulness! Close bosom-friend of the maturing sun; Conspiring with him how to load and bless With fruit the vines that round the thatch-eaves run" (5)
57 Professional Spanish tennis player nicknamed the King of the Clay (5)
58 The solid most dense part of a comet's head (7)
59 Greek epic poem traditionally ascribed to Homer (7)

Down

1 Member of a youth organisation founded by Robert Baden-Powell (5)
2 __ *of the Lost Ark*; 1981 adventure movie starring Harrison Ford as Indiana Jones (7)
3 "Murder most foul, as in the best it is; but this most foul, strange and __." *Hamlet*: Act I, Scene 5 (9)
4 Mathematical instrument also known as a proportional compass (6)
5 The mother-in-law of Ruth in the Old Testament (5)
6 Chemical element in the lanthanide series, atomic number 64 (10)
7 The characteristic language or jargon of a particular group (5)
8 Vast tropical grassland plain to the east of the Andes whose major river is 38 Across (6)
9 West Indian dance involving contorting the body backwards to pass under a progressively-lowering horizontal bar (5)
10 Historian who wrote extensively about the French Revolution (7)
13 English painter and proponent of op art noted for *Movement in Squares* (5)
18 US rock and roll singer-songwriter remembered for *Summertime Blues* (7)
20 Domed Native American hut (7)

18

21 System of symbols used to represent elements in areas such as music, mathematics or chess (8)

23 Variety of cheese-based sauce (7)

24 Form of tubular pasta (8)

25 The largest and most northerly island of the Inner Hebrides (4)

27 Welsh pirate nicknamed Black Bart, said to have captured over 470 ships (7)

29 Nobel Peace Prize-winning statesman who served as the 14th prime minister of Canada (7)

31 Civil rights leader whose profile was depicted on US dollar coins (7)

33 Ridge on the fingerboard of a guitar (4)

35 Mineral also called bloodstone (10)

39 Team game played by skaters with sticks and a puck (3,6)

40 Mythological Greek hunter who was turned into a stag (7)

42 Monetary unit of 5 Across (5)

44 French city on the Loire River (7)

45 Warm-blooded vertebrate such as a bat, cat, whale or human (6)

46 Goldsmith character in Shakespeare's *The Comedy of Errors* (6)

48 Member of a group of Scandinavian poets (5)

49 Norwegian playwright whose notable works include *The Master Builder*, *Peer Gynt* and *A Doll's House* (5)

51 French gold coin that was introduced in 1640 and replaced by the franc in 1795 (5)

53 English theologian who was a leader of the Oxford Movement (5)

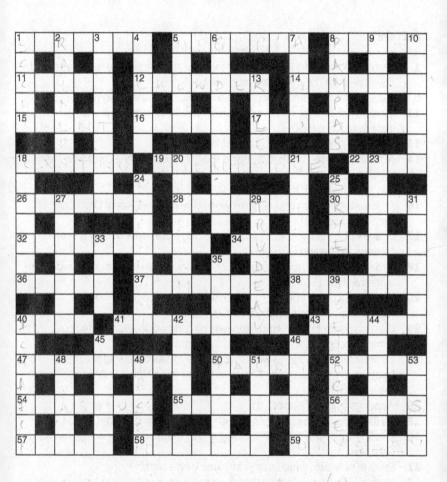

19

Across

1 German-born Nobel Prize-winning theoretical physicist who formulated and developed the theory of general relativity (8)

5 State capital of California, located on the river with the same name (10)

12 Landlocked country bordered by China and India with the prime minister Jhala Nath Khanal (5)

13 One of six children born at a single birth (9)

14 Actor who starred as Rhett Butler in the 1939 epic movie *Gone with the Wind* (5)

15 *The __ in the Rye*; 1951 novel by J. D. Salinger (7)

16 Athenian statesman and lawgiver who reformed the laws of Draco; one of the Seven Sages (5)

17 Village in Cambridgeshire; also a variety of cheese made in only three counties in England (7)

18 Bird of the order Charadriiformes comprising plovers, sandpipers, snipes and oystercatchers (5)

20 Film production company founded in 1912 by Hungarian-born nickelodeon owner Adolph Zukor (9)

24 German poet of the 19th century whose early works were set to music by composers Robert Schumann and Franz Schubert (5)

26 US president who, for his work involving negotiations to end the Russo-Japanese War, became the first American to win a Nobel Prize in any category (9)

28 A species of yucca plant (5,6)

29 1988 comedy film starring Arnold Schwarzenegger and Danny DeVito (5)

30 The Scandinavian hammer-wielding god of thunder and lightning, son of Odin (4)

31 Satellite of Saturn which shares its name with a bird (4)

33 Musical direction indicating that an instrument or voice must remain silent during a particular section (5)

36 Novel by Louisa May Alcott about the lives of the fictional sisters Amy, Beth, Jo and Meg March (6,5)

38 Type of botanical garden devoted to shrubs and trees (9)

40 Common name of a plant in the rose family which includes the species herb bennet, genus *Geum* (5)

41 Town in Kent on the River Medway noted for its Norman castle (9)

42 Astrological sign of a person born between August 23 and September 23, ruled by the planet Mercury (5)

43 Liverpool-born novelist who wrote *The Siege of Krishnapur*, for which he was awarded the 1973 Booker Prize for Fiction (7)

46 Located on the Persian Gulf, one of the seven states of the United Arab Emirates (5)

49 Rectangular case-like bag with a shoulder strap, traditionally used to carry school books (7)

51 Browsing mammal living in the Democratic Republic of the Congo resembling a cross between a giraffe and a zebra (5)

52 Common name of an explosive prepared by saturating a fabric with nitric and sulphuric acids, also called flash paper (3,6)

53 English actor who starred in over 100 movies including *Lolita, 20,000 Leagues Under the Sea* and *Georgy Girl* (5)

54 A type of four-wheeled horse-drawn vehicle formerly used to carry passengers or mail (10)

55 German who founded a famous piano manufacturing firm in New York in 1853 (8)

Down

2 Data or code such as ASCII fed into a computer system (5)

3 Combustible non-metallic element, atomic number 16 (7)

4 Greek island in the Aegean Sea which is the largest of the Cyclades group (5)

5 Bony framework composed of the cranium and the mandible which encloses the encephalon (5)

6 A medicinal preparation of pot marigold flowers used to soothe minor cuts, grazes or scolds (9)

7 A district of the Cordillera Department in Paraguay between San Bernardino and Atyrá (5)

8 Large breed of gun dog with a predominantly white coat with black, grey or blueish points and markings (7,6)

9 Mountainous country known as the "roof of the world" (5)

10 Variety of highly-seasoned German sausage (either spelling) (10)

11 Literally meaning "miller's wife", fish served lightly browned in butter with lemon juice and parsley (8)

13 The first part of an Ancient Greek choral ode (7)

19

19 Poet known as "H. D." who was influenced by Ezra Pound, notable collections include *Sea Garden* and *Helen in Egypt* (9)

21 In mathematics, the quantitative relation between two amounts (5)

22 Old-fashioned beverage of honey fermented with water (4)

23 SI unit of magnetic flux density (5)

25 Flashing-light device on a motor vehicle activated by the driver to show one intends to change direction (9)

27 Genre of tuneful but undemanding popular music (4,9)

30 "He is a traitor; let him to the ___, And chop away that factious pate of his." *King Henry VI, Part II*: Act V, Scene 1 (5)

32 Bodily pump made up of the pericardium, myocardium and the endocardium (5)

34 Gin-based cocktail served with soda and a dash of lemon or lime (3,7)

35 Largest joint of the human body (4)

36 Game for two in which one person vaults over the back of a person who has assumed a crouching position (8)

37 Republic with the capital Skopje (9)

39 French philosopher awarded the 1927 Nobel Prize in Literature (7)

42 Compound such as retinol (7)

44 To cook meat with dry heat (5)

45 Word linking bomb and circuit (5)

47 Composer of *Israel Symphony* (5)

48 Rhythmical or metrical stress (5)

50 Shade-tolerant lily-like plant, much loved by slugs (5)

The Telegraph

20

Across

1 English painter remembered for his depictions of sporting scenes and horses, notably *Whistlejacket* (6)

4 Nocturnal bird resembling a cross between a cuckoo and a kestrel which, according to legend, steals milk from goats (8)

9 The collective noun for a group of goldfinches (5)

13 Country in North Africa which has one of the largest proven oil reserves in the world (5)

14 Fast-moving non-stinging predatory insect, typically with iridescent wings and a brilliantly-coloured body (9)

15 Silicate mineral naturally occurring in a wide range of colours; the traditional birthstone for November (5)

16 *The __ Cat*; short story by Rudyard Kipling about a polo match set in British colonial India (7)

17 A type of fine worsted yarn used for tapestry and embroidery (6)

18 US state with the capital Carson City, largely consisting of desert (6)

19 Inert gaseous element, atomic number 10, discovered in 1898 by Scottish chemist Sir William Ramsay (4)

21 Official residence of an ambassador, also called a diplomatic mission (7)

23 "Thou know'st that all my fortunes are at sea; Neither have I money nor commodity to raise a present sum: therefore go forth; Try what my credit can in ___ do." Shakespeare (6)

28 In ballet, a move in which a dancer raises one of their legs above their waist in a vertical position (9)

29 Member of a body of trained assassins in feudal Japan, skilled in the art of espionage (5)

30 A fabric woven with a pattern of diagonal parallel ribs, such as chino, denim or tweed (5)

31 Italian operatic composer noted for his tragedy *Lucia di Lammermoor* and his comedy *Don Pasquale* (9)

32 Common name for odontalgia (9)

37 English scientist who formulated the law of elasticity and is said to be one of the most neglected natural philosophers (5)

38 Taxonomic category ranking between family and genus (5)

40 2000 historical movie directed by Ridley Scott which stars Russell Crowe as the Roman general Maximus Decimus Meridius (9)

41 Long-handled tool with a blade for cutting grass or corn (6)

43 "I have had a perfectly wonderful ___, but this wasn't it." Groucho Marx (7)

44 Drury Lane comedienne and long-term mistress of King Charles II who was originally an orange-seller (4)

47 Fly-fishing feathers collectively; also a plume in a military headdress worn by a member of the Black Watch regiment or a 58 Across (6)

49 According to the Book of Genesis, the mountain on which Noah's Ark landed after the waters of the great flood receded (6)

51 French army officer who was falsely accused of providing military secrets to the Germans, placed in solitary confinement on Devil's Island and later exonerated (7)

54 English car manufacturer who made his name designing vehicles including the Silver Ghost with Charles Stewart Rolls (5)

55 Colourless flammable gas, used in welding due to the high temperature of the flame (9)

56 Popular street dance performed in Brazilian carnivals, especially in Rio de Janeiro (5)

57 Textile with a highly glossy surface, used to make evening gowns, ballet shoes and neckties (5)

58 Historically, a soldier armed with a light flintlock musket (8)

59 ___ the Great; king who saved southern England from Viking occupation and is credited with the foundation of the English Navy (6)

Down

1 Legendary lizard-like creature said to inhabit and endure fire (10)

2 A type of inflorescence characteristic of wild carrot, dill, fennel and parsley (5)

3 Style of jacket striped in the colours of a school or rowing club (6)

5 Biblical father of Jacob and Esau (5)

6 Music show hosted annually by Jools Holland (10)

7 The third president of the US (9)

8 The radial arms of a starfish (4)

9 Common name for chrysoberyl (4,3)

10 First letter of the Greek alphabet (5)

11 Variety of white Italian cheese popular as a pizza topping (10)

12 Latin phrase literally meaning "to the matter" (2,3)

20

20 The scientific study of bones (9)

22 Artist noted for *Water Lilies* (5)

24 Traditional dish of mutton or lamb cooked with potatoes and onions (5,4)

25 Mediterranean bitter-leaved plant in the chicory genus (6)

26 Square cap with three or four projections worn by Roman Catholic clergymen (7)

27 US inventor of photographic equipment including roll film (7)

30 Mythical Greek muse of comedy (6)

33 Keyboard wind instrument (5)

34 Chemical element which ignites spontaneously in air and glows in the dark, atomic number 15 (10)

35 Plant in the mint genus once used in folk medicine and tea infusions (10)

36 Television sports show that was originally presented by Peter Dimmock in 1958 (10)

39 City in northern Scotland situated on the mouth of the River Ness (9)

42 German painter and engraver noted for his *Dance of Death* woodcut and miniature *Anne of Cleves* (7)

45 The only species of poisonous snake found in Britain (5)

46 Astronomer and mathematician who determined the positions of more than 50,000 stars (6)

48 Vault beneath a church (5)

50 Any of the 29 administrative divisions of the Byzantine empire (5)

52 Bone responsible for articulating the hip and the knee (5)

53 Offspring of any bovine animal (4)

20

1 2 3 4 5 6 7 8 9 10 11
12
13 14 15
16 17 18
19 20 21 22 23 24
25 26 27
28 29 30
31 32 33
34 35 36
37 38 39 40
41 42 43 44
45 46
47 48 49 50 51 52
53
54 55 56
57 58 59

21

Across

1   Welsh-born journalist and explorer who was sent in search of David Livingstone in 1869, finding him two years later in Tanzania (7)

5   Pullein-___; any of three sisters who wrote a series of popular books for children including *Six Ponies, Janet Must Ride and The Lost Pony* (8)

9   Silvery-white, grey or pale green-coloured pliable mineral composed of hydrated magnesium silicate (4)

13   Superhuman-sized mythical being with great strength, appearing in fairy tales and folklore (5)

14   General term for a vigorously-climbing species of cottage garden rose with a mass of delicate clustered flowers throughout the summer (7)

15   1986 Oliver Stone Vietnam War film with the theme *Adagio for Strings* composed by Samuel Barber (7)

16   Crochet stitch made with three loops of yarn on the hook at a time; also a showjumping fence consisting of three elements (6)

17   Tailless amphibian which absorbs oxygen through its skin when submerged in water (4)

18   Flavoursome garnish consisting of chopped parsley, lemon zest and garlic, served drizzled over the veal dish osso buco (9)

20   Branch of science concerned with the bodily structure of living things (7)

21   A person skilled in the scientific study of plant life (8)

22   Danish Nobel Prize-winning physicist noted for his studies in atomic structure and quantum mechanics (4)

24   Hormone produced in the pancreas; a lack of which causes a form of diabetes (7)

26   An equilateral parallelogram (7)

29   Scottish architect whose notable works include the St Martin-in-the-Fields church near Trafalgar Square and Radcliffe Camera in Oxford (5)

31   Taxonomic category ranking above phylum (10)

33   Antibiotic discovered by Alexander Fleming in 1928 (10)

36   Community ___; set of cards in the standard London edition of Monopoly with directions such as: It is your birthday, collect £10 from each player (5)

37   County bordered by Cambridgeshire, Lincolnshire, Suffolk and The Wash; site of Sandringham House (7)

38   System of ropes and chains employed to support a ship's masts and extend the sails (7)

40 Historical term for a variety of fortified white wine imported into Britain from Spain and the Canary Islands (4)

42 Informal term for an ornithologist or a birdwatcher (8)

45 Protective wall or ditch built along the top of a trench to protect soldiers on the front line from enemy fire (7)

48 Science concerned with the properties of sound (9)

49 Type of shelter for birds, especially doves or pigeons (4)

51 King of the fairies and husband of Titania in Shakespeare's *A Midsummer Night's Dream* (6)

53 US city in the Great Lakes region, home of the General Motors, Ford and Chrysler headquarters (7)

54 Mythological daughter of King Minos who helped Theseus escape from the Minotaur's labyrinth (7)

55 Even-toed ungulate related to alpacas, guanacos and vicuñas (5)

56 Scottish neoclassical architect who designed Pulteney Bridge in Bath (4)

57 Profession of creating, regulating and blazoning coats of arms (8)

58 National emblem of Scotland (7)

Down

1 From the Latin literally meaning "archer", a constellation said to represent a centaur drawing a bow (11)

2 A type of poplar-lined promenade in Spanish-speaking countries (7)

3 Small bird of prey introduced to the UK in the 19th century, commonly spotted hunting and perching during daylight hours (6,3)

4 Unit of linear measure equal to 0.9144 metres (4)

5 Largest of the Lesser Sunda Islands (5)

6 Day of ___; in the Catholic Church, a day on which all are required to attend mass (10)

7 Flawless diamond of 100 carats or more, considered to be perfect (7)

8 ___ *Descending*; play by Tennessee Williams based on a modern account of the mythological husband of Eurydice (7)

10 Main ingredient of guacamole (7)

11 One of the largest constellations (9)

12 Irish figurative painter noted for his distorted depictions of human figures such as *Study after Velázquez's Portrait of Pope Innocent X* (5)

19 Colourless poisonous gas with a pungent almond-like odour (8)

21

21 British clothing manufacturer noted for green waxed jackets (7)
23 Tradename of a tangelo (4)
25 Mammal in the weasel family (5)
27 Term for a person who interrupts a conversation on a CB radio (7)
28 Footrests attached to a saddle (8)
30 Mild curry cooked and served in a pan with the same name (5)
32 Ninth letter of the Greek alphabet (4)
34 English nurse and medical reformer nicknamed the Lady with the Lamp (11)
35 German financier who founded a banking house in Frankfurt towards the end of the 18th century (10)
36 Mythological cursed prophetess (9)
39 Italian patriot and Risorgimento leader who played a key role in the establishment of a united kingdom of Italy (9)
41 European country with the capital and largest city Zagreb (7)
43 English RAF engineer who invented the turbojet aircraft engine (7)
44 A toasted or deep-fried Mexican tortilla or pancake typically topped with meat, beans, cheese and salsa (7)
46 Dessert served in a tall glass (7)
47 Style of silk cravat-like necktie with wide square ends (5)
50 Beverage consisting of spirits, hot water, sugar and sometimes spices (5)
52 Vertical slit in the lower part of a suit jacket or coat (4)

21

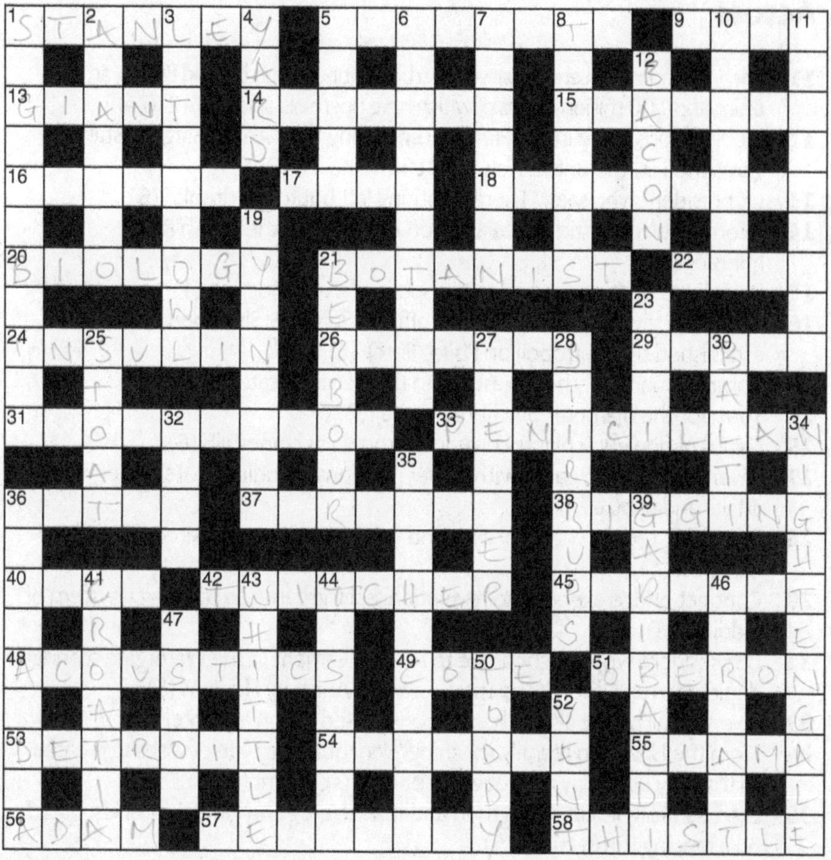

Across

11 *The* ___; name of a series of adventure books for children by Enid Blyton, an estimated 100 million copies of which have been sold since 1942 (6,4)

12 Mountainous route in the Hindu Kush linking Pakistan and Afghanistan, garrisoned by the British between 1839 and 1842 (6,4)

13 US president who said: "There's nothing left but to get drunk." (6)

14 Informal term for the official London residence of the British Prime Minister (6,3)

15 Perforated nozzle attached to the spout of a watering can (4)

16 Nickname given to a British police officer soon after Sir Robert Peel established the Metropolitan Police Force (5)

18 Common name of the largest city in the German state of Hesse (9)

21 Term for the diameter of a fibre or wire (5)

25 Genus of flowering plants commonly known as cranesbills (8)

27 Seven-a-side team game with player positions including goal shooter, wing attack and centre (7)

28 Burrowing rodent with tiny eyes and velvet-like fur, considered by many to be a pest (4)

29 Contract bridge expert who revolutionised the game by devising a system of bidding (10)

31 US president who resigned due to his involvement in the Watergate scandal, depicted in an Oliver Stone movie starring Anthony Hopkins (5)

33 A very small brook; also a channel constructed to convey water (4)

34 From the Hawaiian literally meaning "very quick", a type of website created so that any user may add, develop or edit its content (4)

35 Exercise designed to strengthen and tone the leg and gluteal muscles, based on a fencing thrust move (5)

37 Athletic contest based on five events, originally discus, javelin, jumping, running and wrestling (10)

38 *King* ___; 2005 Peter Jackson fantasy movie starring Naomi Watts and Jack Black, based on a gigantic ape-like monster (4)

39 One of the Leeward Islands, native name Wadadli (7)

41 Person who delivers a commentary accompanying a documentary or other broadcast (8)

43 Positively charged conductor through which electrons flow into an electrical device (5)

45 Side of a ship opposite port (9)

47 Japanese art of swordsmanship, practised with a bamboo weapon called a shinai (5)

50 Mythological Greek hero who fought against Troy in the *Iliad,* proverbial for his great size, strength and courage (4)

52 A red or blush wine produced from a variety of grapes chiefly grown in California (9)

55 NASA space telescope named after an astronomer noted for his studies and findings on the big bang theory, red shift and the Doppler effect (6)

57 Cambodian communist guerrilla movement which, under the leadership of Pol Pot, claimed the lives of around 2.5 million people between 1975-79 (5,5)

58 Low-pitched musical instrument in the clarinet family which features in Beethoven's work *The Creatures of Prometheus* (6,4)

Down

1 Adult male singing voice between bass and tenor (8)

2 Term for a male badger, hedgehog, guinea pig or 28 Across (4)

3 Ski resort in Colorado, originally founded as a mining camp (5)

4 Director of the movies *Hannibal Brooks, The Sentinel* and *The Big Sleep* (6)

5 The main stem of a stag's antler, an anchor or a plough (4)

6 Hebridean island connected to mainland Scotland by a road bridge (4)

7 1987 album by the English rock band Def Leppard with the tracks *Rocket, Animal* and *Love Bites* (8)

8 Alloy that was originally chiefly composed of lead and tin (5)

9 Ancient Greek city which is depicted in the 2006 movie *300* (6)

10 Egyptian goddess who was the daughter of Geb and Nut (4)

17 Woodland- and farmland-dwelling bird which may be observed interacting within flocks of chaffinches (9)

19 A lightweight sheer silky fabric (5)

20 Japanese-style sofa bed (5)

22 Italian physicist and astronomer who discovered the constancy of the swing of a pendulum and was the first to use a telescope to study the stars (7)

23 British overseas territory which is the site of two monolithic promontories formerly called the Pillars of Hercules (9)

24 Highlander's traditional boat-shaped hat with ribbons at the back (9)

26 Craftsperson who is skilled in working with stone (5)

The Telegraph

22

28 Tea-party character in *Alice's Adventures in Wonderland* (5,4)

30 Historically, a carriage pulled by a trio of horses (7)

32 Chemical element, atomic number 54, used in modern car headlights (5)

36 English composer who wrote the choral work *The Dream of Gerontius* (5)

37 National museum of Spain, located in Madrid (5)

40 Corrosion-resistant metal discovered by William Gregor (8)

42 Nickname for the "Stars and Stripes" (3,5)

44 English author noted for his series of *Inspector Morse* novels (6)

46 General term for any piquant condiment made from chopped vegetables or fruits (6)

48 Heraldic term for the colour blue (5)

49 A rotating firework; also a disc-shaped truckle of cheese (5)

51 Former Welsh rugby union player nicknamed "The King" (4)

53 The Greek war god with the Roman counterpart Mars (4)

54 US union leader and socialist who co-founded the Industrial Workers of the World organisation (4)

56 Basic monetary unit of Thailand (4)

N_Frankfort

Isis

22

Famous four;
charlot
Thor
Kong Ajax
Khuper Zindfaidel
Galileo Hedlou
tri athelon
Gibraltar Kamer
Rnge

Across

11 Pulitzer Prize-winning short story writer, novelist and journalist whose notable works include *Pale Horse, Pale Rider* and *Ship of Fools* (6)

12 Brass instrument used for military signals (5)

13 Traditional British roulade-like pudding of jam encased in suet pastry, steamed or baked (4-4)

14 Italian composer and conductor remembered for his orchestral trilogy of symphonic poems comprising *Fountains of Rome, Pines of Rome* and *Roman Festivals* (8)

15 Informal name for a short-legged breed of terrier, typically with a black-, brindle- or wheaten-coloured coat (7)

16 The ninth and smallest letter of the Greek alphabet (4)

17 Irish pianist credited with the origination of the nocturne, later popularised by Chopin (5)

19 US movie studio founded in 1912 by Carl Laemmle; early productions include *The Hunchback of Notre Dame, Tarzan the Mighty* and *Show Boat* (9)

21 A group of grain sheaves arranged in a field (5)

24 A person who imports or exports goods without paying duties (8)

26 Colourful live-bearing freshwater fish introduced to some countries to control mosquito larvae, a popular choice with aquarium owners (5)

27 French phrase literally meaning "to the fact, to the point" (2,4)

30 An adult male red deer, especially one over five years old (4)

32 German-born British biochemist who was a co-recipient of the 1945 Nobel Prize in Physiology or Medicine with Howard Florey and Alexander Fleming for work on penicillin (5)

33 Canadian singer-songwriter and guitarist whose best-selling 1972 album *Harvest* featured the hit singles *Heart of Gold* and *Old Man* (5)

35 US form of motor racing contested on a banked oval-shaped circuit (4)

36 A type of curved or S-shaped architectural moulding (4)

37 Dessert of ice-cream or mousse frozen in a dome-shaped mould of the same name (5)

39 A loop or series of loops used as an ornamental edging on fabrics (5)

40 Section of a Roman basilica, where the praetor's chair stood (4)

41 Reign of ___; period of extreme violence and bloodshed in the French Revolution, during which thousands were executed by guillotine (6)

42 Beryl the ___; *The Topper* comic character whose male counterpart was *The Beano's* Dennis the Menace (5)

43 Type of water-thinnable wall paint consisting of pigment bound in a synthetic resin (8)

45 Either of a pair of bladed boots designed for travelling over ice (5)

48 Scientific study of nutrition and food planning (9)

50 *High Noon* and *Rear Window* actress who married Prince Rainier III of Monaco in 1956 (5)

53 Actor who starred in the 1990 movie *Treasure Island* as Jim Hawkins and the 2005 movie *Batman Begins* as Bruce Wayne/Batman (4)

54 The capital, largest city and chief port of Sri Lanka (7)

56 Term for any of the German motorways; around 65 per cent of which have no speed limit (8)

58 Lyre-shaped musical instrument played between the teeth (4,4)

59 Major Scottish river which flows through Glasgow, once important for trade and ship-building (5)

60 Antibody- and protein-rich colourless part of blood in which corpuscles are suspended, produced by the immune system to fight diseases (6)

Down

1 Radioactive rare earth chemical element, atomic number 102, named after the inventor of dynamite (8)

2 Each of a series of movements which make up a dance (4)

3 English physicist who shared the 1915 Nobel Prize in Physics with his son for contributions towards developing X-ray crystallography (5)

4 Pen name of the Irish novelist and satirist who wrote *At Swim-Two-Birds* and *The Third Policeman* (1'5)

5 "Kill not the goose that lays the golden ___." English proverb (4)

6 Statistical study of human population, especially births, deaths and income (10)

7 One of the 22 regions of France (8)

8 Group of ships sailing together (5)

9 Short, fast race in which competitors typically run a distance of 100, 200 or 400 metres (6)

10 One of the three mythological Greek Fates (6)

18 Unit of astronomical distance equal to just under 10 trillion km (5-4)

20 A person who does not eat or use any animal-based products (5)

22 1968 song by The Beatles which features on *The White Album* (9)

23 From the French literally meaning "eat all", a variety of pea eaten when the pod is young and flat (9)

25 Domain ruled by a king or queen (5)

28 Dish of fried or stewed poultry or rabbit served in a thick white sauce (9)

29 Southern constellation near Telescopium and Tucana (5)

31 To fish with a line and hook (5)

34 ____ Tom Cobley; phrase that originated from the Devon folk song *Widecombe Fair* (5)

38 Pop-rock duo who released *Sweet Dreams (Are Made of This)* in 1983 (10)

39 A type of navigational handbook for use when travelling at sea (5)

42 Screwdriver with a cross head (8)

44 US state, north of Texas (8)

46 Legendary sea monster said to appear off the coast of Norway (6)

47 Belief in the existence of a god (6)

49 Co-presenter of *Countryfile* (6)

51 Singer who co-wrote the hit singles *Caribbean Queen* and *When the Going Gets Tough, the Tough Get Going* (5)

52 Dome-shaped Buddhist shrine (5)

55 Banded variety of chalcedony used to make cameos (4)

57 "I am a ____ of Very Little Brain, and long words bother me." *Winnie-the-Pooh*, A.A. Milne (4)

23

Handwritten margin notes:

Bugle

O'Brien   Young

Barboroni   Stap   O neill

Gugle   Provance

dieteris

Columba   OKLAHOMA

fricasse

picoti

24

Across

1 North African country with the largest city Casablanca, situated on the coastlines of the Atlantic Ocean and the Mediterranean Sea (7)

5 The final *Miss Marple* novel written by Agatha Christie (7)

9 Common name of a plant in the mallow family; the lightweight wood of which is used to make rafts, floats and model aeroplanes (5)

12 Basic monetary unit of Nigeria, equal to 100 kobo (5)

13 The largest moon of Uranus, named after the queen of the fairies in *A Midsummer Night's Dream* (7)

14 "Much have I travell'd in the realms of gold, And many goodly states and kingdoms seen; Round many western ___ have I been Which bards in fealty to Apollo hold." John Keats (7)

15 With an average wingspan of 3.5 metres, one of the largest species of birds in existence (9)

16 North American species of solitary mammal, *Ursus arctos horribilis* (7,4)

17 Hole in the hull of a ship through which an anchor cable passes (5)

18 Silicate mineral with polarising properties, known as the rainbow gemstone because of an Ancient Egyptian legend (10)

20 Biblical son of Adam and Eve who was murdered by his brother (4)

23 Tool with movable jaws, used to clamp an object to a workbench (4)

25 1995 hit single by Simply Red on their album *Life* (10)

29 Traditional fur-lined Inuit coat (5)

30 The study of numbers and their supposed occult significance and influence on human affairs (10)

32 In botany, a compound leaf with three leaflets (10)

35 Workplace of a blacksmith, farrier or other metalworker (5)

36 *The ___*; ballet in two acts with a score composed by Tchaikovsky, based on a story by E. T. A. Hoffmann (10)

37 Nobel Peace Prize-winning US civil rights leader remembered for his "I have a dream" speech, assassinated in 1968 (4)

39 Large antelope with long spear-like horns and conspicuous facial markings, living in regions of Africa and Arabia (4)

40 A person whose profession involves setting-up type for printing (10)

43 Royal dynasty that ruled England from the accession of Henry VII in 1485 until the death of Elizabeth I in 1603 (5)

46 In the late 19th century and early 20th century, a woman seeking the right to vote through organised, often extreme protest (11)

49 Person who is responsible for promoting and popularising a product, service, company or client's profile (9)

51 Irish singer-songwriter who covered the Prince song *Nothing Compares 2 U* in 1990 (1'6)

52 Three-pronged long-handled tool for spearing salmon (7)

53 Musical term meaning "very" (5)

54 Epsom ___; flat race for horses during which Emily Davison threw herself under the horse of George V in 1913, dying four days later (5)

55 Medical condition characterised by a lack of red cells or haemoglobin in the blood (7)

56 Of or like a sister (formal) (7)

Down

1 International organisation founded by Lancelot Ware in 1946, open to the members of the general public with a high IQ rating (5)

2 Children's television series that ran for 20 years with the characters Bungle, George and Zippy (7)

3 City in northern France on the river Eure, noted for its Gothic cathedral (8)

4 Small military camp stationed away from the main body of the troops (7)

5 The keys of a piano or other instrument (5)

6 Canadian novelist who wrote *Anne of Green Gables* and *Anne of Avonlea* (10)

7 Type of gun dog with breeds including the Cavalier King Charles, cocker and springer (7)

8 US swimmer who won seven gold medals in the 1972 Munich Olympics, setting a world record (5)

9 The second wife of Henry VIII (6)

10 Pole weapon used in jousting (5)

11 2008 historical movie directed by Baz Luhrmann, starring Nicole Kidman and Hugh Jackman (9)

17 Small harbour, port or inlet providing shelter for ships or boats during stormy weather (5)

19 Piano with vertical strings (7)

21 Indian dish of highly-seasoned basmati rice served with meat and/or vegetables and hard-boiled eggs (either spelling) (7)

24

22 The traditional birthstone for people born under the sign of Libra, once thought to bring good luck (4)

24 Medicinal herb in the borage and forget-me-not family (7)

26 Director and actor who wrote and starred in the 1972 movie *Play It Again, Sam* (5)

27 City in the central Netherlands (7)

28 English author of an 18th-century novel inspired by the real-life castaway Alexander Selkirk (5)

31 Jagged ridge of coral, rock or sand at or near the surface of water (4)

33 King of England 959-975 (5)

34 In theatre, a wall or portal dividing the auditorium from the stage (10)

35 Nickname of the mineral pyrite (5,4)

38 Powered hand-held machine with a rapidly-rotating nylon cord for cutting grass and weeds (8)

41 Anatomical term for the kneecap (7)

42 Actress who starred in *Pretty Woman* and *Notting Hill* (7)

44 German engineer and manufacturer who founded a motor company with Wilhelm Maybach in 1890 (7)

45 *Looney Tunes* character who often featured with Sylvester and Tweety (6)

47 Powdery substance used to make bread, cakes, pastry and pasta (5)

48 ___ Síochána; police force of the Republic of Ireland (5)

49 Brilliantly-coloured tropical bird (5)

50 Ugly, bad-tempered, cave-dwelling creature, either a dwarf or a giant (5)

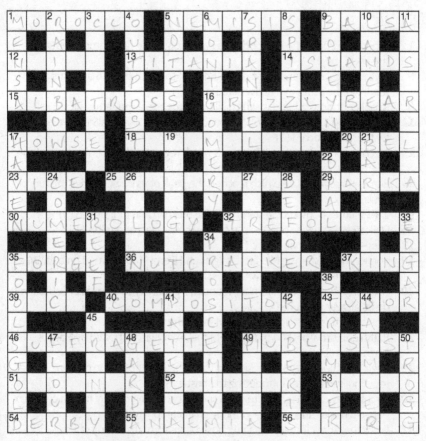

The Telegraph

25

Across

1 Whig statesman who is regarded as having been the first Prime Minister of the UK (7)

5 Mythological Arabian bird said to burn itself to death every 500 years and rise from the ashes in a rejuvenated form (7)

9 In poker or brag, a hand in which all the cards are of the same suit (5)

12 Unit of weight equal to 1/16 of a pound avoirdupois; also an alternative name for the snow leopard (5)

13 Mechanical device in an SLR camera which regulates the opening time of the aperture to expose the photographic film (7)

14 European royal house which reached the peak of its power under the rule of Louis XIV (7)

15 1995 James Bond movie starring Pierce Brosnan and Judi Dench (9)

16 Delicatessen which specialises in cooked cold meats and pâtés (11)

17 A leg-of-mutton-style sleeve (5)

18 Thriller movie starring Michael Douglas and Demi Moore, based on a 1994 novel by Michael Crichton with the same name (10)

20 Second largest city of Colombia, founded by Spanish conquistador Sebastián de Belalcázar in 1536 (4)

23 One of Earth's most abundant elements, symbol Fe (4)

25 British quiz show devised by Bill Wright that was originally hosted by Magnus Magnusson (10)

29 English fashion designer considered to be the father of haute couture, noted for crinolines and for introducing the bustle (5)

30 Circular device in a typewriter with spokes extending radially from a central hub, each with an individual printing character or glyph (5,5)

32 From the Greek literally meaning "love of wisdom", the study of the fundamental nature of knowledge and existence (10)

35 The sequence of cards forming a single round of play in bridge and whist, taken by the winner (5)

36 Common name for the clavicle (10)

37 One of the mythological Greek Oceanids, mother of 43 Across (4)

39 British nobleman ranking between a viscount and a marquess (4)

40 A proposal submitted directly to the vote of the entire electorate, also called a plebiscite (10)

43 Mythological Greek Titan who was forced by Zeus to bear the weight of the heavens on his shoulders (5)

46 Petroleum distillate used to thin paint and clean paintbrushes (5,6)

49 *Flight of the ___*; orchestral interlude in the opera *The Tale of Tsar Saltan* by Nikolai Rimsky-Korsakov (9)

51 The capital and largest city of Kenya, known locally as the green city in the sun (7)

52 Style of music that originated in Trinidad and Tobago (7)

53 *28 Days ___*; 2002 British horror movie directed by Danny Boyle based on chimpanzees infected with a rage-inducing virus (5)

54 Alternative name for the abalone, harvested for food and mother-of-pearl-lined shells (5)

55 The traditional gemstone gift for a 55th wedding anniversary (7)

56 English painter and engraver noted for his series of works depicting "modern moral subjects" such as *A Rake's Progress* (7)

Down

1 "Submission to one ___ brings on another." Latin proverb (5)

2 In cricket, a fielding position far behind the batsman on the boundary (4,3)

3 Dish of beaten eggs cooked in a frying pan, served plain or with cheese, ham or herbs (8)

4 District of central London stretching from the edge of the city to the River Lee (4,3)

5 Decorative arrangement of feathers; also a long column of smoke or vapour (5)

6 The unabbreviated name of a form of abstractionism based on the creation of illusions, exponents of which include Bridget Riley and Victor Vasarely (7,3)

7 Members of a Scandinavian people who conquered England in 1066 (7)

8 Three-masted sailing ship formerly used by the Barbary Pirates (5)

9 "Kind hearts are gardens, kind thoughts are roots, kind words are blossoms, kind deeds are ___." Henry Wadsworth Longfellow (6)

10 Natural clay used as a pigment (5)

11 German composer and violinist noted for his Gebrauchsmusik orchestral work *Mathis der Maler* (9)

17 Medieval association of craftsmen sharing a particular trade (5)

19 English poet and critic who wrote *Façade*, a group of poems recited to music composed by William Walton (7)

21 One of the three Fates (7)

22 Predacious birds collectively known as a parliament (4)

24 English actor who starred in the 1940 film *Rebecca* as Maxim de Winter (7)

26 Latin term meaning "to this" (2,3)

27 ___ Crane; fictional character in *The Legend of Sleepy Hollow* (7)

28 English name of the rabbit character in *The Magic Roundabout* (5)

31 Shoulder section of a garment (4)

33 Nobel Prize-winning Irish poet who wrote the 1928 collection *The Tower* (5)

34 Group of reptiles comprising the lizards; also a northern constellation (10)

35 Karate-like Korean martial art (3,4,2)

38 Tradename of a plastic fastener used to fix screws into masonry (8)

41 Common name for otalgia (7)

42 Extinct species of elephant (7)

44 Marine crustacean with stalked eyes and limbs modified as pincers, boiled alive before being eaten (7)

45 French film director of *La Grande illusion* and *La Règle du jeu* whose father created the masterpieces *Luncheon of the Boating Party* and *The Theatre Box* (6)

47 The largest bone of the pelvis (5)

48 A group of lions; also one of the seven deadly sins (5)

49 Animal with two feet (5)

50 Electrical connection to the ground; also the lair of a fox (5)

25

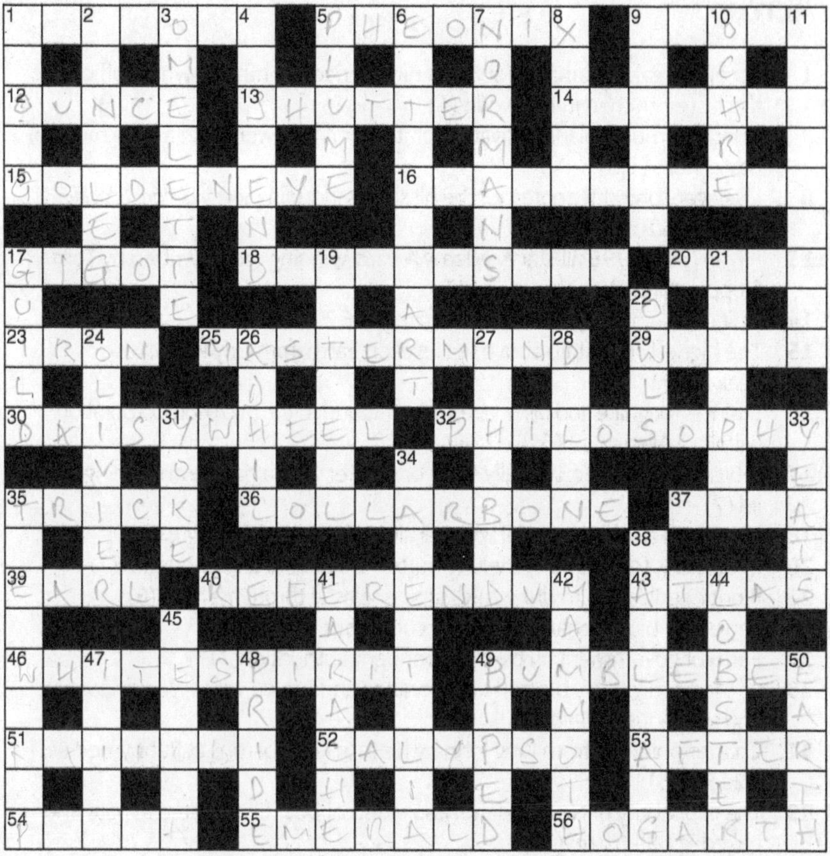

26

Across

1 Record-breaking Jamaican sprinter nicknamed "Lightning" who is officially the fastest human in the world (4)

3 Annual climbing plant cultivated for its fragrant flowers with a wide range of pastel hues (5,3)

8 US singer-songwriter noted for the hit singles including *Solitary Man, Cracklin' Rosie* and *Sweet Caroline* (7)

13 ___ *in Love*; 1998 all-star Academy Award-winning movie written by Tom Stoppard and Marc Norman (11)

14 Unit of distance equal to approximately 0.621 miles (9)

15 The highest mountain above sea level on earth, formerly known as Peak XV (7)

16 Business magnate and billionaire who co-founded the Microsoft Corporation with Paul Allen in 1975 (5)

17 A type of beer mug, typically silver or pewter with a handle and a hinged lid (7)

18 The capital and largest city of Portugal, situated on the River Tagus (6)

20 In cookery, technique of melting butter to separate any impurities (7)

22 Blunt needle used to draw cord, tape or elastic through a hem (6)

26 Terrestrial biome characterised by coniferous forests (5)

27 Form of government by two independent authorities (7)

29 ___ lady; migratory butterfly with orange and brown wings, genus *Vanessa* and subgenus *Cynthia* (7)

31 Charter obtained from King John by his rebellious barons at Runnymede in 1215 (5,5)

33 The capital city of New Zealand; also a dish of beef fillet coated in pâté and baked in puff pastry (10)

36 Enclosed garden of fruit- or nut-producing trees (7)

37 Variety of sheer and delicate fabric made from silk, cotton or synthetic fibres, used to make evening gowns and lingerie (7)

38 In tennis, an extended series of successive strokes between players (5)

39 Historically, a light open-topped carriage for one or two people, typically drawn by a single horse (6)

41 In geometry, a plain figure with six sides and six angles (7)

43 An alloy of copper and nickel, used in electrical resistance wire (6)

47 North American marsupial noted for playing dead as a form of defence (7)

26

49 Form of lyric poem invented by the Greek poet Archilochus; also the third section of a choral ode (5)

50 Class of creatures representing around 80 per cent of all the animal life forms on earth (7)

52 Norwegian anthropologist who, in 1947, travelled 4,300 miles across the Pacific Ocean from Peru to Polynesia on his balsa wood raft, Kon-Tiki (9)

53 A person who studies or collects relics and items of the past (11)

54 Lever worked by the foot in order to impart motion to a machine (7)

55 Type of sports car with two seats and a retractable roof, or formerly no roof (8)

56 Luminous path following a comet; also the caudal fin of a fish (4)

Down

1 Scottish author who was the biographer of the lexicographer Samuel Johnson (7)

2 Contract letting a house, office or other building for a specified term in return for a periodic payment (5)

4 One of the largest species of deer, more commonly called an elk (6)

5 Any of the four Gospels in the New Testament (7)

6 Island of the Greater Antilles, capital city San Juan (6,4)

7 *The King's* ___; the ninth story in Kipling's *The Second Jungle Book* (5)

8 The fourth letter of the Hebrew alphabet (6)

9 Capital and largest city of Jordan (5)

10 The currency of the former German Democratic Republic, equal to 100 pfennig (7)

11 Style of porcelain ware typically with delicate flower or fruit designs, originally made in a German city that was subjected to heavy Allied bombing in 1945 (7)

12 Second-brightest star in the constellation Leo, around 36.2 light years from earth (8)

19 Stage name of Gordon Sumner, singer with The Police, whose hits included *Message in a Bottle* and *Every Breath You Take* (5)

21 Blank page(s) at the beginning or end of a book (7)

23 According to Greek mythology, a giant Boeotian hunter who was slain by the goddess Artemis (5)

26

24 English athlete who has held the world record in triple jump since 1995, when he broke the 18 metre barrier (7)

25 The point in a spacecraft's orbit when it is furthest from the moon (7)

26 Italian word for time (5)

28 A separate clause in a legal document typically outlining a specific rule or regulation (7)

30 Brand of die-cast miniature toy cars and other vehicles (5)

32 The sixth president of the US (5)

34 Accent placed over Spanish n (5)

35 Cocktail of rum, pineapple juice and coconut cream served over ice (4,6)

38 French self-taught painter in the naïve style who was known as le Douanier (the customs officer) (8)

39 Handicraft of creating decorative lace-like fabric from yarn and a long hook-like tool (7)

40 Person employed to assist a priest or minister during church services (7)

42 Brother of Electra who killed his mother Clytemnestra and her lover (7)

44 London-based Premier League football club nicknamed the Gunners (7)

45 In heraldry, to display two coats of arms side by side on a single shield (6)

46 Thick and creamy shellfish soup (6)

48 Indian lute-like musical instrument with four or five main strings (5)

49 Swiss mathematician who contributed to infinitesimal calculus, geometry, algebra and trigonometry (5)

51 The most populous country in the world (5)

26

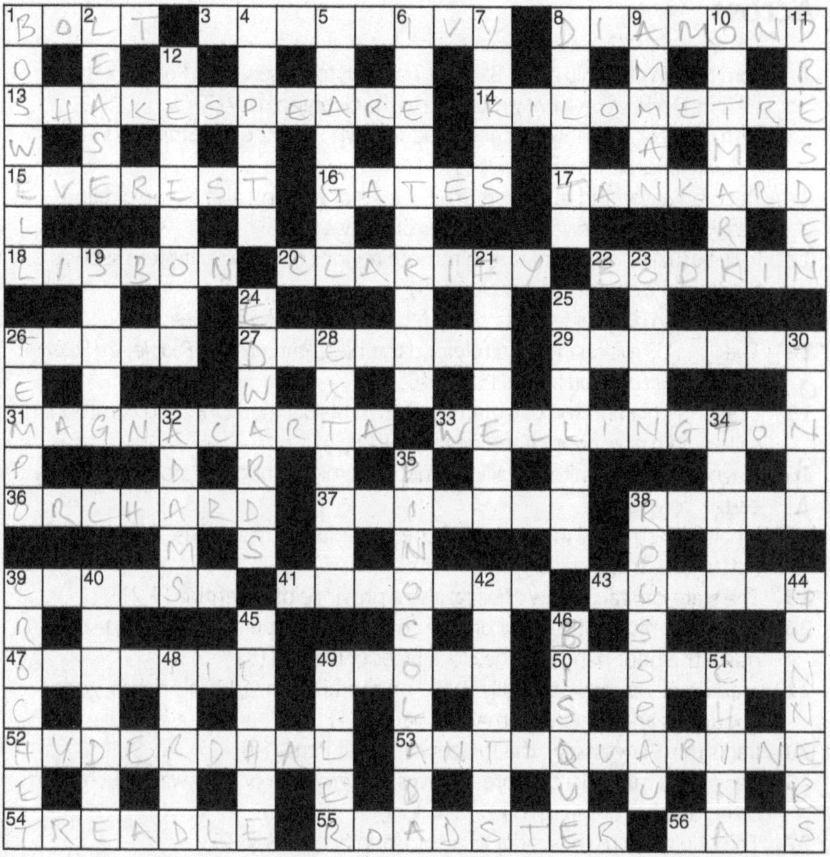

Across

1 Lord Nelson's flagship at the Battle of Trafalgar, today serving in Portsmouth Historic Dockyard as a living museum to the Georgian navy (7)

5 Film director, screenwriter and producer who created the *Star Wars* and *Indiana Jones* series of movies (5)

8 Decorative garland of flowers, fruit, leaves or ribbons; also a type of blind designed to be drawn up in a series of ruches (7)

12 Icy celestial body originating in remote regions of the solar system such as the Kuiper belt or the Oort cloud (5)

13 Type of gun dog trained to find and fetch game shot by a hunter (9)

14 The ___; US rock band who released the hits *Light my Fire*, *People Are Strange* and *Hello, I Love You* in the 1960s (5)

15 Flowering plant in the daisy family used in herbal medicine, also commonly called old man's pepper and devil's nettle (6)

16 Magnetic silvery-white metallic element, atomic number 28, abundant in the earth's core (6)

17 Small four-stringed instrument in the guitar family, popularised in Hawaii by Portuguese travellers (7)

19 The state capital of New Mexico; also a province of Argentina (5,2)

20 Corrosion-resistant form of bronze containing copper, tin and zinc, used to make the hour hands on the clock faces of Big Ben (8)

21 Traditional narrative typically based on moral themes, heroic deeds, gods, goddesses and other supernatural beings (4)

23 Iran's third-largest city; the former capital of Persia (7)

25 Term for a mammal that breeds, lives and grows in or near water such as an otter, dolphin or sea lion (7)

27 The title given to the leader of a community of monks (5)

29 Cartilaginous structure behind the root of the human tongue (10)

31 Debut album by the English rock band Coldplay with the hits *Don't Panic*, *Shiver*, *Yellow* and *Trouble* (10)

35 Kir ___; cocktail comprising champagne with a measure of crème de cassis (5)

36 Chief sanctuary of Zeus, site of an ancient series of athletic competitions that included pentathlon, chariot racing and wrestling (7)

37 Large seed of a tropical palm, cultivated for coir and copra (7)

39 German baroque composer and father of 20 who wrote masterpieces including *The Musical Offering* and *The Well-Tempered Clavier* (4)

41 Skiing on tracks away from the prepared ski runs (3-5)

43 16th-century Italian sculptor and artist in the Mannerist style, said to be the greatest goldsmith of his day (7)

46 The second novel in the *Twilight* series by Stephenie Meyer (3,4)

47 Spanish F1 driver for Ferrari, and former double world champion (6)

49 Strengthening material sewn into the inner sections of a garment, typically in a contrasting colour (6)

51 Registered trade name of a synthetic fibre created by Dupont in 1941, used to make crease-resistant textiles (5)

52 Large mass of snow, rocks and ice descending the side of a mountain at speeds of around 80 mph, typically destroying all in its path (9)

53 Short Japanese poem consisting of 17 syllables, or morae (5)

54 Painting or carving on two wooden panels hinged together like a book (7)

55 The 19th president of the US (5)

56 Ancient Greek beverage of wine mixed with honey (7)

Down

1 Creamy leek and potato soup, traditionally served cold (11)

2 Canadian director, producer and screenwriter whose movies include *The Terminator*, *Aliens*, *The Abyss*, *Titanic* and *Avatar* (7)

3 Practitioner trained to treat medical conditions through manipulation and massage of the bones and musculature (9)

4 Circular tent-like dwelling used by Turkic and Mongolian nomads (4)

5 Long stick-like weapon used by Indian police for crowd control (5)

6 *Hugh's___*; Hugh Fearnley-Whittingstall's *Food Fight* television campaign encouraging consumers to buy free-range poultry (7,3)

7 The capital city of Andalusia (7)

8 Containing an established set of words (9)

9 Atomic number 11, symbol Na (6)

10 Geological process in which part of the earth's crust folds resulting in the formation of a mountain (7)

11 A type of prefabricated building used during the Second World War (6,3)

18 Small Spanish horse (6)

20 Natural force attracting a body towards the centre of the earth (7)

22 Ratio of the speed of a moving object to the speed of sound (4)
24 Mythical being such as Titania (5)
26 Currant confection served toasted and buttered, similar to a hot cross bun (7)
28 Item passed from runner to runner in a relay race (5)
30 Stage name of the Scottish singer Marie McDonald McLaughlin Lawrie (4)
32 English Aviator who, in June 1919, made the first non-stop transatlantic flight with Sir Arthur Whitten Brown (6)
33 Sioux chief who led his people into the Battle of Little Bighorn, killing General Custer and his troops (7,4)
34 Collective body of bishops (10)
35 Legendary medieval outlaw (5,4)
36 German composer who wrote the operetta *Orpheus in the Underworld* (9)
38 UK prime minister from 1976–79 (9)
40 Common name of *Primula veris* (7)
42 Title of the kings of ancient Egypt (7)
44 Atomic number 77 (7)
45 *Mutiny on the* ___; 1935 film starring Charles Laughton and Clark Gable (6)
48 Actor who starred in *Fawlty Towers* as the Barcelonian waiter Manuel (5)
50 Captain ___; fictional character in Jules Verne's novel *Twenty Thousand Leagues Under the Sea* (4)

acquatic

New Town abastolic
Callaghan   Giberti
Chicken, ?on   Gb bertbeacon
Gulvinise

28

Across

1 English novelist who wrote the classics *The Story of the Treasure Seekers*, *Five Children and It* and *The Railway Children* (6)

4 Cocktail named after a Venetian painter, consisting of Prosecco or another variety of sparkling wine with peach purée and/or schnapps (7)

8 Tottenham Hotspur and England international striker who was the second top-scorer in the 2006–07 UEFA Champions League (6)

13 Name of the water vole character in Kenneth Grahame's novel *The Wind in the Willows* (5)

14 English organic chemist awarded the 1947 Nobel Prize in Chemistry for his research on plant alkaloids (8)

15 Strong band of fibrous collagen tissue connecting muscle to bone (6)

17 Agricultural science dealing with the structure of soils, especially in relation to the production of crops (8)

18 The world's second-largest and second most populous continent (6)

19 Musical term indicating that a composition, movement or passage must be performed in a very slow and dignified manner (5)

20 T-shaped device on a ship for securing a rope (5)

22 Large flat stone slab used for paving; also a common name of some species of iris plants (4)

24 The former name for a vehicle registration certificate (7)

28 Military commander during the American Civil War who served as the 18th president of the US (5)

29 Large-scale musical work performed without scenery or costumes, such as Handel's *Messiah* or Haydn's *The Creation* and *The Seasons* (8)

30 Sixth and last wife of Henry VIII (4)

35 1990 drama movie starring Robert De Niro and Robin Williams, based on the memoirs of English neurologist Oliver Sacks (10)

36 Earth's southernmost continent, most of which is covered by ice caps around a mile deep (10)

38 The size of a piece of land (4)

39 A blind made from angled slats; also a type of louvred window (8)

40 Hungarian composer and piano virtuoso noted for symphonic poems (5)

43 Any one of a large group of Baleen marine mammals ranging in size from the blue whale to the minke whale (7)

45 Flightless extinct bird on the coat of arms of Mauritius (4)

46 Codeword used in radio communication between November and papa (5)

49 According to the Book of Genesis, a great tower built in an attempt to reach heaven (5)

50 US sharpshooter born Phoebe Ann Mosey who starred in Buffalo Bill's Wild West Show for 17 years (6)

52 System of pipes and fixtures designed to provide a building with water, heating and drainage (8)

55 Hand-tool with a bevelled steel blade used in carpentry and stonemasonry (6)

56 Timed team games on horseback, typically including pole bending, chase me Charlie and egg-and-spoon racing (8)

57 Mound of stones built as a landmark or memorial; also a Scottish breed of terrier developed to hunt around such formations (5)

58 English novelist who created the characters Elinor and Marianne Dashwood (6)

59 Plant in the carrot family, genus *Sium sisarum*, cultivated in some countries for its sweet potato-like roots (7)

60 Southern constellation in the Milky Way which contains Canopus, the second-brightest star in the night sky (6)

Down

1 European country nicknamed the land of the midnight sun, noted for fjords and mountainous scenery (6)

2 The second-largest planet in the solar system (6)

3 Short poem on pastoral subjects (5)

5 Tuscan island where Napoleon Bonaparte was first exiled following his forced abdication in 1814 (4)

6 US poet who wrote *The Wreck of the Hesperus* and *The Village Blacksmith* (10)

7 Biblical mother-in-law of Ruth (5)

9 Branch of physics concerned with the deformation and flow of matter (8)

10 To cook meat inadequately (7)

11 English comedian who featured in *Educating Archie* before being given his own radio series in 1954 (7)

12 Character in Edmund Spenser's epic poem *The Faerie Queene* (11)

16 The woolly grip of a campanologist's bell rope (5)

21 German monk and theologian who led the Protestant Reformation and was later excommunicated at the Diet of Worms (6)

23 English actor who starred as Obi-Wan Kenobi in *Star Wars* (8)

25 Herbivorous lizard with a spiny crest along its back (6)

26 Bite-sized appetiser served with drinks before a main meal (6)

27 The foremost part of an advancing army (8)

31 Buddhist, Hindu and Jainist doctrine advocating non-violence and respect for all living things (6)

32 Island of Venice noted for its bridge over the Grand Canal (6)

33 Literally meaning "haven of peace", the largest city in Tanzania (3,2,6)

34 Six-headed sea monster said to devour sailors trying to escape the whirlpool Charybdis (6)

37 Tree-boring species of bird (10)

41 Central target of a dartboard (5-3)

42 Bodily fluid circulating in the veins and arteries of humans (5)

43 1938 novel by Daphne du Maurier (7)

44 US dancer who choreographed numerous musicals including *West Side Story* and *Fiddler on the Roof* (7)

47 Atoll in the Marshall Islands that was used as a site for testing nuclear weapons between 1948-56 (6)

48 Country with the capital Kampala (6)

51 Traditional Inuit canoe (5)

53 Coffee drink flavoured with cocoa (5)

54 Herb used to flavour Lincolnshire sausages and other pork dishes (4)

28

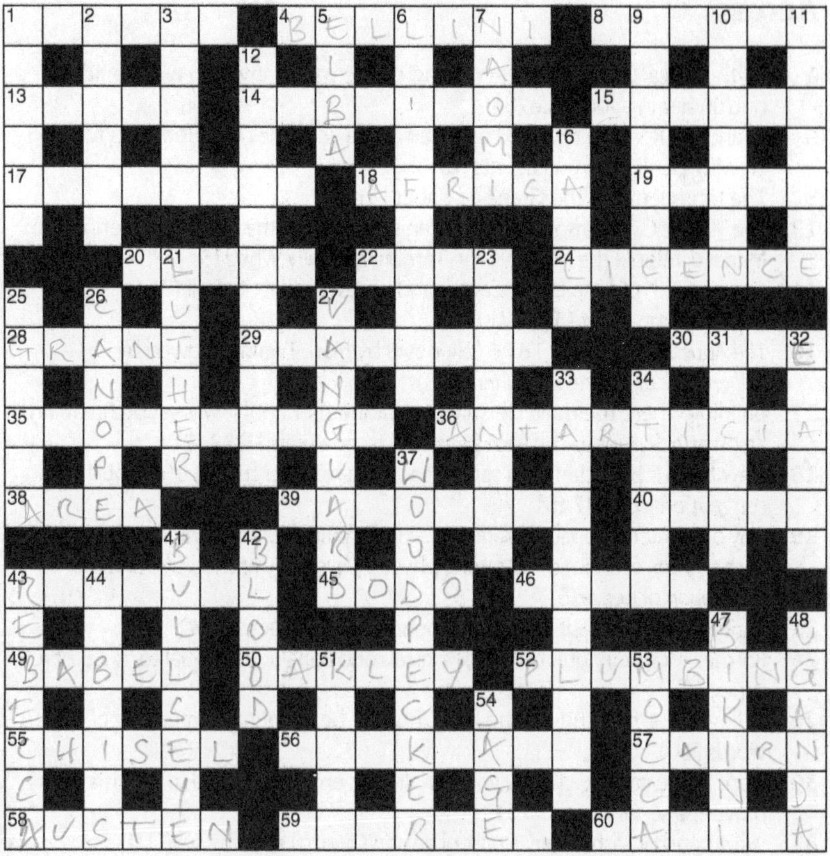

29

Across

1 Mythological Greek huntress who agreed to marry any man who could outrun her in a foot race (8)

5 In ancient Rome, a rounded open-air arena with lines of tiered seats for viewing public sporting events (6)

9 The tenth letter of the Greek alphabet (5)

13 *The* ___; D. C. Thomson & Co children's comic with the characters Dennis the Menace, Minnie the Minx, Ivy the Terrible and Billy Whizz (5)

14 Country with the capital city Zagreb and largest coastal city Split (7)

15 English county east of The Wash (7)

16 *The Adventures of* ___; 1876 folk novel by Mark Twain, followed by *Adventures of Huckleberry Finn* (3,6)

17 Building where the main German legislature met until it was set on fire in an arson attack prior to the Nazi accession to power in 1933 (9)

18 New Labour politician who served as prime minister from 1997 until his resignation in 2007 (5)

19 Any of six international accolades awarded annually for outstanding work in chemistry, economics, literature, physics, physiology or medicine and the promotion of peace (5,5)

21 Variety of tubular pasta resembling penne or large macaroni (4)

24 Former monetary unit of India, Pakistan and Bangladesh equal to 1/16 of a rupee (4)

26 In linguistics, the study of the form, history, behaviour and meaning of words (10)

30 Plant in the cabbage family with small pungent leaves, used to garnish egg mayonnaise sandwiches (5)

31 Waistband or sash worn as part of a man's formal evening suit (10)

33 Area of unoccupied ground between the trenches or front lines of two opposing armies (2-4-4)

36 Constellation and sign of the zodiac represented by the scales (5)

37 English architect who designed the London National History Museum and Manchester Town Hall (10)

38 Stage name of the rock musician who released the tracks *Hot in the City* and *White Wedding* in the early 1980s (4)

40 Defensive water-filled or dry ditch encircling a castle (4)

41 In ancient Egypt, a stylised picture of an object used to represent a word or sound (10)

45 Hungarian choreographer and dancer who developed a system of dance notation and movement analysis in the 1920s (5)

48 Leader of a tribe or clan (9)

49 Island situated south of Cape Cod and east of Martha's Vineyard (9)

51 US lawyer and author who created the *Perry Mason* series of detective novels (7)

52 *The* ___; bronze and marble sculpture by Auguste Rodin (7)

53 Ancient region of central Anatolia or Asia Minor, in present-day Turkey (5)

54 Card game based on forming sets or sequences of cards (5)

55 Stage name of the actor and *Crystal Maze* presenter who wrote *The Rocky Horror Show* (1'5)

56 In chess, gaining a rook in return for a bishop or a knight (8)

Down

1 English comedian who starred in a television series with the theme tune *Songs of Joy* (5)

2 Medical condition characterised by a deficiency of red cells and haemoglobin in the blood (7)

3 Italian chemist and physicist who, in 1811, formulated a system to obtain molecular and atomic weights (8)

4 Hypothetical elementary particle travelling faster than light (7)

6 Latin phrase meaning "among other people" (5,5)

7 Any musical instrument with a keyboard, especially the harpsichord and the fortepiano (7)

8 Venezuelan terrorist nicknamed Carlos the Jackal, serving life imprisonment in France (7)

9 Literally meaning "empty hand", traditional Japanese martial art originally developed by Gichin Funakoshi (6)

10 Any one of the tines of a fork (5)

11 Organic compounds derived from plants, such as atropine, morphine, quinine and strychnine (9)

12 Non-SI unit of pressure equivalent to one millimetre of mercury in an old type of barometer (4)

18 The French word for white (5)

20 Doughnut-like confection consisting of deep-fried ball or square of choux pastry, sprinkled in sugar (7)

22 EU country with the highest peak Carrauntoohil (7)

23 Book of the New Testament (4)

25 Country in southern Africa that gained independence in 1990 after a 25-year-long bush war (7)

27 Either one of a pair of cubital joints of the human body (5)

28 Branch of medicine concerned with conditions and anatomy of the ear (7)

29 Irish poet and dramatist awarded the 1923 19 Across in literature (5)

32 Town in the Netherlands (4)

34 US singer and songwriter born Robert Allen Zimmerman who wrote *The Times They Are a-Changin'* (5)

35 Two-masted sailing ship (10)

36 Soft pale cheese with a pungent odour but a mild taste (9)

39 Lively fanfare played on brass instruments (8)

42 The first part of Dante's epic poem *Divine Comedy*, followed by *Purgatorio* and *Paradiso* (7)

43 Word linking chemical, fusion and nuclear (7)

44 Rock guitarist and singer who wrote *Purple Haze* and *Voodoo Chile* (7)

46 Russian anarchist who was a member of the International Workingmen's Association until his expulsion in 1872 (7)

47 English poet who wrote *Arcadia* (6)

48 A read-only optical memory device for a computer (2-3)

49 The winged goddess of victory (4)

50 In Anglo-Saxon England, a man granted land by a king (5)

30

Across

1 Prime minister who was forced to abandon his policy of appeasement following Hitler's invasion of Czechoslovakia and the outbreak of the Second World War (11)

7 Statesman and diplomat awarded the 1973 Nobel Peace Prize for his part in negotiating the withdrawal of US troops from South Vietnam (9)

12 The derived SI unit of electrical charge, equal to the quantity of electricity conveyed when a current of one ampere flows for one second (7)

13 Italian dish of small pockets of pasta filled with meat or cheese, served with a tomato-based sauce (7)

14 According to Greek myth, the prince of Troy who abducted Helen from her husband Menelaus, provoking the Trojan War (5)

15 The final decision of a law court or independent arbitrator (5)

16 The capital city of Cyprus, now the only divided capital in the world (7)

17 Any one of the mythical sea nymphs such as Asia or Calypso (7)

18 Style of hat originally made in Ecuador from the dried leaves of the toquilla palm (6)

20 A type of upholstered seat without a back or arms which may also serve as a storage chest (7)

22 The ___ Queene; unfinished epic poem by Edmund Spenser (6)

25 Carnivorous mammal related to badgers, ferrets and weasels; known collectively as a bevy, family, romp or, when in water, a raft (5)

26 The ___; 2000 movie about the American Revolutionary War, starring Mel Gibson and Heath Ledger (7)

28 English composer, conductor, pianist and life peer whose operas include *Peter Grimes*, *A Midsummer Night's Dream* and *Death in Venice* (7)

31 Another name for Asteroid 433, noted for travelling closer to earth than any celestial body except the moon (4)

32 Mortar-like substance for filling gaps between tiles (5)

33 Small naturally-formed hillock (5)

34 Gambling card game in which players place bets on the order in which certain cards will appear (4)

38 Turkish dessert of layered filo pastry with chopped nuts, soaked in honey (7)

39 Mythological Greek huntress and goddess of the moon whose Roman counterpart is Diana (7)

40 Any one of a number of savage brutish beings in Jonathan Swift's *Gulliver's Travels* (5)

41 The largest monolithic statue in the world (6)

43 Quality cut of beef from the lower part of the ribs (7)

45 Term for out-of-date computer software or hardware (6)

48 Dried stigmas of a species of crocus used as a food colouring and a spice (7)

49 Actor and singer who won an Academy Award for his role in the 1953 movie *From Here to Eternity* (7)

50 "If you don't ___ the mountain, you can't view the plain" Chinese proverb (5)

53 Formation of frost on an aircraft (5)

54 The common name for thetympanic membrane (7)

55 The ___; band who released *Manic Monday* and *Eternal Flame* in the 1980s (7)

56 US cyclist who won the Tour de France seven times consecutively (9)

57 Either one of a pair of lecterns in the House of Commons where ministers stand when addressing the Chamber (either spelling) (8,3)

Down

1 Beans obtained from the tropical evergreen tree *Theobroma cacao* (5)

2 Island in the Caribbean Sea off the coast of Venezuela that had a gold rush for a century until the reserves were exhausted (5)

3 Nickname of the queen and eldest daughter of Henry VIII who ordered more than 280 Protestants to be burnt at the stake (6,4)

4 Flemish Baroque painter renowned for his depictions of history and mythology such as *Samson and Delilah* and *Venus and Adonis* (6)

5 Fruit in the almond, cherry, peach, plum and rose family (7)

6 Canadian province south of Prince Edward Island (4,6)

7 Basic monetary unit of Sweden, equal to 100 öre (5)

8 *Miss ___*; West End and Broadway musical by *Les Misérables* writer Claude-Michel Schönberg (6)

9 Person responsible for organising the finances of an opera, concert or play (10)

10 US actress who starred in *The Killers* and *The Night of the Iguana* (7)

11 Indian-born British novelist, subject of a fatwa in 1989 (7)

18 Short familiar saying expressing a moral lesson or piece of advice (7)

19 Number of inter-linked computers (7)

21 In semantics, a word opposite in meaning to another (7)

The Telegraph

30

23 Pouch worn as part of the male Scottish Highland dress (7)
24 Garden structure for growing sweet peas, clematis, runner beans or other climbing plants (7)
27 Cataclysmic wave caused by movements in the sea floor during an earthquake or volcanic eruption (7)
29 Technical name for the windpipe (7)
30 A newly coined word or phrase (7)
35 A person who builds wagons (10)
36 Former name of an industrial Russian city on the Volga River (10)
37 Speeds of more than five times the speed of sound, Mach 5 (10)
41 Structured poem with six six-line stanzas having the same end-words in different sequences (7)
42 Atomic number 72 (7)
44 ___ of Panama; narrow strip linking North and South America (7)
46 Name of the goldsmith in Shakespeare's *The Comedy of Errors* (6)
47 Spanish explorer who crossed the 44 Down in 1513, becoming the first European to have seen and reached the eastern shores of the Pacific Ocean (6)
49 Bolero-style knitted garment (5)
51 Abbreviation of a Latin phrase meaning "at one's pleasure" (2-3)
52 Home county bordering Cambridgeshire, Hertfordshire, Kent and Suffolk (5)

netbank

bank

30

C	H	A	M	B	E	R	L	A	I	N		K	I	S	S	E	N	G	E	R
O			L		V		P		O		R		A			E				U
C			O		B		R	A	V	I	O	L	I			P				S
O			O		E		I		A		N		G							H
A			D		N	I	C	O	S	I	A		O							D
			Y		S		O		C				N							I
P	A	N	A	M	A		O	T	T	O	M	A	N		F	A	I	R	I	E
R			A						T		I									
O	T	T	E	R		P	A	T	R	I	O	T						R		
V			Y			O		S		A		O								
E				G	R	O	U	T		N		L			A					
R			R		R		N		S		Y		I		C					
B	A	K	L	A	V	A		A	R	T	I	M	I	S						
				N		M		A						H						
					S	I	R	L	O	I	N			E	A					
								I						L						
S	A	F	F	R	O	N		N	G	R	A			S	C	A	L	E		
								G						O	D	S				
								R			B	A	N	G	L	E	S			
A	R	M	S	T	R	O	N	G		D	I	S	P	A	T	C	H	B	O	X

PRIO
Suroguni
Straite
THREA
act the
verb artimis aphrodism
antonyn Tia chea
coulomm
aire

Across

11 English astronomer and mathematician who, using Newton's laws of motion, was the first to calculate the orbit of a comet that was later named after him (6)

12 Musical form with a recurring principal theme, typically in the final movement of a sonata or concerto (5)

13 Any one of the thousands of rocky or icy bodies orbiting the sun between Mars and Jupiter (8)

14 Capital and chief port of the African country Sierra Leone (8)

15 The pen name of the English science fiction author who wrote *The Day of the Triffids*, *The Chrysalids*, *The Midwich Cuckoos* and *Chocky* (7)

16 The nest of a squirrel (4)

17 Full-bodied variety of black tea (5)

19 Situated on the banks of the Orange River, the capital of the Northern Cape which has served as a diamond-mining centre since the early 1870s (9)

21 Skulking wading bird related to allies and sandpipers; both sexes of which have mottled brown plumage (5)

25 Mythological Greek daughter of Oedipus and his mother Jocasta, who was the subject of one of the tragedies written by Sophocles (8)

27 Trick-taking card game originally from Spain; also fabric dyed so that the colour is graduated from light to dark (5)

28 The Roman goddess of fruits and abundance (6)

30 Scottish engineer who coined the word "horsepower" and whose improvements in the efficiency of the Newcomen steam engine led to its wide use in industry (4)

32 The spherical seed head of the dandelion after the flower dries out (5)

33 Name of the group of chemical elements that includes argon, helium, krypton, neon, radon and xenon (5)

35 English comedian remembered for his television partnership with Dudley Moore in *Beyond the Fringe* and *Not Only... But Also* (4)

36 Formal deliberative legislative assembly in certain countries (4)

37 In phonetics, an unstressed central vowel represented by the symbol   (5)

39 The first letter of the Hebrew alphabet, said to depict an ox's head (5)

40 ___ Sally; character in Barbara Euphan Todd's series of *Worzel Gummidge* stories, depicted by Una Stubbs in the television adaptations (4)

41 French word for a type of enclosed arena in which horses and riders are schooled (6)

42 City in north-eastern European Russia formerly called Vyatka (5)

43 In mathematics, the fractional part of a logarithm after the decimal point (8)

45 Italian Romantic composer noted for his operas including *La traviata*, *Aida*, *Otello* and *Falstaff* (5)

47 A pigment made from soot (9)

49 Style of cravat-like necktie with wide square ends (5)

52 Enclosure of stakes set in a river or stream to catch fish (4)

54 Goat-like antelope native to mountainous regions of Europe from Spain to Romania to the Caucasus (7)

56 Carbonaceous residue of wood that has undergone combustion with exclusion of air (8)

58 Variety of curry from Goa (8)

59 US film director who worked with Ismail Merchant on the films *Heat and Dust*, *A Room with a View*, *Howards End* and *The Remains of the Day* (5)

60 The Greek muse of astronomy (6)

Down

1 Academy Award-winning English stage and screen actor who starred in the films *Cleopatra*, *My Fair Lady* and *Doctor Dolittle* (8)

2 Fruit of the blackthorn (4)

3 English poet who joined the fight against the Ottoman Empire in the Greek War of Independence but died from malaria before seeing action (5)

4 Oil-rich sultanate on the coast of Borneo which became independent from the UK in 1984 (6)

5 English author and physicist who wrote the *Strangers and Brothers* series of 11 novels (4)

6 A type of petition with signatures written in a circular formation so that no one appears to be a ringleader (5,5)

7 Highly-esteemed wool used to make pashmina shawls (8)

8 Item collected by a philatelist (5)

9 English dramatist and literary critic of the Restoration who wrote the 1678 work based on *Antony and Cleopatra*, *All for Love* (6)

10 Small piccolo-like instrument used in military marching bands (4)

18 Greek philosopher who taught Alexander the Great (9)

20 English theatre director noted for Royal Shakespeare Company productions including *King Lear* (5)

22 Each of a pair of boat-like floats attached to a seaplane (7)

23 Cathedral city that has been a centre of porcelain manufacture since 1751 (9)

24 *The __*; 1990s television sitcom starring Joe McGann, Diana Weston and Honor Blackman (5,4)

26 The eldest son of Cain (5)

29 Branch of physics dealing with motion, dynamics and kinetics (9)

31 Sighting device used in surveying to measure angles (7)

34 20th-century English classical guitarist and lutenist (5)

38 An extreme fear of heights (10)

39 Heavy iron block for shaping horseshoes and other metal objects with a hammer (5)

42 Island that in 1883 was the scene of one of the most violent volcanic eruptions in recorded history (8)

44 Country with the capital Bratislava (8)

46 Southern constellation symbolised by the Swordfish (6)

48 Final part of the vertebral column (6)

50 Small spoon-bladed oar (5)

51 The current British Foreign Secretary and First Secretary of State (5)

53 Title of various independent rulers in Muslim countries (4)

55 A stroke, throw, hit or kick in sports such as tennis, golf or football (4)

57 World record-breaking Olympic gold medallist nicknamed the "Jarrow Arrow" (4)

Krakatoa

clytemestra   c_

31

Across

1 Radioactive metallic element, atomic number 84, discovered by Marie and Pierre Curie in 1898, for which they were jointly awarded the 1903 Nobel Prize in Physics (8)

5 Either one of the two versions of the body of Jewish civil and ceremonial law comprising the Mishnah and the Gemara (6)

9 Small porous vessel used by goldsmiths to refine and assay precious metals (5)

13 1897 novel by the Irish author who also wrote *The Primrose Path* and *The Jewel of Seven Stars* (7)

14 French explorer who made three voyages to Canada between 1534 and 1542, and who was the first to establish France's claim to North America (7)

15 Tough, fibrous tissue responsible for connecting muscle to a bone, tendon or ligament (5)

16 Anatomical term for the middle of the three muscular layers which form the wall of the heart (10)

17 UK television series with contenders who included Amazon, Jet, Hunter, Lightning and Wolf (10)

19 Middle Eastern paste prepared from ground sesame seeds and olive oil, used to flavour hummus (6)

21 Deep-blue mineral of basic copper carbonate, often found interwoven with malachite (7)

22 John F. Kennedy's alleged assassin who was shot and killed by Jack Ruby before he could be brought to trial (6)

27 Mountainous country with a coastline on the Black Sea (7)

29 Member of a Jamaican religious movement worshipping the former Ethiopian emperor Haile Selassie I (11)

32 English clergyman who invented the power loom in 1784 (10)

33 Character in Robert Southey's fairy tale *The Story of the Three Bears* (10)

35 Traditional soup of lamb or mutton with pearl barley and various chopped root vegetables (6,5)

36 Sum paid to an author for each copy of a book sold (7)

38 Urban area south-west of Johannesburg consisting of several townships (6)

40 Large fruit of the tropical tree in the cinnamon, spicebush and bay laurel family, *Persea americana* (7)

43 A popular house plant with colourful variegated leaves (6)

47 *All Creatures Great and Small* actress who featured as the Oxo mum in a series of advertisements throughout the 1980s and 1990s (10)

49 Collective body of people in a country or region entitled to vote (10)

52 Hindu religious teacher (5)

53 Sweet or savoury dish of sponge cake or meat spread with a filling, rolled into a spiral and sliced (7)

54 "O, wonder! How many goodly creatures are there here! How beauteous __ is! O brave new world, That has such people in't!"
The Tempest: Act V, Scene 1 (7)

55 The side edge of a sail; also a creature used in bloodletting since ancient times (5)

56 Medium-sized pig, lighter than a baconer but heavier than a porker (6)

57 Card game in which a player holding cards totalling 10 or less may end the game (3,5)

Down

1 Instrument which calculates the approximate distance walked by counting the amount of steps taken (9)

2 In South America, one of the vast grassy steppes or plains (5)

3 Von __; Hungarian-born US mathematician and polymath who contributed to the development of the digital computer (7)

4 Republic known as the Pearl of Africa despite its former dictatorial regime of Idi Amin, high mortality rate and being one of the world's poorest countries (6)

6 Mythological Greek Titan goddess and personification of the breeze (4)

7 Jersey worn in cycle racing; also tights worn by ballet dancers, gymnasts and circus performers (7)

8 Style of traditional Alpine dress (6)

9 French-born Brazilian architect who designed and developed the city of Brasília in 1956 (5)

10 Woman who was created by Hephaestus to avenge Prometheus with her jar of evils (7)

11 US track and field athlete who won nine Olympic gold medals (5)

12 Creator of the *Peanuts* comic strip (6)

18 Ornamental plaque for the harness of a draught or shire horse (5)

20 Human bone of the upper arm (7)

23 1849 novel by Charlotte Brontë (7)

24 Artist noted for his depictions of dancers, nudes and racehorses (5)

25 Starch obtained from cassava (7)

26 ___ *Salad*; the third episode of the second series of *Fawlty Towers*, followed by *The Kipper and the Corpse* (7)

28 Largest town in Monmouthshire (7)

29 The first track on the *Back to Black* album by Amy Winehouse (5)

30 Alchemist's name for mercury (5)

31 Streamlined enclosure housing an aircraft engine (7)

32 Large constellation said to represent a sea monster (5)

34 Irish novelist who wrote *Dubliners* (5)

37 1965 song by The Beatles (9)

39 Knight and Scottish national hero depicted by Mel Gibson in *Braveheart* (7)

41 Bridge-like structure formed in a series of arches which carries a railway or road over a valley (7)

42 Megalithic tomb of upright stones supporting a horizontal capstone (6)

44 Entertainer who hosted a daytime television series with Melanie Sykes from 2002-06 (1'6)

45 Fly ___; common name of the red- and white-capped hallucinogenic fungus *Amanita muscaria* (6)

46 Norway lobsters coated in breadcrumbs and deep-fried (6)

47 Herb used to make pesto (5)

48 One of the Goidelic languages (5)

50 The genus name of a family of plants that includes celery (5)

51 The title of a lady of the same rank as a knight (4)

mastermind

32

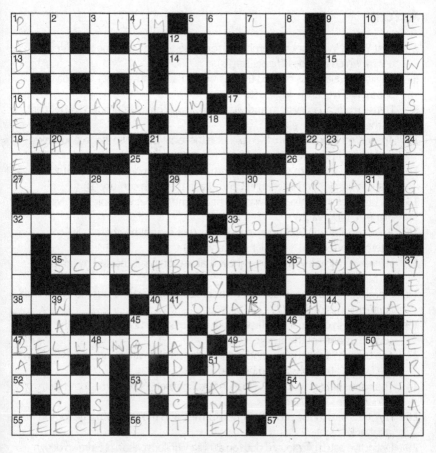

Villette

Tahini   myocardia   Torah

zepr   Zephr

Plutonium

Leotard

Across

1 First World War poet remembered for his series of five sonnets entitled *1914* which includes *The Soldier* (6)

5 English novelist who created the characters Paul Pennyfeather, Brenda Last, Sebastian Flyte and Aloysius (5)

8 Dense tropical ecosystem and vital habitat which covers around six per cent of the Earth's surface (6)

13 The second-largest known dwarf planet in the solar system; also the second-largest body in the Kuiper belt (5)

14 City on the southern shore of the Firth of Forth that developed around a castle built by King Malcolm III Canmore in the 11th century (9)

15 US business magnate who was married to the former Olympic skier Ivana Marie Zelníčková (5)

16 Any one of over 100 known substances that cannot be chemically interconverted into a simpler substance (7)

17 *Winner ___ All*; television game show that was originally hosted by Jimmy Tarbuck (5)

18 Member of the *Goon Show* cast who starred as Inspector Clouseau in the *Pink Panther* series of films (7)

19 In the Jewish calendar, the first month of the ecclesiastical year and the seventh month of the civil year (5)

21 The branch of technology and industry concerned with aviation and flight in the Earth's atmosphere and beyond (9)

24 The name of Bert Baxter's Alsatian in Sue Townsend's book *The Secret Diary of Adrian Mole, Aged 13¾* (5)

26 Flightless bird in the order Sphenisciformes; also the former name for the great auk (7)

29 Distinctive patch of coloured cloth on a military uniform; also a pre-drawn design template for a tattoo (5)

31 An official ban on commerce and trade with a specific country (7)

33 Nickname for the City of London, the Bank of England and the surrounding areas collectively (6,4)

34 Dry-cured Italian ham served paper-thin in a course of antipasti (10)

36 The Corps of Her Majesty's Royal ___; branch of the Navy in which personnel are rigorously trained to serve as commandos (7)

37 Rope attached to the clew of a sail to control or alter its direction (5)

38 Glandular organ of a flower which secretes a sugary fluid (7)

39 US poet who wrote the strangely-spelled *Little Orphant Annie* (5)

41 System of communication based on signalling with a pair of flags (9)

44 Large nest of a bird of prey, especially an eagle (5)

47 Spanish-born tenor noted for his many concert performances with Carreras and Pavarotti (7)

50 In human anatomy, the toughened plates of keratin growing from each of the distal phalanges (5)

52 Dense dark cloud of gas and cosmic dust in a star formation, observed against a brighter background (7)

54 Country with the national anthem *Bilady, Bilady, Bilady* (5)

55 Violent storm measuring 12 on the Beaufort Scale, also called a tropical cyclone (9)

56 Post-Freudian Austrian-born psychoanalyst and pioneering child psychologist (5)

57 English novelist and playwright who wrote *Brighton Rock, The Power and the Glory* and *The Heart of the Matter* (6)

58 Ancient Hebrew unit of liquid volume equal to 10 baths (5)

59 Transition metal in the platinum family which is the densest natural element known, atomic number 76 (6)

Down

2 Global news agency founded in London in 1851 by the telegraphy pioneer born Israel Beer Josafat (7)

3 Toxic gas and allotropic form of oxygen present in the atmosphere (5)

4 Greek tragedy by Sophocles (7)

5 Trick-taking card game for four players, two against two (5)

6 Landlocked country with the capital and largest city Tashkent (10)

7 Spicy paste of ground chilli peppers, paprika and olive oil used in North African cuisine (7)

8 US sculptor, print-maker and pop artist who depicted universally recognised images such as flags (5)

9 English actor noted for his lead roles in *Bergerac* and *Midsomer Murders* (7)

10 Jeweller's and watchmaker's magnifying glass, either hand-held or worn in one of the eye sockets (5)

11 Abdominal organ responsible for removing old red blood cells (6)

33

12 The theory of knowledge (12)
20 Subatomic particle present in all atomic nuclei, with the exception of ordinary hydrogen (7)
22 British statesman born off the coast of Jamaica who founded Singapore (7)
23 US transcendentalist and New Thought pioneer who wrote *Nature* (7)
25 Square cap worn by Roman Catholic clergy (7)
26 Latin phrase literally meaning "after noon" or "after midday" (4,8)
27 Description of a substance with a pH close to 7.0 (7)
28 Goddess of divine retribution (7)
30 Character in *Hamlet*, present in the grave-digger scene (7)
32 Soft French roll or loaf containing a high content of butter and eggs (7)
35 Traditional cottage garden plant with striking spikes of purplish-blue flowers, sometimes called larkspur (10)
40 The longest river in Asia (7)
42 __ of the Glen; drama series which takes its name from a painting by Sir Edwin Landseer (7)
43 Nickname of the Cretan-born Spanish painter Doménikos Theotokópoulos (2,5)
45 Cylindrical pile of coins (7)
46 Stage direction literally meaning "they go out" (6)
48 __ of London; official title of Alexander Boris de Pfeffel Johnson (5)
49 Earthy pigment composed of clay and iron oxide (5)
51 Drummer for The Beatles who replaced Pete Best in 1962 (5)
53 A type of loose fibre obtained by untwisting old rope (5)

?

bareta

Horatio   Yangse

Prosciutto

Across

1 Pulitzer Prize-winning novelist and activist whose notable works include *The Color Purple* and *Possessing the Secret of Joy* (6)

4 B anglore-born cricketer who captained England and Kent, scoring 107 centuries in his career, 22 of them being in Test cricket (7)

8 Compact group of terrestrial or underwater mountains (6)

14 Playwright, dramatist and leading exponent of the Theatre of the Absurd who wrote *The Bald Soprano*, *The Killer* and *Rhinoceros* (7)

15 South American country with a national flag consisting of horizontal bands of yellow, blue and red with a coat of arms bearing a condor (7)

16 The highest adult male singing voice; also the largest and deepest-pitched bell in a full peal (5)

17 Highly unstable, artificially synthesised chemical element, atomic number 109 (10)

18 Mediterranean dish of diced cucumber and tomatoes with feta cheese, Kalamata olives and thinly-sliced red onion (5,5)

20 Plant of a genus that includes catmint or catnip (6)

22 The son of Henry III who was known as "Longshanks" and the "Hammer of the Scots" (6,1)

24 __ *Woman*; 1990 movie starring Richard Gere and Julia Roberts featuring a number one hit by Roy Orbison (6)

27 Nobel Prize-winning poet and short story writer whose notable works include *Rikki-Tikki-Tavi*, *If*, *Gunga Din* and *Just So Stories* (7)

28 Capital nicknamed "The City of a Thousand Minarets" (5)

29 British chemist born in 28 Across who was awarded the 1964 Nobel Prize in Chemistry for determining the structures of penicillin, vitamin B12 and insulin using her X-ray techniques (7)

32 Any one of the keys of a piano (4)

33 Labour politician who served as Home Secretary from 1997-2001 and Foreign Secretary from 2001-06 (5)

34 US dancer and choreographer remembered for his performances in the film musicals *An American in Paris* and *Singin' in the Rain* (5)

35 Rack-like trough or manger for animal fodder (4)

39 SI derived unit of electrical conductance equal to one reciprocal ohm, named after a German-born British inventor and industrialist (7)

40 English poet who spent much of his life in an asylum, where he composed *I Am* (5)

41 Protective glass over a watch face; also a piezoelectric material used as an oscillator or transducer (7)

42 Bread roll-like food typically sliced in two, toasted and buttered (6)

44 Small bunting formerly eaten as a delicacy in parts of France (7)

46 English novelist whose pen name was Acton Bell (6)

50 The art of engraving on wood (10)

52 The science of numbers (10)

55 Synthetic fibre used to make sportswear, hosiery and other garments in which stretch is desirable (5)

56 __ *Den*; entrepreneurial series with venture capitalists including Deborah Meaden and Theo Paphitis (7)

57 Word linking history, law, science and theology (7)

58 Member of an Athabaskan-speaking Native American people who lived in New Mexico and Arizona (6)

59 Russian-born French painter noted for his use of rich colours (7)

60 Australian swimmer who won the Olympic gold medal for the 100 metres freestyle three times successively (6)

Down

1 Author of the *Leaves of Grass* poetry collection which included his verses *I Sing the Body Electric*, *Song of Myself* and *America* (7)

2 The Hawaiian "Pineapple Island" (5)

3 Soviet-Russian film-maker who directed *The Battleship Potemkin* (10)

5 Swedish strait also called The Sound (7)

6 Inner part of a washing machine (4)

7 Shrub or tree in the honeysuckle family, genus *Sambucus* (5)

9 The national system of motorways in Italy and parts of Sicily (10)

10 A quantum state with zero spin (7)

11 English physicist who discovered electromagnetic induction (7)

12 English artist noted for his depictions of life in Salford (5)

13 Constellation between Taurus and Pisces, said to represent the Ram (5)

19 French avant-garde pianist noted for his *Gymnopédies* series of compositions (5)

34

21 Laboratory instrument for transferring and measuring small, precise amounts of liquids (7)

23 The jurisdiction of a bishop (7)

25 An exaggerated opinion of one's own importance (7)

26 Character in Shakespeare's *The Merchant of Venice* (7)

27 Title of two historical books of the Old Testament (5)

28 Author of *Troilus and Criseyde* (7)

30 Fibrous substance forming the main structural constituent of claws, feathers, hair, hoofs and horns (7)

31 Chemist who bequeathed his entire fortune to fund a series of prizes (5)

36 Signalling device which employs the use of a mirror and sunlight (10)

37 One of the six noble gases (5)

38 Instrument for measuring the humidity of the air (10)

42 The human jawbone, especially the upper half (7)

43 Small sailing boat used on the Nile and in the Mediterranean (7)

45 Colloidal suspension of fine particles in a gas such as air (7)

47 Elongated fish also called a snake mackerel (7)

48 Container for storing tea leaves (5)

49 US actress who starred in *Total Recall*, *Basic Instinct* and *Casino* (5)

51 Conservative politician who served as prime minister from 1970-74 (5)

53 *Who Stole the __?*; the eleventh chapter of Lewis Carroll's *Alice's Adventures in Wonderland* (5)

54 Instrument used to signal that a meal is about to be served (4)

Across

11 Austrian composer of over 600 works including around 16 operas, more than 40 symphonies, 26 string quartets and 27 piano concertos (6)

12 __ the Great; king of Macedon and student of Aristotle who created one of the largest empires in ancient history before his 30th birthday (9)

13 Any one of the 16 least powerful chess pieces (4)

14 Period of time during June 6, 1944, when the Allied forces invaded Normandy (1-3)

15 Name by which the Dutch painter who created *The Anatomy Lesson of Dr Nicolaes Tulp*, *Belshazzar's Feast* and *Night Watch* is known (9)

16 Irish physician whose collections of specimens, books and curiosities formed the foundation of the British Museum and the Natural History Museum (6)

17 English Romantic painter of landscapes and seascapes whose notable works include *Rain, Steam and Speed* and *The Fighting Temeraire* (6)

20 Imaginary kingdom in adventure novels by Anthony Hope (9)

23 Traditional Arab lateen-rigged vessel used in the Indian Ocean (4)

24 The capital and most populous city of Norway, formerly known as Christiania (4)

26 The world's largest existent land carnivore, *Ursus maritimus* (5,4)

28 In physics, the capacity of a material body or of radiation to perform work (6)

30 Use of unnecessary or redundant words to convey a meaning (8)

32 Mountain first successfully climbed in 1953 by Sir Edmund Hillary and Tenzing Norgay (7)

34 The female of the ferret; also a section of the underside of a toadstool or mushroom (4)

36 Endangered species of miniature water buffalo native to the Indonesian island Sulawesi (4)

37 Resort in central Switzerland; also another name for alfalfa (7)

38 Collective body of freeholders (8)

39 One of the wives of Henry VIII who was beheaded (6)

42 A book of the New Testament ascribed to Saint Paul the Apostle (9)

44 British novelist who created Oompa-Loompas and snozzcumbers (4)

45 British explorer and naval officer who, in 1831, located the position of the north magnetic pole and later headed an expedition to the Antarctic (4)

47 Title of any great Hindu sage (9)

49 The largest city of the US Garden State and Essex County (6)

51 Drummer character in Jim Henson's *The Muppet Show* (6)

52 Natural harbour in the Orkney Islands that was used as a British naval base during the First World War (5,4)

55 Historical television drama series which begins with a depiction of Julius Caesar's conquest of Gaul (4)

57 The lowest female singing voice (4)

58 Bavarian city where Nazi war criminals were tried by the International Military Tribunal in 1945 and 1946 (9)

59 The mythological Greek god of darkness, son of Chaos (6)

Down

1 Historical measure of land area equal to a quarter of an acre or 40 square perches (4)

2 An Indian fig tree; also a style of loose silk or cotton gown worn by men in the 18th century (6)

3 ___man; 1972 hit by David Bowie (4)

4 Style of brimless bonnet or cap worn as part of the traditional Scottish Highland dress (8)

5 Pomaceous fruit in the rose family with varieties including Comice, Conference, D'Anjou, and Williams (4)

6 Highly-prized wood used by gun and cabinet makers (6)

7 Horizontal passage into a mine (4)

8 Capital of Queensland, Australia (8)

9 In computing, to transfer data from a local system to a larger remote one (6)

10 English name of a collection of posthumously-published songs by Franz Schubert (4,4)

18 The letter of the Greek alphabet between tau and phi (7)

19 Common name of the painter and architect of the High Renaissance who created *Sistine Madonna* (7)

21 The name of a group of elements in the lanthanide series that includes atomic numbers 57 through to 71, plus scandium and yttrium (4,5)

22 ___ Stakes; a race for two-year-old thoroughbred horses (7)

25 Order of slender-bodied predatory insects comprising dragonflies and damselflies (7)

27 Informal term for a short break with light refreshments taken between breakfast and lunch (9)

29 Country with the motto Dieu et mon droit, literally meaning "God and my right" (7)

31 Shakespearean character who says: "I dare do all that may become a man; Who dares do more is none." (7)

33 English atomic physicist who discovered isotopes and electrons, for which he was awarded the 1906 Nobel Prize in Physics (7)

35 Type of dog which is typically bred from crossing a greyhound with a collie or retriever (7)

40 Irish nationalist leader who was known as "The Liberator" (1'7)

41 Small savoury ball typically made with suet, cooked and served in casseroles, soups and stews (8)

43 The study of the ultimate nature and significance of values (8)

46 Israelite leader whose supernatural strength lay in his uncut hair (6)

48 Dominions of a king or queen (6)

50 The Chief Justice of the US who headed a commission into the assassination of John F. Kennedy (6)

52 Brownish-red-coloured variety of chalcedony similar to carnelian (4)

53 The Greek god of war with the Roman counterpart Mars (4)

54 English architect who redesigned St Paul's Cathedral following the 1666 Fire of London (4)

56 Heavy beetle-like hammer (4)

35

Howard   Thor   onyx

Victoria   Dhau   Dahl

clan   Lucerne

Across

1 Novelist who wrote the children's classics *Little Lord Fauntleroy*, *A Little Princess* and *The Secret Garden* (7)

5 English composer who set William Blake's poem *And did those feet in ancient time* to music, today known as *Jerusalem* (5)

8 Jockey who penned more than 40 internationally best-selling crime and thriller novels in his retirement (7)

12 Metalloid chemical element, atomic number 14, used to make transistors and electronic circuits (7)

13 Art form such as Richard Hamilton's work *Just What Is It That Makes Today's Homes So Different, So Appealing?* (7)

14 A lobster trap, a bobbin rack on a spinning machine or a wicker basket for holding fish (5)

15 Containing the ace, king, queen, jack and 10 all in the same suit, the highest-ranking standard poker hand (5,5)

16 Branch of medicine specialising in the study and treatment of disorders of the mind (10)

18 Musical composition for eight instruments or voices (5)

20 Band of tissue above a horse's coffin bone; also section of a deer's antler (7)

22 Cell transmitting nerve impulses to the brain and spinal cord (6)

27 Loose garment worn in ancient Greece and Rome (5)

28 According to legend, the castle where King Arthur held his court (7)

30 Resinous substance formerly used to make gramophone records (7)

32 The capital of the Mogul empire from 1526 to 1658 (4)

33 US president who was preceded by Andrew Johnson and succeeded by Rutherford B. Hayes (5)

34 Heavy block found in a forge (5)

35 Primeval giant of Norse mythology who was slain by Odin and his brothers (4)

39 In Italian cuisine, small dumplings made from flour, potatoes or semolina, typically served with a sauce (7)

40 National monetary unit of Paraguay that was formerly equal to 100 céntimos (7)

41 Rock group noted for tracks including *I Feel Free*, *Sunshine of Your Love* and *Crossroads* (5)

42 Scottish outlaw and folk hero who is the subject of a historical novel with the same name by Sir Walter Scott (3,3)

44 County town in the West Midlands on the River Avon (7)

46 Finch closely related to the linnet, Latin name *Carduelis flavirostris* (5)

50 Temperature at which a combustible liquid gives off sufficient vapour to ignite in air (10)

52 Inlet where the British under Nelson defeated the French fleet in the Battle of the Nile (7,3)

55 Dish of marinated meat and vegetables cooked and served on a large skewer (5)

56 Swedish chemist who discovered oxygen, chlorine, glycerol, tungsten and a number of other chemicals (7)

57 French post-impressionist painter who created *Rideau, Cruchon et Compotier* and *The Bathers* (7)

58 German mathematician and pioneer of differential geometry (7)

59 Revolutionary and journalist who was stabbed to death in his bath by Charlotte Corday, depicted in a painting by Jacques-Louis David (5)

60 The shortened surname of the Indian novelist who wrote *Swami and Friends*, *The Man-Eater of Malgudi* and *A Tiger for Malgudi* (7)

Down

1 Warm brownish-yellow-coloured pigment obtained from the soot of burnt wood, especially of the beech (6)

2 An extended unbroken exchange of strokes between tennis players (5)

3 Title or form of address given to some high-ranking officials, usually preceded by "Your", "His" or "Her" (10)

4 Term for any of the brown seaweeds, especially oarweed (6)

5 Painter and sculptor whose *Garçon à la pipe* sold at Sotheby's auction for over $104 million in 2004 (7)

6 Small loaf of bread; also an official register of names (4)

7 Nobel Prize-winning poet who wrote *The Tower* and *The Winding Stair* (5)

8 Comedienne who portrayed the character Reverend Geraldine Granger from 1994 to 2007 (6)

9 P hysicist, mathematician and inventor who discovered the laws of buoyancy and displacement (10)

10 City on the River Dee (7)

11 *Mustang* __; song that featured in the 1991 film *The Commitments* (5)
17 *Britain's Got Talent* contestant who released her debut album *I Dreamed a Dream* in 2009 (5)
19 Musical direction indicating that a piece must be played with spirit and vigour (3,4)
21 Baltic republic on the south coast of the Gulf of Finland (7)
23 Trademark name of an alloy of atomic numbers 24 and 28, used in electrical heating elements (8)
24 Any person who is not a member or official of either the House of Commons or the House of Lords (8)
25 The eighth sign of the zodiac (7)
26 Synthetic compound used as a mild analgesic and an anti-coagulant (7)
29 Nicaraguan capital that was almost completely destroyed by an earthquake in December 1972 (7)
31 A former unit of luminance (7)
36 An extreme fear of heights (10)
37 One of the islands of Vanuatu (5)
38 Nobel Peace Prize-winning polymath who established a hospital in Gabon (10)
43 The fruit of the blackberry (7)
45 Surrey-born radical agriculturist who wrote *Rural Rides* (7)
47 English actress who portrayed Elizabeth I in *Fire Over England* (6)
48 Roman blacksmith god of fire (6)
49 Two-legged heraldic dragon with a barbed tail and wings (6)
50 Muslim religious ascetic living solely on alms (5)
51 A minor Hebrew prophet (5)
53 US actor and comedian of radio and television noted for his comic timing (5)
54 Kiln or furnace for annealing glass (4)

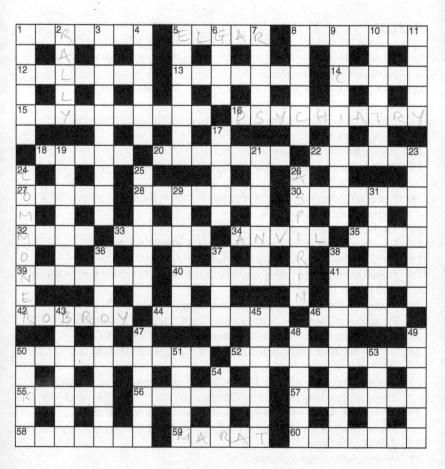

creat anvil marat
Sienna
Warwickewat

37

Across

1 Novelist who wrote *The Once and Future King* tetralogy which begins with *The Sword in the Stone* (5)

4 Rugby union player whose last-minute drop goal secured England's 20-17 win over Australia in the 2003 World Cup (9)

9 Legendary German scholar reputed to have sold his soul to the devil and Mephistopheles (5)

14 The capital city of Tuscany (8)

15 Group of nine musicians; also a composition for nine voices or instruments (5)

16 Protestant bishop and martyr who was burned at the stake for opposing the Catholic policies of Mary I (6)

17 The head of a university faculty (4)

18 French philosopher who was one of the founders of sociology (5)

19 An Israeli monetary unit; also a marketplace in ancient Greece (5)

20 English painter of both world wars whose notable works include *The Ypres Salient at Night* and *Totes Meer* (4)

21 Electrophysiologist who was co-awarded the 1932 Nobel Prize for Physiology or Medicine for his work on the functions of neurons (6)

22 Cricketer who captained the Yorkshire team from 1971-78 (7)

24 Society Island that was popularised by Paul Gauguin and Robert Louis Stevenson (6)

27 Fabulous half-man half-bull, human flesh-eating creature that was slain by Theseus in the labyrinth built by Daedalus (8)

29 From the Italian literally meaning "jest", a light, vigorous and playful movement in a symphony or sonata, typically in triple time (7)

31 Row of a chessboard (4)

32 Amino acid found in vegetables (10)

35 Substance traditionally used to treat and coat cricket bats (7,3)

36 A loosely-clumped mass of fine woolly particles (4)

37 Highly-seasoned spicy Spanish pork sausage eaten as tapas (7)

38 *The Curious ___ of the Dog in the Night-Time*; 2003 mystery novel by Mark Haddon based on the investigations of a character with Asperger's syndrome (8)

41 "___ we stand, divided we fall." *The Four Oxen and the Tiger*, Aesop (6)

42 Old World shrub with highly-fragrant flowers used to flavour some varieties of tea (7)

44 *Stuart* ___; 1945 children's novel by *Charlotte's Web* author E. B. White (6)

46 Musical instrument that was developed from the shawm (4)

49 Capital and largest city of Ghana (5)

51 Nocturnal mammal with a short proboscis, whose closest relations include rhinoceroses and horses (5)

53 According to Chinese philosophy, the opposite to yin (4)

54 The smallest country in the world by size after Vatican City but the most densely-populated (6)

55 In computing, to detect and remove errors in a programme or piece of source code (5)

56 The ___; headquarters of the US Department of Defence that was badly damaged in the September 11 terrorist attacks (8)

57 Serve-like shot delivered with force in tennis and badminton (5)

58 Roulade-like type of cake based on sponge, jam and buttercream (5,4)

59 Wood used to make piano keys (5)

Down

2 Two-handed weapon in the form of a spear combined with an axe (7)

3 Film director, screenwriter and actor whose works include *Reservoir Dogs*, *Pulp Fiction* and *Kill Bill* (9)

5 Metal girder or joist used in construction (1-4)

6 Classical and rock violinist who released an album in 1999 based on the music of Jimi Hendrix (7)

7 Secret agent of feudal Japan (5)

8 Small military camp positioned at some distance from the main army (7)

10 Pulitzer Prize-winning poet who penned *Look, Stranger!*, *Another Time* and *The Age of Anxiety* (5)

11 Saint-___; composer, conductor and organist noted for *The Carnival of the Animals*, *Danse Macabre* and *Samson and Delilah* (5)

12 Non-venomous snake native to tropical South America; one species of which may grow up to nine metres (8)

13 Common name for the sternum (10)

22 Mexican dish of a flour tortilla folded around meat and beans (7)

23 Shakespearean character who says: "Keep up your bright swords, for the dew will rust them." (7)

25 King of Judea who, according to the New Testament, ordered the Massacre of the Innocents (5)

26 Device which regulates the tautness of stitches created by a sewing machine (7)

28 Protein hormone produced in the pancreas by the islets of Langerhans (7)

29 One of the basic units of taxonomic classification (7)

30 Scottish engineer noted for his contributions towards thermodynamics (7)

33 Horse-racing town in Berkshire; also a style of necktie (5)

34 Ecclesiastical dignitary ranking below a bishop (10)

39 Pale greenish-coloured toxic gas, atomic number 17 (8)

40 In ancient Greece, a wild choral hymn dedicated to the god of wine, Dionysus (9)

42 Silvery-headed pale-eyed bird, noted for thievery (7)

43 In mathematics, any positive or negative whole number (7)

45 President of the US who was assassinated by John Wilkes Booth in a theatre box (7)

47 Shrub related to gorse (5)

48 English actress remembered for her role as Lady Bracknell in the 1952 film adaptation of Oscar Wilde's *The Importance of Being Earnest* (5)

50 Statesman elected President of the Palestinian National Authority following the death of Yasser Arafat (5)

52 Aperture in the centre of the iris (5)

37

diagio Epsom allegro volute

Jabot lyre

menateur artic

slub

Banquo Jackdaw outpost

nipan

Across

1   English textile designer, craftsman and poet who established a decorative arts firm with Edward Burne-Jones, Dante Gabriel Rossetti and others in 1861 (6)

5   Empress __; also known as Maud, daughter of Henry I, mother of Henry II, and leader of an unsuccessful civil war against Stephen of Blois (7)

9   The common name of a small crab apple-like fruit that requires bletting before it is suitable to eat (6)

12 1993 novel by Sebastian Faulks, based during the First World War (8)

13 Growth-promoting hormone present in plants (5)

14 Early Jesuit missionary to India and the Far East (6)

15 Metal neck ornament worn by the ancient Celts (4)

16 Device in or attached to a photographic camera for producing a period of sudden illumination (5)

17 The US "Witch City" (5)

18 Area of central London, site of Carnaby Street (4)

19 Book of the Bible concerning the Israelite of the same name who led his people into the Promised Land (6)

20 Horse-drawn vehicle that was used in ancient warfare and racing (7)

22 Upper tower of a medieval castle; also a section of a lathe (6)

25 Architectural style prevalent during the reign of James I (8)

27 Academy Award-winning actress who starred in the musical films *Mary Poppins* and *The Sound of Music* (7)

29 Ninth letter of the Greek alphabet (4)

30 Traditional British dish of minced beef topped with mashed potato (7,3)

33 Former unit of pressure that was equal to 101,325 pascals (10)

34 Actor who starred in the *Road* series of movies with Bing Crosby (4)

35 Country with a national flag consisting of two horizontal red stripes and one white (7)

36 Shrub or fruit tree with branches trained to grow flat against a wall (8)

39 Ancient Roman boxing glove, typically loaded with iron or lead; also Aphrodite's girdle (6)

40 Katherine __; Welsh mezzo-soprano who recently released the album *Daydream* (7)

42 Type of roof constructed from straw, sedge, water reeds, heather or any other similar natural material (6)

44 A cooked mixture of butter and flour used to thicken various classic sauces (4)

47 Novelist who wrote: "We seek him here, we seek him there, those Frenchies seek him everywhere. Is he in heaven?—Is he in hell? That damned, elusive Pimpernel." (5)

49 The Welsh name for Wales (5)

51 In cricket, either of the two crosspieces bridging the stumps (4)

52 Root vegetable in the cabbage family resembling a large radish (6)

53 Statesman and soldier who served as prime minister of the Union of South Africa from 1919-24 and later from 1939-48 (5)

54 In zoology, the scientific study of animal behaviour (8)

55 Person skilled in the construction of the wooden elements of a house (6)

56 Country that was suspended from the Commonwealth for over three years following the execution of the activist Ken Saro-Wiwa in 1995 (7)

57 Life-supporting gaseous element forming around 20.8 per cent of the earth's atmosphere (6)

Down

2 Great river spanning between Venezuela and Colombia; also the name of one of Elisabeth Beresford's Womble characters (7)

3 Purple-leaved variety of chicory (9)

4 One of many frozen, crystal-like conglomerations studied and photographed by Wilson Bentley (9)

5 Molten material below or within the earth's crust (5)

6 Anatomical term for what is commonly called the windpipe (7)

7 The total stock of words and phrases in a language (5)

8 Architectural fillet or listel encircling a column; also a heraldic charge in the form of a ring (7)

9 Highly infectious disease of rabbits, called "white blindness" in the 1972 classic *Watership Down* (11)

10 Professional snooker player nicknamed "The Nugget" who won six world championships in the 1980s (5)

11 Hebrew letter based on a hieroglyph depicting an ox's head (5)

20 Supergiant which is the second-brightest star in the night sky (7)

21 US state bordered by Kentucky, Illinois, Ohio and Michigan (7)

23 Scottish broadcasting executive who played a pivotal role in the development of the BBC (5)

24 The mythological Greek muse of music, lyric poetry and flutes (7)

26 In linguistics, the omission of the final sound or syllable of a word (7)

27 Department in southern France in the Midi-Pyrénées region (7)

28 The swineherd of Odysseus (7)

31 River that rises in Staffordshire, unites with the Ouse and empties into the North Sea (5)

32 *The Ant and the __;* fable by Greek story-teller Aesop (11)

37 The male romantic lead character in Shakespeare's comedy *The Taming of the Shrew* (9)

38 Familiar name of a folk and blues musician who played the twelve-string guitar and the accordion (4,5)

40 Academy award-winning English actress and politician who starred in *Women in Love* and *A Touch of Class* (7)

41 One of the teeth at the front of the mouth adapted for cutting (7)

43 In sailing, a metal eyelet through which rope may pass (7)

45 City in western Bolivia that was once an important silver and tin mining region (5)

46 Colourless, odourless noble gas, atomic number 54 (5)

48 Singer-songwriter who released the album *Harvest* in 1972 (5)

50 Hound of Icarius's daughter Erigone that was turned into the dog star Procyon (5)

38

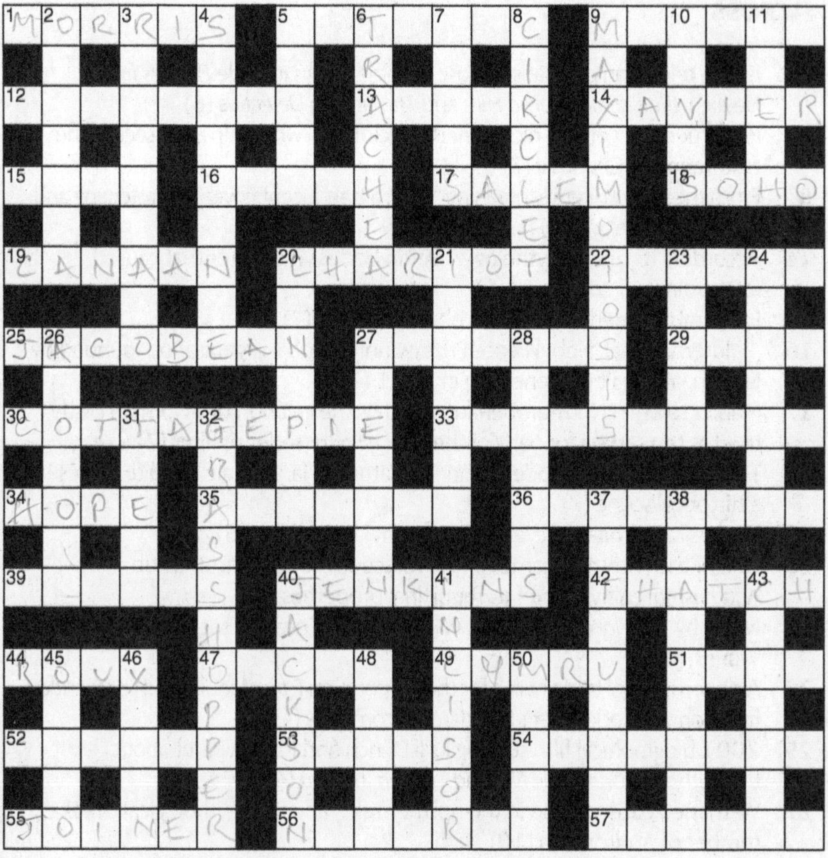

39

Across

1 British television dramatist whose notable works include *Pennies from Heaven*, *Blue Remembered Hills* and *The Singing Detective* (6)

4 Parliamentary general nicknamed "Black Tom" who helped to secure the restoration of Charles II (7)

8 From the French literally meaning "bell", a translucent cover for protecting and forcing young plants (6)

14 According to Greek mythology, river in Hades with water that caused forgetfulness if consumed (5)

15 Favourable omen drawn from observing birds (7)

16 __ International; Nobel Peace Prize-winning global organisation founded by English lawyer Peter Benenson in 1961 (7)

17 Market town in Northumberland which is the location of a Norman castle used as the setting for parts of the *Harry Potter* series of films (7)

18 Three-dimensional model, either miniature or large-scale, used to represent a historical scene (7)

19 In Classical architecture, a rounded convex moulding (5)

20 One of the common names of the rutaceous South African shrub *Agathosma*, cultivated for its medicinal properties (5)

21 Novel by the *Horatio Hornblower* author C. S. Forester, set during the Great War (3,7)

23 An international trade name for the corporation ExxonMobil which descended from John D. Rockefeller's Standard Oil company (4)

25 2001 biographical film starring Judi Dench and Kate Winslet about the author of *Under the Net* and *The Sea, the Sea* (4)

27 W-shaped constellation in the northern sky; also the mythological Greek mother of Andromeda (10)

30 English clergyman and author who created the *Thomas the Tank Engine* series of children's books (5)

32 Aria that was composed by George Gershwin for the 1935 opera *Porgy and Bess*, today a popular jazz standard (10)

34 *The __*; 1939 musical film starring Judy Garland, based on a 1900 novel by L. Frank Baum (6,2,2)

37 Auditory device typically used to signal danger or an emergency situation (5)

38 Duty-free tourist destination on the north coast of Jamaica (7,3)

3

39

39 Socialist and reformer who co-founded the London School of Economics; both he and his wife were members of the Fabian Society (4)
41 The wife or widow of a knight (4)
43 Military fortification which protects the end of a causeway-like structure nearest the enemy's position (10)
46 An uninvited guest who arrives with an invited one; also the darkest, most central part of a sunspot (5)
49 The second-largest bone in the human body (5)
50 Legendary Spanish nobleman and libertine who is the central subject of a play by Molière, a poem by Byron and an opera by Mozart (3,4)
52 Term for an adult wild hawk caught for training (7)
54 The mother of King Arthur (7)
55 King of Great Britain and Ireland from 1714-27 (6,1)
56 The anglicised name of the Roman statesman Marcus Cicero, whose murder was ordered by his enemy Mark Antony (5)
57 Pessimistic donkey character created by A. A. Milne (6)
58 Variety of medium-sweet sherry (7)
59 Protein substance functioning as a catalyst to increase or decrease the rate of specific biochemical reactions (6)

Down

1 Lively dance of Bohemian origin (5)
2 The name of the passenger liner that struck an iceberg on her maiden voyage and sank with the loss of over 1,500 lives almost 100 years ago (7)
3 Title applied to an honourably retired or discharged professor, minister or bishop (8)
5 The name of two Syrian presidents since 1971 (5)
6 Ungulate mammal that has been hunted by man to the point of near extinction in recent decades (10)
7 Material used to make transparencies for use in an overhead projector (7)
9 Novelist born John Griffith Chaney who wrote *Call of the Wild* and *White Fang*, both of which were set during the Klondike Gold Rush (6)
10 Authorities responsible for collecting duties on imported goods (7)
11 The study of the origin of words (9)
12 In computing, a unit of coded data transmitted across a network (6)

The Telegraph

39

13 Pinkish-coloured dip made from fish roe, olive oil and seasoning, typically served with grissini or crudités (1,2)

20 English composer who wrote the orchestral work *A Colour Symphony* (5)

22 Inventor of photographic roll film (7)

24 In telecommunication, a unit of data transmission speed for a modem equal to one bit per second (4)

26 The third-largest city in Turkey (5)

28 Latin phrase literally meaning "before noon" (4,8)

29 Part of a literary or dramatic work (7)

31 The author of *Moll Flanders* (5)

33 Evil ___; the witch character in the *Willo the Wisp* series (4)

35 African equid that was related to the now extinct quagga subspecies (5)

36 French existentialist philosopher who had a lifelong relationship with Jean-Paul Sartre (2,8)

37 A single diamond set in a ring (9)

40 Chemical element, symbol W (8)

42 Courtier and maîtresse-en-titre of Louis XV who was guillotined during the French Revolution (2,5)

44 Town in the north of the Republic of Ireland; also a type of tweed (7)

45 Tuberous Mexican plant named after a Swedish botanist (6)

47 18th-century Astronomer Royal who discovered the aberration of light (7)

48 Scottish mathematician who invented logarithms (6)

51 Historically, title of the king or supreme ruler of Ethiopia (5)

53 Mrs ___; character in *Father Ted* (5)

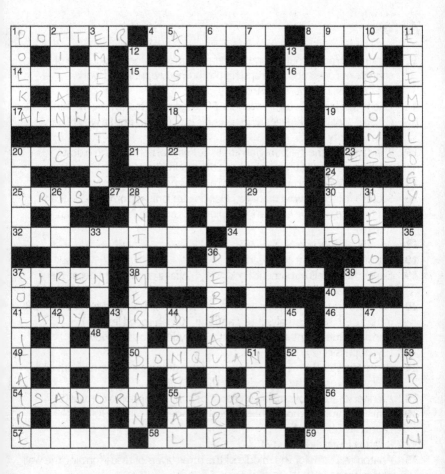

The Telegraph

40

Across

1 Elizabethan poet, courtier and soldier remembered for his sequence of sonnets *Astrophel and Stella* and his posthumously-published work *The Countess of Pembroke's Arcadia* (6)

4 Chemical element, atomic number 69, used in portable X-ray machines (7)

8 Guido __; political blogger who takes his pseudonym from a would-be revolutionary (6)

14 The capital of the Italian region Emilia-Romagna, home to the oldest continuously operating university in the world (7)

15 __ of Love; West End production with music by Andrew Lloyd Webber (7)

16 Scottish footballer who managed Manchester United from 1945-69 and led them to win five League Championships and the 1968 European Cup (5)

17 An official stoppage of trade (7)

18 Lettuce also called a crisphead (7)

19 Department for Environment, Food and __ Affairs; government department formed in 2001 (5)

20 Baroness and Labour politician who, as Minister of Transport from 1965-68, introduced the breathalyser test and the 70mph speed limit (6)

22 German experimental psychologist and physicist who founded psychophysics (7)

24 Prime Minister from 1945–51, noted for instituting a modern health and welfare system in the UK, including the NHS (6)

28 Architectural console supporting or appearing to support a cornice (5)

30 Sea __; champion thoroughbred racehorse depicted in a 2001 book by Laura Hillenbrand (7)

32 Relating to earthquakes (7)

35 Anatomical term for the middle of the three layers of tissue forming the wall of the heart (10)

36 The scientific study of insects (10)

38 Medical term for what is more commonly called German measles (7)

39 Italian sports car manufacturer with the "prancing horse" logo (7)

40 One of the ingredients used to make Lyonnaise-style potatoes (5)

41 *Black* __; novel written by Anna Sewel during her last year of life (6)

43 __ & *Makepeace*; 1980s television crime drama series that starred Michael Brandon and Glynis Barber (7)

45 Deep-red variety of garnet (6)

49 Corn-based type of Mexican crisp, typically served with dips or various toppings (5)

51 Anglicised name of the King of the Scots 1040-57 who was also nicknamed the "Red King" (7)

53 An instrument for measuring the flow of electric current (7)

56 African mammal which looks similar to a dog but acts like a cat (5)

57 German composer who produced the opera *Der Rosenkavalier* with the librettist Hugo von Hofmannsthal (7)

58 Latin term literally meaning "in the next month" (7)

59 International distress signal in voice procedure radio communication (6)

60 *The __;* Shakespeare play which ends: "As you from crimes would pardon'd be, Let your indulgence set me free." (7)

61 Satellite of Saturn discovered in 1684 by the Italian-born French astronomer Giovanni Domenico Cassini, who studied in 14 Across (6)

Down

1 An artist's paintbrush made from the fur of marten of the same name; also the colour black in heraldry (5)

2 French organist and composer of operas and ballets who wrote *Coppélia*, *Sylvia* and *Lakmé* (7)

3 English Romantic composer who wrote *The Dream of Gerontius* (5)

5 A colourless variety of opal (7)

6 According to Irish folklore, a shoe-making sprite that hides its coins in a pot of gold at the end of a rainbow (10)

7 *The Man from __;* US spy-fi, espionage television series that starred Robert Vaughn (1,1,1,1,1)

9 Of traffic lights, the colour of the cautionary signal between stop and go, and vice versa (5)

10 Type of falcon depicted in the Ken Loach film with the tagline: "They beat him. They deprived him. They ridiculed him. They broke his heart. But they couldn't break his spirit." (7)

11 Colour also called azure (3,4)

12 English name of the Italian explorer who sailed from Bristol to North America in the caravel Matthew in 1497 (5)

13 Tributary of the Missouri River (5)

The Telegraph

40

20 A leader of the English Reformation who helped negotiate Henry VIII's divorce from Catherine of Aragon and was later condemned to death (7)

21 Motor car with a folding top (9)

23 Baltic country with a blue, black and white horizontally-striped flag (7)

25 In mechanical engineering, the study of friction, wear and lubrication (9)

26 Largest city of the Ivory Coast (7)

27 In chemistry, the diffusion of molecules through a semi-permeable membrane (7)

29 Former measure of volume equal to four bushels; also a hollow in a hillside, especially in southern England (5)

31 Light cooked dish based on adding egg yolks to beaten egg whites (7)

33 Polynesian language of the aboriginal people of New Zealand (5)

34 The capital of French Guiana (7)

37 Athletic event associated with Jonathan Edwards (6,4)

41 English jurist and philosopher who was the first major proponent of utilitarianism and animal rights (7)

42 Sport studied by a toxophilite (7)

44 Ancient Greek city, site of one the Seven Wonders of the Ancient World (7)

46 The largest living bird (7)

47 Of or belonging to a strict US Mennonite sect founded in 1693 (5)

48 Square in an Italian town (5)

50 The largest city in Nebraska (5)

52 Nobel Prize-winning physicist and radioactivity pioneer who discovered polonium and radium (5)

54 Footballer who captained the England team that won the 1966 World Cup (5)

55 Television mini-series based on a 1976 novel by Alex Haley (5)

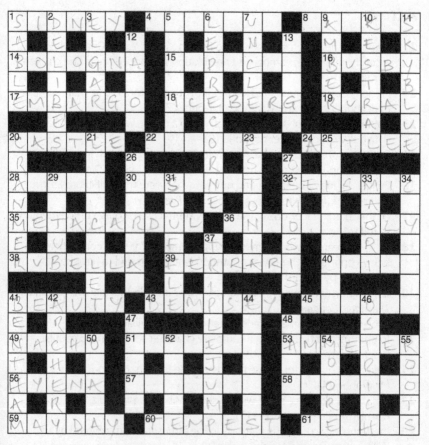

41

Across

11 Celebrity chef and restaurateur also known as the "Naked Chef", who was recently involved in campaigns to revolutionise school dinners and chicken farming (6)

12 French painter, sculptor and leading fauvist noted for his *Blue Nudes* series of découpées, also known as the "cut-outs" (7)

13 Rotating power tool used in carpentry; also a device which directs packets of data between computer networks (6)

14 Drummer of rock band The Who from 1964 until his death in 1978 (4)

15 Nut-like cupule fruit of the tree in the beech family, genus *Quercus* (5)

16 Pulitzer Prize-winning poet and novelist who wrote the collections *Earth Triumphant*, *The Charnel Rose* and *Selected Poems* (5)

17 Of the colour wheel, one of the primary subtractive colours, complementary to red (4)

18 __ V; 12 year-old who reigned as King of England for two months before being confined to the Tower of London where he is said to have been murdered by Richard III (6)

20 English horror novelist whose notable works include *The Rats*, *The Fog* and *The Magic Cottage* (7)

22 Type of rural settlement, generally smaller than a village (6)

23 In printing and typography, a complete character set within a particular typeface family (4)

25 Enid Blyton character whose friends include Big Ears, Mr Plod and Mr Wobbly Man (5)

27 Salsa verde-like sauce made with crushed basil, garlic, pine nuts, olive oil and Parmigiano-Reggiano cheese (5)

29 Inert noble gas occurring naturally in the atmosphere, discovered by Sir William Ramsey and Morris Travers (4)

31 Yellow supergiant which is the brightest star in Cygnus (5)

32 Dated term for a female pilot (8)

34 Rustic type of seat in the form of a high-backed wooden bench (6)

37 The largest city in Syria (6)

38 In Kantian philosophy, a thing as it is in itself, as opposed to as it is known through perception (8)

39 Elizabethan sea captain and navigator who, in his ship the Golden Hind, was the first Englishman to circumnavigate the globe (5)

41 English composer and organist of the Chapel Royal who was granted a monopoly in music printing with Thomas Tallis for 21 years from 1575 (4)

43 Type of periodical published in electronic form (1-4)

44 The nickname of the recording artist born Salvatore Phillip Bono who made up part of a pop duo with Cher (5)

45 Queen ___; architectural style characterised by red brickwork (4)

46 Items collected and/or studied by a philatelist (6)

48 Provençal salad of young green leaves, shoots and flowers, typically chicory, fennel, rocket and spinach (7)

50 Greek island in the Aegean Sea, once the site of one of the tallest statues of the ancient world (6)

52 Any one of the 23 layers of fibrocartilage separating adjacent vertebrae in the human spine (4)

53 A girth for a Western saddle (5)

55 Archaic name for the blackbird (5)

56 Singer-songwriter who released the album *Piano Man* in 1973 (4)

57 English director who co-founded The Archers film company with Emeric Pressburger, where they produced *A Matter of Life and Death* and *The Red Shoes* (6)

58 Logarithmic unit of sound intensity (7)

59 Sacred Hindu river that rises in the Himalayas and empties into the Bay of Bengal, where it forms the world's largest delta (6)

Down

1 Soft Cell vocalist who released *Tainted Love* with David Ball in 1981 (6)

2 Door-to-door cosmetics sales company founded in 1886 (4)

3 National dog of Germany, originally used to hunt wild boar (5,4)

4 ___ *Criminal*; Michael Jackson hit single from his best-selling album *Bad* (6)

5 1960s children's television series with the characters Captain Troy Tempest and King Titan (8)

6 One of the mythological daughters of Oceanus and Tethys (4)

7 Archbishop of Canterbury who was assassinated as a result of opposing Henry II's attempts to control the clergy, canonised by Pope Alexander III soon after (6)

8 Another name for eggy bread (6,5)

9 Flying ___; legendary ghost ship (8)

41

10 The chief witch in *Macbeth* (6)

19 Port city in northern Belgium (7)

21 Law term literally meaning "from one side only" (2,5)

24 Transparent sheet placed on top of a piece of artwork for extra detail (7)

26 *The __ Code*; Dan Brown novel (2,5)

28 Deep, mellow-sounding musical instrument used in military bands (7)

30 Heavy, waterproofed cotton cloth (7)

33 Charms or trinkets worn to ward off negativity (7)

35 Destructive funnel-shaped vortex of violently-rotating winds (7)

36 Climbing shrub with highly-fragrant cream- and pinkish-coloured flowers (11)

40 Scientific study of the properties of the earth's water (9)

42 Greek courtier who was seated beneath a sword suspended by a single hair by Dionysius I (8)

44 Town in Devon situated near the mouth of the Kingsbridge Estuary (8)

47 A hand-knitted woollen fabric (6)

48 In Greek tragedy, an ode sung by a single actor (6)

49 Spout-like device attached to the end of a hose for directing the flow of water (6)

51 *Ocean's __*; remake of the 1960 Rat Pack movie with the same name (6)

54 Inexpensive variety of white wine (4)

56 Swiss psychologist who originated the concept of the introvert and extrovert personalities (4)

Noddy   Aleppo   Jung

disc   osso

        franossona

Pica

The Telegraph

42

Across

1 Victorian novelist and playwright noted for his detective and mystery stories such as *The Woman in White, The Moonstone* and *No Name* (7)

5 A type of internet message board (5)

8 Humorist and cartoonist whose collection *My World __ and Welcome to It* contains the story *The Secret Life of Walter Mitty* (7)

12 Swiss Reformed theologian and Christian thinker who wrote the 1919 commentary *The Epistle to the Romans* and *Church Dogmatics* (5)

13 Around 10 metres in length, a herbivorous dinosaur that had a broad heavy tail, lizard-like teeth andthumbs which developed into spikes (9)

14 A small arm leading from a larger body of water; also a passage between peninsulas (5)

15 Region lying north of London (4,6)

16 Sociological and statistical study of elections and trends in voting (10)

18 A celebration for a special event, especially a 25th, 50th, 60th or 70th anniversary (7)

21 In computing, a hand-held mechanical or optical device used in conjunction with a mat to move a cursor around a VDU (5)

23 A miner's pick; also a clamp-like section of a lathe to which work is fixed while being turned (7)

25 Painting applied directly to a wall (5)

27 Scarlet textile dye that was chiefly obtained from madder, but today is synthesised chemically (6,3)

29 Italian actress born Sofia Scicolone who, in 1960, starred in the comedy *The Millionairess* and the wartime drama *Two Women* (5)

31 An early name for a type of nuclear reactor (6,4)

32 Naturally occurring hallucinogenic compound found in many species of mushrooms and toadstools, notably the liberty cap (10)

34 Capital city which gave its name to an ancient kingdom traditionally founded by the Mesopotamian king Sargon the Great (5)

35 Common name of a small reddish-coloured insect in the Formicidae family which captures the young of other similar insects to raise as slaves (6,3)

36 In dressmaking, to draw fabric into a series of gathered rows using specialised elastic thread to create a puckered effect (5)

37 The true name of an author (7)

40 Represented as half-man, half-fish, the national god of the Philistines (5)

42

42 Located on the Danube River, the second-largest city in Serbia after Belgrade (4,3)

44 Post-apocalyptic science fiction novel by the *Uplift Universe* series creator David Brin (3,7)

47 *Goodnight* __; sitcom that starred Nicholas Lyndhurst as the time-travelling double life-leading character Gary Sparrow (10)

52 Spanish word for "friend" (5)

53 The traditional condiment to accompany roast lamb (4,5)

54 The UK's heaviest but fastest-flying duck, *Somateria mollissima* (5)

55 The brightest star in the constellation Canis Minor (7)

56 Jarvis __; elderly bank manager character in Charles Dickens's novel *A Tale of Two Cities* (5)

57 Soviet chess grandmaster who held the title of world chess champion from 1969-72 (7)

Down

1 Secretary of State for Business (5)

2 The common name of a slow-moving strepsirrhine nocturnal primate with large eyes (5)

3 According to the Old Testament, the son of Abraham and Hagar who was cast out after the birth of Isaac (7)

4 A sideways deviation of the ball in cricket; also a style of jazz (5)

5 Short-lived style of highly-colourful expressionistic painting that flourished in Paris from around 1900-1910 (7)

6 Any one of the letters of the ancient Germanic alphabet (4)

7 According to Greek mythology, the greedy king of Phrygia whose ears were turned into those of an ass by Apollo (5)

8 Informal term for a person who is fond of travelling at speeds of 100mph or more (3-2)

9 Historical term for a carriage drawn by three horses (7)

10 Conservative statesman who served as prime minister from 1902-05 (7)

11 Kenneth Grahame's water vole character whose friends include Mole, Mr Badger and Mr Toad (5)

17 British rock band whose songs formed the basis of the jukebox musical *We Will Rock You* (5)

The Telegraph

42

18 Spicy Creole or Cajun dish of rice cooked with seafood, chicken, smoked sausage and vegetables (9)

19 Thistle-like plant in the daisy family used with dandelion to flavour a traditional British soft drink (7)

20 The clear granule-free outer layer of a living cell (9)

22 Term used to describe the total land mass of the largest and second-smallest continent combined (7)

23 The maiden name of Catherine, Duchess of Cambridge (9)

24 Former name for St Petersburg (9)

26 Estate landowner in Scotland (5)

28 Recipient of the 1915 Nobel Prize in Literature (7)

29 Comedian and actor who created *Little Britain* with David Walliams (5)

30 Author who wrote the best-sellers *The Carpetbaggers* and *The Betsy* (7)

33 Cosmetic for the lips and cheeks (5)

38 Golfer known as "Supermex" (7)

39 The science of intellect (7)

41 Principal town in Berkshire (7)

43 An early Spanish instrument (7)

44 *Lady and the __*; 1955 Walt Disney animated film production (5)

45 Legendary Athenian misanthrope (5)

46 Chronicle of the events of one year (5)

48 The father of Hermia in *A Midsummer Night's Dream* (5)

49 The world's longest continental mountain range (5)

50 Fabric used for towelling (5)

51 Old term for a Russian emperor (4)

42

disraeli   Terry   tom up

Lemur   andes

Leningrad   bright

Balisteros

43

Across

11 Actress born Norma Jean Mortenson, a week of whose life is portrayed in a film starring Michelle Williams, Kenneth Branagh, Emma Watson and Judi Dench (6)

12 Genus of numerous species of mainly spring-flowering plants that includes auricula, cowslip, oxlip and polyanthus (7)

13 Formal item of neckwear for men that was the forerunner of the tie (6)

14 Central picture on a postage stamp; also the illustration on a banknote (8)

15 Letter of the Greek alphabet between tau and phi (7)

16 In motor sports, the point when the vehicle is closest to the edge of the track when turning a corner (4)

17 Any one of the 150 lyrical poems or songs in the Old Testament ascribed to David (5)

19 French term for a decorative item considered to be collectable (5,1'3)

21 Residence provided for a minister, especially one of the Scottish Presbyterian Church (5)

25 Woollen or woven garments collectively (8)

26 Elongated enclosure for skittles and tenpin bowling (5)

27 Former monetary unit of Greece that was equal to 1/100 of a drachma; also any of a group of subatomic particles with weak interactions (6)

29 Venetian explorer of Central Asia and China who is said to have served the court of Kublai Khan (4)

31 US-born British poet and dramatist who wrote *The Waste Land*, *The Hollow Men* and *Four Quartets* (5)

32 Fruit with cultivars including Discovery, Jazz and Pink Lady (5)

34 __ earth; group of chemical elements that includes 15 lanthanides plus scandium and yttrium (4)

35 Engineer who invented the first four-stroke internal-combustion engine (4)

36 City in Oneida County, New York (5)

38 Irish playwright whose work *The Playboy of the Western World* provoked riots at the Dublin Abbey Theatre on its opening night in 1907 (5)

39 Polish-born US biochemist who formulated the concept of vitamins and indicated the diseases caused by a deficiency of them in the diet (4)

40 Dr __; Robert Louis Stevenson character with an evil alter ego (6)

41 English term for a boulangère (5)

42 System of beliefs of a particular political or economic group (8)

44 Discovered by Clyde Tombaugh in 1930, the former most remote known planet in the solar system (5)

46 Wife of King Arthur whose love affair with Sir Lancelot is said to have caused the downfall of the Knights of the Round Table (9)

47 US golfer nicknamed the "Hawk", who in 1953 won the Open, the US Open and the Masters (5)

50 Mistress of Charles II (4)

52 Any one of the 12 peers of Charlemagne's court (7)

53 Highly toxic chemical element, atomic number 81, also known as the "poisoner's poison" (8)

55 Bird in the Columbidae family, used for racing and homing (6)

56 *The __*; 1924 play written by the actor Arnold Ridley who later played Private Godfrey in *Dad's Army* (7)

57 Powerful and prominent city-state in ancient Greece (6)

Down

1 Romanian-born actor noted for his gangster roles in films including *Little Caesar*, *Key Largo*, *Double Indemnity* and *The Ten Commandments* (8)

2 English architect who redesigned St Paul's Cathedral following the 1666 Fire of London (4)

3 The capital of Western Australia; also a town in central Scotland on the banks of the River Tay (5)

4 Architectural recess in a church with a domed roof (4)

5 In the British Army, an officer ranking below a captain (10)

6 Corn tortilla filled with cheese and other ingredients, folded and grilled or fried (10)

7 Delicate but distinctive variety of tea flavoured with bergamot (4,4)

8 Type of plain cake traditionally served with clotted cream and jam (5)

9 The southernmost country of Central America; also a style of hat (6)

10 Side of the moon towards the observer; also the obverse of a coin (4)

18 The scientific study of the physical characteristics of rocks as mineral masses (9)

20 Italian baroque sculptor and painter noted for his works at St Peter's Basilica in Vatican City (7)

22 Ornamental type of pouch worn as part of the traditional Scottish Highland dress for men (7)

23 Oil-rich republic on the coastline of the Caribbean Sea with the capital city Caracas (9)

24 International maritime signal flag hoisted by a ship about to sail (4,5)

28 Set of creative works stored in a flat case of the same name (9)

30 Neutral colour similar to ecru (7)

33 One of a pair of baskets carriedby a packhorse or donkey, or attached to the sides of a bicycle (7)

37 System of weight loss based on forcing the body into a state of ketosis by eating minimal amounts of carbohydrates (6,4)

38 Composer, pianist and conductor who wrote the Ballets Russes *The Firebird*, *Petrushka* and *The Rite of Spring* in the early 20th century (10)

41 In some parts of the US, strict rules preventing entertainment, shopping or leisure activities on Sundays (4,4)

43 Sum of money given to an employee at the end of a period of their employment (8)

45 A type of wheeled vehicle powered by a pair of riders (6)

48 The common name for the human vertebral column (5)

49 The narrow middle section of a violin; also part of a ship (5)

51 Political party official appointed to maintain parliamentary discipline (4)

53 Weight of a vehicle without cargo, fuel or passengers (4)

54 Clay-, sand- and humus-rich soil (4)

munroe

Citadel (Watt) Plotonium

epsilon

douglass

Worsted

Geophysics

Venus? togy

Veniezula

44

Across

11 English actor who starred as Bertie Wooster in the most recent adaptation of P.G. Wodehouse's novels (6)

12 A joint for coupling for pipes; also section of a national flag (5)

13 Latin phrase used as an inscription on a bookplate followed by the name of the owner (2,6)

14 Canadian jazz pianist and composer noted for his appearances with Ella Fitzgerald (8)

15 Plane figure with six straight sides and six angles (7)

16 Variety of pinkish-coloured wine (4)

17 Inventor who said: "Many of life's failures are people who did not realise how close they were to success when they gave up." (6)

19 The name of the mountain in the Black Hills of South Dakota with the giant relief carvings of the presidents Washington, Jefferson, Lincoln and Theodore Roosevelt (8)

22 Alternative name for any of the Jacks in a deck of playing cards (5)

25 Highly unstable radioactive chemical element, atomic number 87, discovered by Marguerite Perey in 1939 (8)

27 *The* __; magazine that was launched in 1992 by the former *Private Eye* editor Richard Ingrams (5)

28 __ II; king of England who was defeated by Robert the Bruce at Bannockburn and later deposed by his wife Isabella and her lover Roger de Mortimer (6)

30 English scientist noted for inventions including an electric clock and a circuit for measuring electrical resistance (10)

33 Musical term meaning "very" (5)

35 Side of a ship that is sheltered from the wind (4)

36 Hungarian who invented the ballpoint pen (4)

37 City in England nicknamed the "Knightsbridge of the North" (5)

39 Branch of physics concerned with the measurement of luminous intensity, especially in terms of perceived brightness to the human eye (10)

40 US series of horror movies written by Kevin Williamson and directed by Wes Craven (6)

41 German-born British biochemist who shared the 1945 Nobel Prize in Physiology or Medicine with Howard Florey and Alexander Fleming for work on penicillin (5)

42 Hat resembling a fez (8)

45 Academy Award-winning film director and screenwriter whose works include *Born on the Fourth of July, JFK* and *Natural Born Killers* (5)

47 Vessel in a fleet carrying the commanding admiral (8)

49 Abbreviated name for an examination which is a prerequisite to most degree-level courses (1,5)

51 Scottish engineer who coined the word "horsepower" and also made significant improvements to the efficiency of the Newcomen steam engine (4)

53 Comedian who created the characters Mr Cholmondeley-Warner, Tim Nice-But-Dim and Tory Boy (7)

56 A concealed plastic case containing a reel of magnetic tape for recording or playing sound or video (8)

58 The smallest, most simple structural unit of an element or compound (8)

59 A type of durable twilled or worsted fabric used to make military uniforms (5)

60 Term for a computer which uses a modem rather than broadband to connect to the internet (4-2)

Down

1 Highly-fragrant shrub in the mint family; dried sprigs of which are placed in wardrobes and cupboards to perfume linen and clothing (8)

2 Scottish dialect for a hillside or sloping bank (4)

3 The capital of Finland (8)

4 English landscape painter noted for his treatment of light (6)

5 Semi-retired weather forecaster whose name featured in the 1988 song *John Kettley Is a Weatherman* (4)

6 Woman who served four years in prison for the murder of Meredith Kercher before the case was overturned this year (4)

7 Dish of rice, flaked smoked haddock and chopped hard-boiled eggs served with a sprinkle of cayenne pepper (8)

8 Australian-born film actor known for his swashbuckling roles (5)

9 Moon named after the mythical king of the fairies (6)

The Telegraph

44

10 The 24 long curved bones articulated in pairs to the human spine (4)
18 Republic in south-east Asia comprising 63 islands (9)
20 Pottery in Stoke-on-Trent noted for its popular Blue Italian range (5)
21 Mythological sorceress who helped Jason find the Golden Fleece (5)
23 Dutch painter who created *Girl With a Pearl Earring* (7)
24 Film actor who is generally typecast in tough-guy roles (2,4)
26 The author of *Principia Ethica* (5)
29 Elastic substance also called baleen, formerly used in corsetry (9)
31 __ *One Hundred*; former pop group with the lead singer Nick Heyward (7)
32 Highly-seasoned sausage served sliced in sandwiches (6)
34 Mammal in the weasel family (5)
38 Informal lingo, often vituperative (5)
39 Hook-nosed hunchback character (5)
41 Television comedy drama series by Mike Bullen that starred James Nesbitt, Helen Baxendale, Fay Ripley and Hermione Norris (4,4)
43 __ *in Blue*; 1924 composition by George Gershwin (8)
44 Computer preceded by the ZX81 (8)
46 In football, the instance of playing the ball through an opponent's legs (6)
48 Protester posted outside a place of work during a strike by a union (6)
50 The second planet from the sun (5)
52 One of the 12 minor prophets (4)
54 1977 single by The Commodores (4)
55 Anthropologist who was involved in the discovery of an extinct hominid genus he named *Australopithecus* (4)
57 Cheese-making town in Holland (4)

45

Across

1 Irish novelist, playwright and poet whose notable works include *The Vicar of Wakefield*, *The Deserted Village* and *She Stoops to Conquer* (9)

6 Prolific Russian composer who wrote the ballets *Swan Lake*, *The Sleeping Beauty* and *The Nutcracker* (11)

12 Queen's Park __; Premier League football club owned by Tony Fernandes (7)

13 The lowest British hereditary title (7)

14 Located on the Gulf of Aqaba, the port city and resort which is Israel's only outlet to the Red Sea (5)

15 Former British decimal coin that was first issued in 1971 but withdrawn from circulation in 1984 (9)

16 Informal or common name for a particle accelerator (4,7)

17 Son of a scrap metal merchant who formed a highly-successful film company with Samuel Goldwyn during Hollywood's "Golden Age" (5)

18 Medicine or medical care that relieves pain but does not deal with the cause of the condition (10)

21 Village in western Norway that was the scene of the Battle of Rastarkalv between Haakon the Good and the sons of Eric Bloodaxe (4)

23 Falconer's bunch of feathers swung above the head to recall a hawk; also a type of bait used by anglers (4)

25 Artisan who works with rock (10)

27 Peer of the __; title of an aristocrat who has the right to sit in the House of Lords (5)

29 1986 action fantasy film starring Christopher Lambert as an immortal Scottish swordsman (10)

31 William Shakespeare's play with the line: "Hell is empty and all the devils are here." (3,7)

34 Italian city, site of La Scala (5)

35 In physics, to convert a subatomic particle into electromagnetic radiation (10)

36 Unit of particle interaction cross-section area equal to 10^{-28} square metres; also an agricultural building for storage and livestock (4)

38 The mythological Greek winged goddess of victory (4)

40 Ice cream made in a block of three layered flavours, typically chocolate, vanilla and strawberry (10)

42 Dome-shaped shelter originally built by the Inuit (5)
45 Herbal liqueur that was created by a French monk and later developed by wine merchant and religious art collector Alexandre Le Grand (11)
47 Novel by William Makepeace Thackeray; also the castle in Falmouth built by Henry VIII (9)
50 Sharp ridge of rock found on rugged mountains (5)
51 Any of a large class of organic compounds including the alkaloids, hormones, sterols and vitamins (7)
52 City in California, site of the Disneyland Resort (7)
53 Branch of science concerned with the effects of extremely low temperatures on living organisms (11)
54 Leader of the Greeks in the Trojan War who was murdered by his wife Clytemnestra (9)

Down

1 Courtyard surrounded by cloisters (5)
2 Astronomer and aviation pioneer who invented the bolometer (7)
3 1996 all-star movie based on a novel of the same name by Lorenzo Carcaterra (8)
4 Norwegian playwright and theatre director who wrote *Peer Gynt*, *A Doll's House*, *Ghosts* and *The Wild Duck* (5)
5 Kestrel-sized bird of prey resembling a giant swift, noted for high-speed aerial manoeuvres and for catching birds and dragonflies on the wing (5)
6 Latin phrase literally meaning "solid earth" (5,5)
7 Printed statement or piece of information issued to the press or people attending a lecture (7)
8 In prosody, a rhythmical or metrical stress (5)
9 2009 novel by David Nicholls (3,3)
10 Non-metallic chemical found in the planetary rings of Jupiter, in hot springs, meteorites and volcanoes (7)
11 Element of the lanthanide series, atomic number 70 (9)
17 Mixture of leaves, compost and bark spread around the base of plants to enrich and insulate the soil (5)
18 Autocratic monarch or ruler (9)
19 __ Society of London; organisation concerned with taxonomy, named after a Swedish botanist who devised the binomial nomenclature system (7)

20 French name for the card game twenty-one or blackjack (5-2-2)

22 An electrically-powered passenger vehicle; also a type of cart formerly used in coalmines (4)

24 Blue supergiant and constellation in Orion, around 85,000 times as luminous as our sun (5)

26 River that rises in northern France, flows through Belgium and the Netherlands and empties into the North Sea (7)

28 The name of the wolf in Rudyard Kipling's *Jungle Book* stories (5)

30 Each of a pair of respiratory organs within the rib cage (4)

32 A traditional Japanese sword or dagger; also a musical term meaning "too much" (5)

33 Microcrystalline form of quartz with varieties including agate, carnelian and onyx (10)

34 The highest peak in the Alps (4,5)

37 Large terrier type of dog with a black and tan coat, originally bred to hunt otters (8)

39 US senator who was involved in the Chappaquiddick incident (7)

41 16th-century gambling game that was a forerunner of poker (7)

43 The light chamber at the top of a lighthouse (7)

44 Word used to modify the meaning of another word or sentence (6)

46 Freshwater salmonoid whitefish found in the Great Lakes (5)

47 City in Veneto, birthplace of Galileo Galilei and Livy (5)

48 Southern African antelope (5)

49 Singer-songwriter who made the album *Bridge Over Troubled Water* with Art Garfunkel in the late 1960s (5)

45

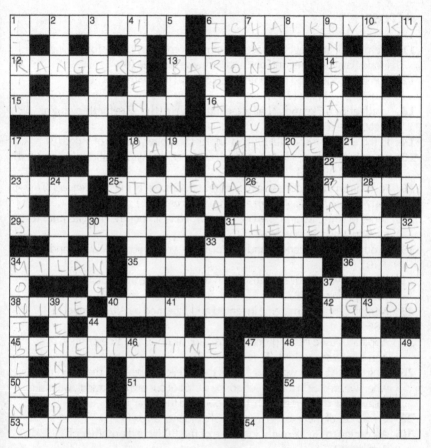

Meyer   Ibex
         disalgesic

         lantern

The Telegraph

46

Across

11 Member of an imaginary race of beings invented by J. R. R. Tolkien including Frodo Baggins, Peregrin Took and Samwise Gamgee (6)

12 Roman goddess and personification of good luck with the Greek counterpart Tyche (7)

13 In athletics, a 7kg metal ball attached to a length of wire for throwing at great force (6)

14 In the UK, the respectful form of address to a peer, bishop or judge (8)

15 Town in Berkshire, site of the royal residence that was significantly damaged by fire in 1992 (7)

16 Nickname of the fictional adventuring archaeologist in the films *Raiders of the Lost Ark*, *The Temple of Doom* and *The Last Crusade* (4)

17 Series of stretches and exercises performed to limber the muscles prior to participating in a match (4-2)

19 Group of nine volcanic islands in Polynesia, governed by New Zealand until 1961 (5)

21 Large red velvet-covered cushion in the House of Lords, upon which the Lord Speaker sits (8)

23 Nitroglycerin-rich material invented and patented by Alfred Nobel in 1867 (8)

25 Apparatus used in the process of creating alcohol; also a description of a non-effervescent drink (5)

26 King Lear character who says: "This is the excellent foppery of the world, that, when we are sick in fortune, often the surfeit of our own behaviour, we make guilty of our disasters the sun, the moon, and the stars." (6)

28 Cheap cut of meat taken from the shoulder of an ox (4)

30 According to Greek mythology, one of the 50 Nereids, mother of Achilles (6)

32 In theology, each of the three main classes of angels as depicted by Pseudo-Dionysius the Areopagite (9)

34 From the German literally meaning "slice", a dish consisting of a pan-fried breadcrumb-coated fillet of veal (9)

36 US president who in 1945 authorised the use of the Little Boy and Fat Man atom bombs against Hiroshima and Nagasaki (6)

38 Hawaiian feast or party, named after the dish served at the event of the same name consisting of octopus, taro and coconut (4)

40 Building such as the Louvre, Paris, or the National Gallery, London (6)

41 *Home* __; Christmas comedy film starring Macaulay Culkin, Joe Pesci and Daniel Stern (5)

42 Dolphin-like cetacean (8)

44 Spitz-like dog resembling a large Pomeranian (8)

46 Hit single by Peter Gabriel from his 1992 album *Us* (5)

47 Agricultural tool for ploughing, removing weeds and covering seeds; also a London borough bordering Hertfordshire (6)

49 Actress who starred in the 1988 film *Hairspray* and later became a television talk-show hostess (4)

51 Form of vitamin A essential for vision and growth, found in cod liver oil, egg yolks and spinach (7)

54 Traditional British pudding consisting of suet pastry with strawberry jam (4-4)

56 Second wife of Henry VIII, depicted by Miranda Raison in a play at Shakespeare's Globe in 2010 (6)

57 Densely-populated city on the Chao Phraya waterway, Thai name in its truncated form Krung Thep (7)

58 Capital of Albania since 1920 (6)

Down

1 Relating to the arteries surrounding and supplying the heart (8)

2 Latin word meaning "in the same place", used to refer to a previously cited textual reference (6)

3 US state bordering New Mexico (4)

4 Away from the prepared runs or tracks in skiing (3-5)

5 The family name of a group of birds that includes the jackdaw, jay, magpie, raven and the rook (4)

6 Common name of a domesticated cavy, used extensively in scientific research (6,3)

7 2006 animated film by *Toy Story* creators Pixar, based on a world populated by anthropomorphic vehicles (4)

8 __ of Delphi; ancient Greek statue (10)

9 Digital messages sent via addresses which use the @ sign (6)

10 Combination of cards in canasta (4)

18 Prong of an antler; also a unit of weight for diamonds equal to 2mg (5)

20 Lightweight cotton cloth used to make bouquet garni bags (6)
21 *Just __*; the first in a series of children's books by the English author Richmal Crompton (7)
22 Alternative name for the Greek goddess of the moon Artemis (7)
24 Italian phrase used to describe pasta cooked "to the bite" (2,5)
27 Cherry used to make kirsch (7)
29 Educational discourse to an audience of degree students (7)
31 Traditional birthstone for May (7)
33 English novelist who wrote *Brighton Rock*, *The Power and the Glory* and *The Heart of the Matter* (6)
35 Percussion instrument resembling a shallow drum encircled with pairs of zills (10)
37 Prime minister nicknamed "Boreas", who served a 12-year term ending in losing Britain's American colonies (5)
39 Speech sound other than a vowel (9)
42 Welsh town that was the birthplace of Henry VII (8)
43 Country with a blue national flag bearing a white saltire (8)
45 Monetary unit of modern-day Israel, equal to 100 agora (6)
48 Mary Tourtel's bear character who lives in the fictional locale Nutwood (6)
50 Acronym describing a member of a military organisation who has absconded from duty (1,1,1,1)
52 Type of beer mug in the form of a seated man wearing a tricorn (4)
53 The third of the four Gospels (4)
55 Pen name of the French novelist and naval officer who wrote *Matelot* (4)

Across

1 In Scotland, New Year's Eve and all the associated traditional customs and celebrations throughout the night until the following day (8)

5 1982 hit single by Toto which features on their Grammy Award-winning album with the opening track *Rosanna* (6)

9 The daughter-in-law of Naomi in the Book of Ruth (5)

13 Any one of the 17 sacred hymns attributed to the Persian prophet Zoroaster (5)

14 Greek name of a text written by Porphyry of Tyre introducing Aristotle's *Categories*, now sometimes used to describe an academic introduction to a subject (7)

15 An old Chinese table game for four people with a set of 136 or 144 tiles (3-4)

16 Area of heath and woodland in southern England that was reserved as the royal hunting ground for William I in 1079 and has remained Crown property since (3,6)

17 Calcutta-born British author who wrote a novel which opens at Miss Pinkerton's academy for young ladies (9)

19 Mythological tree or wood nymph; also a brownish butterfly in the Nymphalidae family (5)

20 Island country whose capital is named after the title of the duke who defeated Napoleon at the Battle of Waterloo (3,7)

22 The thin strip of cardboard in a cracker that creates a sharp bang when pulled apart (4)

24 *The Jewel of the* ___;the sequel to the 1984 film *Romancing the Stone* which stars Michael Douglas and Kathleen Turner (4)

26 Casino resort and home of the Monaco Grand Prix street circuit (5,5)

28 A type of puzzle in which words are represented by a combination of individual letters, pictures and symbols (5)

30 English painter and caricaturist whose watercolours and drawings feature in William Combe's *Tour of Dr Syntax* series of books (10)

32 County town associated with the legends of Robin Hood and his Merry Men (10)

35 English composer and organist who wrote the compilation *Cathedral Music* and the music to *Heart of Oak* (5)

36 Scientific device associated with the chemist Sir William Crookes (10)

37 German-Swiss painter noted for his watercolour *Twittering Machine* (4)

39 Bone of the human body which articulates with the humerus, radius and the distal radius (4)

41 Scottish author who wrote a series of adventure stories for young adults including *The Coral Island* and *The Pirate City* (10)

43 Variety of dessert pear; also a former province in the Loire Valley (5)

46 Nickname given to a member or supporter of Parliament during the English Civil War (9)

47 Also called China red, a pigment made from mercury sulphide or cinnabar (9)

49 Zone of the ocean bed at depths of around 3,000 to 6,000 metres (7)

51 The name of the Marvel Comics character Tony Stark when in superhero mode (4,3,)

52 Outdated communications network that preceded fax and email (5)

53 In diplomacy, a Minister Plenipotentiary; also an author's concluding words (5)

54 Informal name for the Houses of Parliament clock tower where members of the general public gather to hear the "bongs" of the bell of the same name at midnight on New Year's Eve (3,3)

55 According to mythology, the son of the Trojan hero Aeneas (8)

Down

1 Traditional home of the Navajo people, built with the entrance facing east (5)

2 *The __*; 1972 film starring Steve McQueen and Ali MacGraw based on the Jim Thompson novel of the same name (7)

3 One of the world's largest snakes (8)

4 The shortened name of the novel with characters including the White Rabbit, Cheshire Cat and the March Hare (5,2,10)

6 The foremost seats in the House of Commons (5,5)

7 Steep part of a glacier resembling a static avalanche of frozen water (7)

8 In mathematics, either of the lines enclosing an angle (3)

9 *The __*; 2001 film starring Nicole Kidman and Christopher Eccleston (6)

10 The brightest star in the constellation Canis Minor (7)

11 Song performed and popularised by Frank Sinatra in the 1959 comedy film *A Hole in the Head* (4,5)

12 German philosopher who wrote *Critique of Pure Reason* (4)

18 Alternative name for the giant oarfish (4,2,3,8)

19 Name of the basic monetary unitAlgeria and Bosnia-Herzegovina (5)
21 A town in Hertfordshire (7)
23 Nickname given to a member of the Women's Royal Naval Service (4)
25 English artist noted for his depictions of matchstick-like figures set against urban landscapes (5)
27 Breeding colony of penguins, turtles or seals (7)
29 Island to the north of the Mindanao in a province of the same name (5)
31 Birds as a class of vertebrates (4)
33 Freshwater lake between Zambia and Democratic Republic of the Congo (5)
34 __: A Romance of Exmoor; novel by Richard Doddridge Blackmore (5,5)
35 The largest living animal (4,5)
38 Port between the Mediterranean Sea and the 24 Across (8)
40 Ballet dancer who was often the dance partner of Margot Fonteyn (7)
42 Presenter and newsreader whowas a contestant on *I'm a Celebrity... Get Me Out of Here!* in 2006 (7)
44 Game similar to Basque pelota (3,4)
45 __ Bear; the name of the BBC Children in Need mascot (6)
47 Upper part ofshoe or boot (4)
48 Largest island in the Cyclades (5)
50 Underarm bowl in cricket (3)

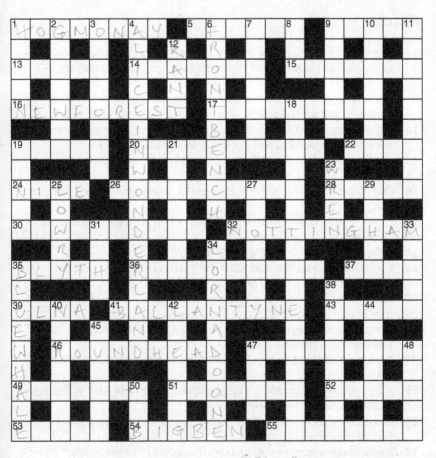

1 HOGMONAY 5 F 9
L 12 R
13 14 A O 15
C N N
16 NEWFOREST 17 T 18
I B
19 20 N 21 E 22
W N 23 W
24 NILE 25 E 26 O C 27 28 29 R
O N H E
30 W 31 D 32 NOTTINGHAM 33
R E 34
35 BLYTH 36 R O 37
L L R 38
39 ULVA 40 41 BALLANTYNE 42 43 44
E 45 N A
W 46 ROUNDHEAD N 47 48
H O
49 A 50 51 O 52
L N
53 C 54 BIGBEN 55

Canne

Nile
blue whale
Ner

Ballantine
Lorna Doone

Lit

48

Across

1   English author who wrote the 1877 children's classic *Black Beauty* (6)
4   The capital and largest city of Wales, originally settled by the Romans in 55 AD (7)
8   In anatomy, a partition which separates a cavity into two chambers, especially the nostrils and the heart (6)
14   City that was almost completely destroyed by troops under the command of William Sherman in a battle of the American Civil War (7)
15   The taxonomic rank in biological classification between phylum and order (5)
16   One of the 12 animals of the Chinese zodiac; also a red-skinned cultivar of Irish potato (7)
17   Crescent-shaped butter-rich French pastry eaten as part of a continental breakfast (9)
18   Latin phrase literally meaning "for this" (2,3)
19   Constellation containing stars including Rigel and Betelgeuse, said to represent the mythological huntsman of the same name (5)
20   Stable subatomic elementary particle which acts as the primary carrier of a form of energy in solids (8)
22   Poetic or literary name for the country that was once referred to in its Latinised form, Hibernia (7,4)
27   The largest and loudest of the gibbons, illegally hunted by humans for the pet trade (7)
29   A group of eggs or a brood of chicks; also one of the three foot-pedals in a motor vehicle with manual transmission (6)
31   Bloodsucking fly which can transmit sleeping sickness in humans and nagana in livestock (6)
33   Elizabethan philosopher, statesman and pioneer of modern scientific thought who wrote *The Advancement of Learning* and *Novum Organum* (5)
34   Mythological Greek youth who rejected the nymph Echo in favour of his own reflection (9)
35   Novelist who wrote *The Once and Future King* tetralogy which begins with *The Sword in the Stone* (5)
36   Button on a clock which temporarily hibernates its alarm, granting a few more minutes of sleep (6)

38 Irish novelist and short story writer who penned *The Country Girls* and the screenplay for the 1964 film *Girl with Green Eyes* (1'5)

39 Pickled herring fillet served folded round slices of gherkin and onion (7)

42 System of gear changingdesigned to match the speed of the intended gear to the speed of the currently selected gear (11)

44 Severe snowstorm with winds over 35mph, often causing white-out (8)

48 Dutch painter born Jheronimus van Aken who created the triptychs *The Garden of Earthly Delights* and *The Haywain* (5)

50 Labour politician who served as Home Secretary from 1997-2001 (5)

52 *The Dance of the __ Fairy;* instrumental piece in Tchaikovsky's *The Nutcracker* (5,4)

54 Creamy-textured Italian dish of Arborio or Carnaroli rice cooked gradually in stock (7)

55 The roe of a scallop (5)

56 __ of hand; another term for prestidigitation (7)

57 Former name of Ho Chi Minh City (6)

58 *I Don't Like __;* 1979 number one single by the Boomtown Rats (7)

59 French Impressionist painter noted for his combinations of complementary colours and technique of broken brushstrokes (6)

Down

1 *The Body __;* 1955 science fiction novel by Jack Finney (9)

2 Whig statesman who is regarded as having been the first Prime Minister of Great Britain (7)

3 Respiratory organs containing around 1500 miles of airways (5)

5 Novelist who wrote *Little Women* and *Little Men* (6)

6 Roman goddess of the hunt and of the moon with the Greek counterpart Artemis (5)

7 Chess Grandmaster who was world champion from 1972-75 after he defeated Boris Spassky (7)

9 Social science concerned with the production, consumption and distribution of goods and services (9)

10 Member of a people living in Rwanda and Burundi (5)

11 Berthing area for yachts and other pleasure boats (6)

12 Complex form of mirage attributed to an Arthurian sorceresswhich can be observed in the Strait of Messina (4,7)

13 Novel by the author who also wrote *The Primrose Path*, *Miss Betty* and *The Jewel of the Seven Stars* (7)

21 "Oh, East is East, and West is West, and never the __ shall meet, Till Earth and Sky stand presently at God's great Judgment Seat." Rudyard Kipling (5)

23 Island with the capital Port Louis (9)

24 The lightest of the alkali metals (7)

25 Ancient Egyptian amulet cut in the shape of a beetle of the same name (6)

26 Part of deoxyribonucleic acid (4)

28 Oily fish used to make Gentleman's Relish (7)

30 1995 Martin Scorsese film starring Robert De Niro and Sharon Stone (6)

32 A person who claims to predict the future by studying the positions of celestial bodies and constellations (11)

33 Winger for Manchester United named the European Footballer of the Year in 1968 (4)

35 Ballroom dance in triple time (5)

37 Roman Catholic cleric's skullcap in various colours depending on rank (9)

40 Device for counting the number of steps taken when walking (9)

41 City in Lancashire, north of Chorley and south of Morecambe (7)

43 North African country (7)

45 Musical term meaning "briskly" (7)

46 Genus name of the candytufts (6)

47 __ Wilkes; character in Margaret Mitchell's *Gone with the Wind* (6)

49 Japanese vinegared rice dish (5)

51 *Tomorrow's* __; science and technology television series (5)

53 Actor remembered for his portrayal of Superman in a series of films (5)

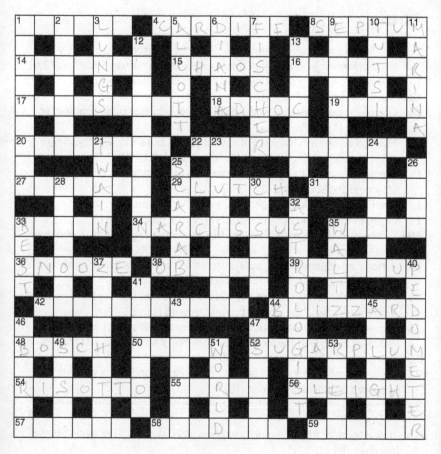

Best
Seville allegro
Scarab actown sleight
Morocco Tension Croissant sardine

49

Across

1 The first in a series of children's novels by Mary Norton about a family of diminutive beings living under the floorboards of a human household (3,9)

7 In Australia, a young male trainee working with cattle or sheep (8)

13 The longest river in France (5)

14 One of the broad, flat limbs of a dolphin, seal, whale or turtle adapted for swimming (7)

15 Mythical creature in the form of a white horse; also a carriage drawn by a team of three horses, two abreast with a single leader (7)

16 Common name of the flag which combines the crosses of St Andrew, St George and St Patrick (5,4)

17 The first name of René Artois's wife in the BBC sitcom 'Allo 'Allo! (5)

18 Organ of the human body enclosed within the pericardium (5)

19 "Stone walls do not a prison make, Nor iron bars a cage; Minds __ and quiet take that for an hermitage." *To Althea, from Prison*, Richard Lovelace (8)

21 A crowned draughts piece, a playing card ranking below ace or either of a pair of the most important chess pieces (4)

23 Animal of the African Savanna which is a member of the "big five" group with the elephant, rhinoceros, lion and leopard (7)

26 Supreme __ of the International Confederation of Wizards; rank or title of Professor Albus Dumbledore in the *Harry Potter* series of books (7)

29 A critique of a novel or film (6)

31 Italian operatic tenor who was one of the first major classical vocalists to be recorded on gramophone discs (6)

33 Geographical television documentary series which began at the White Cliffs of Dover (5)

34 Italian term for freelance photographers who take candid or secret pictures of celebrities (9)

35 Miss __; teacher and niece of headmistress Trunchbull in Roald Dahl's *Matilda* (5)

36 Tidal races in the Orkneys and Shetlands; also resting perches for sleeping hens (6)

38 Athenian gymnasium and public meeting place in which Aristotle taught philosophy (6)

39 From the French literally meaning "heavenly", a keyboard instrument in which hammers strike steel plates attached to wooden resonators (7)

42 Technical term for earache (7)

43 Long strip of ribbon or other material worn round the waist as part of a dress (4)

44 The edible root-tuber of a woodland plant in the parsley family, *Conopodium majus* (8)

48 *Moon__*; third in the James Bond series of novels by Ian Fleming (5)

50 A controlled high-speed skid in motor racing (5)

52 *The Lark __*; composition by Ralph Vaughan Williams (9)

54 To raise a pawn to the rank of queen in chess (7)

55 Floating leaf of an aquatic ornamental plant in the Nymphaeaceae family (4,3)

56 Basic monetary unit of Iceland equal to 100 aurar (5)

57 The second-largest city in Japan by population (8)

58 Snack or lunch dish of a slice of bread covered in various toppings such as cold meat with salad (4,8)

Down

1 Brittle silvery-white tin-like metalloid, atomic number 52, used as a semiconductor (9)

2 Number of identical books, newspapers or magazines published at one time (7)

3 The UK's largest cinema chain (5)

4 Repeated line in a song or poem at the end of each verse (7)

5 Spirit distilled from barley or rye (6)

6 Basic monetary unit of Sri Lanka, the Seychelles and Mauritius (5)

8 The capital and the second-largest city of the United Arab Emirates (3,5)

9 Genus name of the red-hot pokers (9)

10 Variety of full-bodied oak-aged red wine from Spain (5)

11 The scientific study of birds (11)

12 Author whose stories *The Legend of Sleepy Hollow* and *Rip Van Winkle* appear in his book *The Sketch Book of Geoffrey Crayon, Gent* (6)

20 __ bouillon; wine and vegetable stock for poaching fish (5)

22 City in the Scottish Highlands at the mouth of the River Ness (9)

24 Italian philosopher, theologian and Dominican priest who was known as the Angelic Doctor (7)

25 Decorative object given as an award for a victory (6)

The Telegraph

49

27 Muesli-like breakfast dish consisting of rolled oats and honey (7)
28 English poet and satirist who wrote *An Essay on Man* (4)
30 Any of a class of proteins acting as a biological catalyst (6)
32 One of the group 12 elements (4)
33 The science, study and practice of making maps (11)
35 English composer who wrote the orchestral suite *The Planets* (5)
37 Creature called a woolly bear in caterpillar form (5,4)
40 An original musical score or manuscript in the musician's or author's personal handwriting (9)
41 2011 album by Katherine Jenkins; also the English name of Paul César Helleu's 1901 oil painting *Rêverie* (8)
43 Joint of dogs, horses and sheep corresponding to the human knee (6)
45 According to Greek mythology, the home of the god Pan (7)
46 Located north of Mombasa, the capital of Kenya (7)
47 Small type of pole- or oar-propelled wooden boat used in China for fishing and transportation (6)
49 In parts of India, Iran, Pakistan and Turkey, a pavilion or summerhouse (5)
51 Springtime plant with cup-shaped flowers in a range of colours (5)
53 *The __ Chef*, Jamie Oliver's first television cookery series (5)

49

The Telegraph

50

Across

1 Scottish writer of doggerel verse whose works such as *Tay Bridge Disaster* earned him the reputation as the worst poet in the history of the English language (10)

6 English actress who starred as Flora Poste in the 1995 film version of *Cold Comfort Farm* (10)

13 Taxonomic category denoted by a capitalised Latin name (5)

14 1819 novel set in the 12th century written by *Rob Roy* creator Sir Walter Scott (7)

15 The least abundant of the naturally occurring rare-earth elements, atomic number 69 (7)

16 Music and business entrepreneur who managed various bands including The Beatles and Gerry and the Pacemakers before his premature death in 1967 (7)

17 Second-largest country in Europe, which gained independence in 1991 after the collapse of the Soviet Union (7)

18 Edible bulb vegetable related to chives, garlic, leeks, scallions and shallots (5)

19 According to the Book of Genesis, one of the 12 sons of Jacob and one of his four wives, Leah, Rachel, Bilhah or Zilpah (8)

21 Italian Baroque painter whose 1640-45 work *Philosophy* bears a Latin inscription which translates as: "Be quiet, unless your speech be better than silence" (4)

22 Truncated name of Sir Thomas More's book *De optimo reip. statu, deque noua insula Vtopia, libellus uere aureus, nec minus salutaris quam festiuus* (6)

26 Ancient city in Egypt, site of the pyramid complex at Giza, Saqqara and the Great Sphinx (7)

29 Angle-measuring instrument in the form of a graduated eighth of a circle that was used in astronomy and navigation (6)

31 Deadly fire-breathing monster with 100 dragon heads, son of Gaia and Tartarus (6)

33 Constellation in the northern sky that is surrounded by Andromeda, Aries, Perseus and Pisces (10)

34 Breed of draught horse with heavily-feathered fetlocks (10)

37 In fencing, the formal performance before engaging in a bout (6)

39 Musical articulation indicating that notes are to be played smoothly without breaks (6)

40 Genus of annual plants in the buttercup family, also called love-in-a-mist (7)
43 Carbohydrate found in potatoes, corn, rice, wheat and other foods (6)
44 "The mind is always the __ of the heart." François de La Rochefoucauld, *Maxim 102* (4)
45 Sweet Italian liqueur flavoured with sweet almonds or apricots (8)
50 Feisty and territorial little bird with a melancholic song, believed by some to portend unfavourable luck if found in one's home (5)
52 Daphne du Maurier's novel which begins: "Last night I dreamt I went to Manderley again" (7)
53 The female graduates or former students of a school or university collectively (7)
55 Spicy variety of Spanish sausage flavoured and coloured with paprika, served in traditional bean stews (7)
56 From the Chinese literally meaning "lion dog", a breed of canine resembling a Lhasa apso (4-3)
57 Australian cricketing term for a googly or a wrong'un (5)
58 Novel in Robert B. Parker's Spenser series of fictional detective works (6,4)
59 German dish of finely shredded pickled cabbage (10)

Down

1 Alkaline earth metal which burns with a brilliant white flame (9)
2 English group who released the album *Invisible Touch* in 1986 (7)
3 Elizabethan playwright and pamphleteer who wrote *Pierce Penniless's Supplication to the Devil* and *The Unfortunate Traveller* (5)
4 City in south-central Brazil (7)
5 Obsolete unit of land distance that was equal to around three miles (6)
7 __, *or the History of a Young Lady's Entrance into the World*; 1778 novel by Frances Burney (7)
8 Dramatist believed to have been the political informant and agent of Alexander I of Russia who was assassinated by the Germans in 1819 (8)
9 Study of the nervous system (9)
10 Mother of the gods in the Vedas (5)
11 A stoat in its white winter coat (6)
12 Wilbur's arachnid friend in one of E. B. White's classic children's tales (9)
20 Singer-songwriter and poet who wrote *Let Us Compare Mythologies* (5)

50

23 Son of Abraham who was cast out with his mother, Hagar, after the birth of Isaac (7)

24 Book forming part of a series (6)

25 Queen __; architectural style (4)

27 Jersey worn in bicycle racing (7)

28 Tactical ballistic missile (4)

30 British flag officer and war hero whose statue stands on a 151ft tall column in Trafalgar Square (6)

32 Seaport city in Yemen (4)

33 Cupel used in metal refinery (4)

35 __ Kane; character portrayed by Marilyn Monroe in *Some Like It Hot* (5)

36 Italian appetiser of raw beef, venison or salmon served thinly sliced (9)

38 Director who created *Kill Bill* (9)

41 2001 novel by Ian McEwan (9)

42 Forest associated with the legends of Robin Hood (8)

44 French composer who wrote *Prélude à l'après-midi d'un faune* and *Suite bergamasque* (7)

46 Rhythm of a piece of music (7)

47 Republic in North Africa (7)

48 Spring-flowering corm plant (6)

49 Woman's loose gown fashionable in the 17th and 18th centuries (6)

51 Maiden name of Cherie Blair (5)

54 Turkic language of the landlocked country with the capital Tashkent (5)

50

Ivanhoe   saurkraut
file   gorgon   allium
Evalina

51

Across

1   *Little Lord __*; 1886 novel by *The Secret Garden* and *The Little Princess* author Frances Hodgson Burnett (10)

6   Gate in the form of a very strong and heavy latticed grill, used to fortify the entrance of a medieval castle or town (10)

13   Indigenous peoples inhabiting Arctic regions including Alaska, Northern Canada and 12 Down (5)

14   Latin legal term literally meaning "from one party or side" (2,5)

15   English group who released a cover version of *The House of the Rising Sun* and their own song *We Gotta Get Out of This Place* in the 1960s (7)

16   Transparent film for use with an overhead projector (7)

17   Daughter of Agamemnon and Clytemnestra, sister of 7 Down (7)

18   Town in the Runnymede borough of Surrey (5)

19   Another name for the mineral talc, especially as soapstone (8)

21   Historically, charitable deeds or money donated to the poor (4)

22   Creature in the phylum Arthropoda and subphylum Hexapoda (6)

26   Formation of military planes, ships, troops or other vehicles in parallel rows; also the migratory pattern of birds (7)

29   *Moonlight __*; popular name of a piano composition by Ludwig van Beethoven which he wrote for his pupil Giulietta Guicciardi (6)

31   Danish author who wrote the memoir *Out of Africa* under the pen name Isak Dinesen (6)

33   Apartment in some monasteries where relaxation of the rules was permitted; also a dagger used to deliver a death stroke to a wounded enemy (10)

34   From the French literally meaning "sweet note", an old-fashioned term for a love letter (6-4)

37   "Small showers last long, but sudden __ are short" *Richard II*: Act II, Scene 1 (6)

39   Victorian actor and Lyceum Theatre manager born John Henry Brodribb, said to have inspired Bram Stoker to create Dracula (6)

40   In geometry, a quadrilateral with all sides of equal length (7)

43   The most populous city in Australia, site of a famous opera house (6)

44   English dressmaker noted for her timeless "stand-alone" designs (4)

45   Children's television series with the puppet characters Troy Tempest and George Lee "Phones" Sheridan (8)

50 Paula __; *The Tube* and *The Big Breakfast* presenter whose daughters include Fifi Trixibelle, Peaches Honeyblossom and Heavenly Hiraani Tiger Lily (5)

52 Captain Antonio __; protagonist in the 1994 love and war story written by Louis de Bernières (7)

53 Italian bel canto composer who wrote *The Barber of Seville*, *William Tell* and a further 37 operas (7)

55 The capital and chief port of Puerto Rico, founded by Ponce de León in 1508 (3,4)

56 Scottish biographer who wrote *The Life of Samuel Johnson* (7)

57 Provençal garlic-flavoured sauce (5)

58 Silvery-coloured radioactive chemical element in the lanthanide series, atomic number 61 (10)

59 German who was awarded the 1932 Nobel Prize in Physics for creating quantum mechanics and discovering the allotropic forms of hydrogen (10)

Down

1 French dish of chicken or rabbit served in a white gravy-like sauce (9)

2 Musical instrument that was originally popularised in Hawaii by Portuguese immigrants (7)

3 Brightly coloured, often iridescent little tropical fish (5)

4 One of the Seven Summits and eight-thousanders (7)

5 Fish-eating bird of prey mainly inhabiting parts of Scotland (6)

7 Mythical being who was persuaded by his sister, 17 Across, to kill their mother and her lover Aegisthus (7)

8 Coffee- and vanilla-flavoured rum liqueur originally from Jamaica (3,5)

9 *The __*; 1995 hit single by 32 Down (9)

10 English film director whose works include *Cathy Come Home*, *Kes* and *Sweet Sixteen* (5)

11 Tropical plant cultivated for its oil-rich seeds, used to make the hummus flavouring tahini (6)

12 Island which is also known as Kalaallit Nunaat (9)

20 The doorkeeper of a Freemasons' lodge (5)

23 Crest of various birds including chickens, turkeys and pheasants (7)

24 Description of *The Merchant of Venice* character Shylock (6)

25 Variety of chalcedony used to make the dark-coloured sections of a cameo (4)

27 One of the humanities disciplines (7)

51

28 Section of the human body known in Latin as the collum (4)
30 Medical system which assigns degrees of urgency to patients in order to prioritise treatment (6)
32 Britpop band whose popular songs include *Girls & Boys*, *Parklife* and *The* 9 Down (4)
33 Seasoning prepared from soya beans, used to make a traditional Japanese soup (4)
35 __ *in My Side*; 1986 song by the pop duo Eurythmics (5)
36 Fixed annual allowance provided by Parliament to meet the expensesincurred by the Queen in her duties (5,4)
38 The traditional British accompaniment of roast lamb (4,5)
41 Sport of exiting a plane in flight (9)
42 __ Bucket; character portrayed by Patricia Routledge (8)
44 Large scavenging African stork (7)
46 Reptiles of the Testudines order (7)
47 Underground stem of asparagus, ginger, iris and Lilly of the Valley (7)
48 Aromatic herb related to mint, sage, lavender and thyme (6)
49 Warship of the Hellenistic era with two banks of oars (6)
51 Circular painting or sculpture (5)
54 Country that hosted the 1992 Summer Olympics (5)

Fricassee

Hyacinth

52

Across

11 Nanette ___; English actress who starred in various films directed by her husband including the 1975 version of *The Stepford Wives* and *International Velvet* in 1978 (6)

12 Starchy substance extracted from the cassava root used to make a milk-based pudding (7)

13 Constellation bordering 39 Across which, according to mythology, represents the eagle that carried Ganymede to Mount Olympus (6)

14 With over 23 million inhabitants, the most populous city of China (8)

15 Actress married to Clark Gable who starred in Alfred Hitchcock's 1941 comedy *Mr. & Mrs. Smith* (7)

16 The young offspring of a possum, kangaroo, koala or wallaby (4)

17 Powerful hobby-like raptor of coastal regions feeding on pigeons, doves, ducks and other birds (9,6)

21 *Downton* ___; television period drama by Julian Fellowes (5)

23 Dairy dessert manufactured by Häagen-Dazs and Ben & Jerry's (3,5)

25 Chemical element which lies between strontium and zirconium in the periodic table (7)

26 Flatfish with species including Dover and lemon (4)

27 Hallucinogenic compound naturally occurring in liberty caps and related mushrooms (10)

29 Crimean city that was the site of a major wartime conference between the "Big Three" in 1945 (5)

31 Electromagnetic wave discovered and named by Wilhelm Röntgen, for which he was awarded the first ever Nobel Prize in Physics (1-3)

33 The author of *Essays of Elia* and *Tales from Shakespeare* (4)

34 English slapstick stand-up comedian and actor noted for his tours *Big* and *Roadrunner* (5)

36 Roman goddess of springtime, wife of Pluto (10)

37 Ancient Hebrew dry measure equal to one tenth of an ephah (4)

39 Constellation in the Milky Way north of 13 Across, also called the Arrow (7)

41 Everlasting flower said to grow in the mythological meadows of the same name in the underworld (8)

43 A type of covered passageway between the transept and the chapterhouse in some cathedrals (5)

45 1996 science-fiction action film starring Will Smith and Jeff Goldblum, based on an extraterrestrial invasion of Earth (12,3)

48 Italian-Jewish novelist and poet who recounted his experiences as a survivor of Auschwitz in his first book, *If This Is a Man* (4)

49 Bivalve mollusc with a fan-shaped shell and around 100 eyes (7)

51 US president who never married (8)

53 Actor and scientologist whose early films include *Risky Business*, *Top Gun*, *Cocktail* and *Rain Man* (6)

54 Player's turn at batting in cricket (7)

55 German socialist, industrialist, political theorist and philosopher who co-founded Communism with Marx (6)

Down

1 Species of African antelope which shares its genus with the kob, puku and the waterbuck (6)

2 Country bordered by United Arab Emirates, Saudi Arabia and Yemen, capital city Muscat (4)

3 __ - __ race; term for a competition in which one contestant is certain to win (3-5)

4 Small ornamental case for nail scissors, tweezers and sewing items (4)

5 Gemstone naturally occurring in all colours of the spectrum, believed by some to be bad luck following Sir Walter Scott's *Anne of Geierstein* (4)

6 The worship of the world (10)

7 Term for an 18th-century British dandy sporting a style of the same name (8)

8 Austrian composer who wrote the oratorio *The Creation* (5)

9 State in north-west India, site of the Golden Temple (6)

10 Plant in the lily family forming blankets of lavender-coloured flowers throughout woodlands in spring (8)

18 King Arthur's legendary sword (9)

19 Country in southern Africa with the capital Windhoek, comprising large parts of the Kalahari Desert (7)

20 Australian-born US actor noted for roles as Captain Blood, Robin Hood and Don Juan (5)

22 Term meaning to adjoin two coats of arms on the same shield (6)

24 Architect who designed Brazil's new capital, Brasilia, in the 1950s (5)

26 Musical instrument that was played by Charlie "Yardbird" Parker (9)

28 Monty Python member who co-wrote *Fawlty Towers* (6)

30 Skintight garment named after a French acrobat and trapeze artist (7)

32 1970s Broadway and West End musical with the songs *Tomorrow* and *Hard Knock Life* (5)

35 Former Scottish county which became part of the Highlands in 1975 (10)

36 Carpenter's hand tool for smoothing and shaping wood (5)

38 Deciduous tree related to fig, cultivated for its dark purplish fruit (8)

40 Poem by Rudyard Kipling about an Indian water bearer who saves the life of a soldier but dies himself (5,3)

42 Chilean general and dictator who assumed power in a coup d'état in 1973 and was replaced in 1990 by a democratically-elected president (8)

44 Prince ___, Duke of Edinburgh; UK's longest-serving consort, patron of over 800 organisations (6)

46 System of farming based on the cultivation of crops and cereals (6)

47 English actress who now runs a successful cake-decorating business (5)

50 The __ Ladies; female counterparts of the T-Birds in the 1978 musical film *Grease* (4)

51 Indian physicist who, with Albert Einstein, described the fundamental particles that were later to be named after him (4)

52 Simple non-flowering autotrophic organism such as seaweed (4)

53

Across

1 Satirist, poet and close friend of Percy Bysshe Shelley who wrote the novels *Headlong Hall*, *Nightmare Abbey* and *Crotchet Castle* (7)

5 Mary __; English cookery writer who co-judges *The Great British Bake Off* television series (5)

8 Pythagoras' __; rule which states that the square on the hypotenuse of a right-angled triangle is equal in area to the sum of the squares on the other two sides (7)

12 *The __ Suspects*; 1995 film which takes its name from a quote in the 1942 classic *Casablanca* (5)

13 New York __; major league baseball team whose batsmen included Babe Ruth and Mickey Mantle (7)

14 Any one of the 3,000 daughters of the mythological Greek sea goddess Tethys and her brother and husband (7)

15 First aired in 1958 and presented by Christopher Trace and Leila Williams, the world's longest-running children's television series (4,5)

16 Taxonomic category between genus and family, zoological names of which typically end in "ini" while botanical names end in "eae" (5)

17 __ *Who's Coming to Dinner*; 1967 Stanley Kramer drama film starring Spencer Tracy, Sidney Poitier and Katharine Hepburn (5)

18 Capital of the Greek region Epirus (8)

20 British television game show which featured Anneka Rice as the skyrunner from 1982-88 (8,4)

23 Pop duo who released various hit singles including *Sometimes*, *Ship of Fools* and *A Little Respect* (7)

26 English television chef and restaurateur who wrote the cookery books *Mediterranean Escapes*, *Coast to Coast* and *Far Eastern Odyssey* (5)

28 Food eaten on Shrove Tuesday (7)

30 Group of mythological nymphs who guarded Hera's golden apples with a 100-headed, firey-eyed, non-sleeping dragon (10)

31 Dish consisting of cubed feta cheese, tomatoes, red onion, cucumber and Kalamata olives (5,5)

34 __ & *Makepeace*; 1980s crime drama starring Michael Brandon and Glynis Barber who later married in real life (7)

36 Three-tiered jewelled crown worn by the Pope (5)

37 Hand tool used in plumbing, engineering and car maintenance (7)

39 Collection of classical Greek sculptures that were taken from the Parthenon by Thomas Bruce in the 19th century (5,7)

43 County bordered by Devon, Dorset, Gloucestershire and Wiltshire (8)

47 Marketplace or assembly point in Ancient Greece (5)

48 English pop artist who designed the *Sgt. Pepper's Lonely Hearts Club Band* album sleeve for The Beatles (5)

49 Sacred banner of the Abbey of St Denis that was traditionally given to French kings setting out for war (9)

51 Jane __; wife of Henry VIII who died 12 days after the birth of their son Edward VI (7)

52 Variety of long grain Indian rice with a delicate fragrance (7)

53 Pembroke Welsh __; breed of dog with a fox-like face, several of which are owned by Elizabeth II (5)

54 In Christianity, a district under the pastoral care of a bishop (7)

55 Medieval association of craftspeople in a particular trade (5)

56 19th-century art movement characterised by the representation of things as they actually are (7)

Down

1 Instrument used to determine the depth of a body of water or the vertical on an upright surface (5,4)

2 Another name for the plant rocket (7)

3 Species of the genus *Primula* (5)

4 Chemical element of the noble gas series, atomic number 36 (7)

5 Word linking code, digit and star (6)

6 Early type of tape recorder (4-2-4)

7 Orthodox Jewish school or seminary for the study of religious scripture, especially the Talmud (7)

8 US philosopher and transcendentalist who wrote *Walden, or Life in the Woods* (7)

9 Term for a tree or plant with leaves throughout all the seasons (9)

10 Form of French poetry with 10, 13 or 15 lines, written on two rhymes (7)

11 Mythological king of Phrygia with donkey's ears whose touch turned all to gold (5)

19 Succession of notes to be sung on a single syllable (5)

21 Cloth used to make plus fours, hacking jackets and flat caps (5)

53

22 In astrology, the relative angle between two celestial bodies (6)
24 Full-bodied variety of black tea (5)
25 The first in a series of romance novels by Jilly Cooper, followed by *Bella*, *Harriet* and *Octavia* (5)
27 Novelist and critic who presented *The Film Programme* from 1972-98 (6)
28 __ Corner; section of Westminster Abbey where Chaucer is buried (5)
29 Film director and actor who starred in the 1977 film *Annie Hall* (5)
30 *Brambly* __; series of illustrated books for children by Jill Barklem (5)
32 Cartilaginous fish with a diamond-shaped body, related to sharks (5)
33 Pianist and composer who served as the second prime minister of the Republic of Poland (10)
35 Island country on the southern tip of the Malay Peninsula (9)
38 Rare metal in the platinum group, naturally occurring in the Ural mountains (9)
40 Soviet foreign minister during the Cold War nicknamed "Mr Nyet" (7)
41 French word for an inn (7)
42 Large type of floor cushion with a filling of polystyrene beads (4,3)
44 English actor who starred as Heathcliff in William Wyler's version of *Wuthering Heights* (7)
45 Member of a military caste in feudal Japan (7)
46 Country with the capital Warsaw (6)
47 President of Syria from 1971-2000 (5)
50 Tuscan city west of Florence, birthplace of Puccini (5)

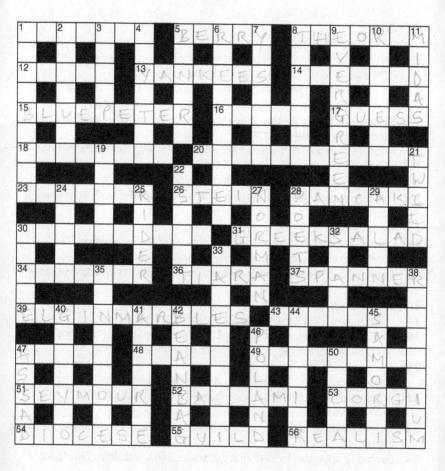

Floyd
Rider

Yankees

54

Across

1 Irish dramatist, novelist and poet who wrote *The Canterville Ghost*, *The Picture of Dorian Gray* and *Lady Windermere's Fan* (5)

4 Typically spotted in woodlands, hedgerows and orchards, the common name of the bird *Pyrrhula pyrrhula*, known collectively as a bellowing (9)

9 Mythological Roman goddess of agriculture; also the first body identified as an asteroid (now a dwarf planet) (5)

12 Ancient Greek architect who is believed to have designed the Parthenon with Callicrates (7)

13 Collective noun for a group of goldfinches (5)

14 Traditional colour of a hunting pink and the name of the cloth from which it is tailored (7)

15 The underground lair of a fox (5)

16 Layered Italian dish made with sheets of pasta of the same name (7)

17 Priest's assistant or candle-bearer during a church service or procession (7)

18 Track and field event formerly contested by multiple world record-breaking athlete Sergey Bubka (4,5)

20 The 12th sign of the zodiac (6)

22 Sharp spike on the legs of some male galliformes (4)

26 1997 James Cameron epic starring Leonardo DiCaprio and Kate Winslet, based on one of the biggest maritime disasters in history (7)

29 Anti-apartheid activist who served 27 years in prison and went on to become South Africa's first democratically-elected president (7)

31 Any one of the mountains in Scotland over 3,000 ft tall such as Ben Nevis (5)

32 Crumbly type of biscuit traditionally baked in the form of a petticoat-tail or finger (10)

34 Gymnastic apparatus for performing straddles, pikes, seat drops, twists and somersaults (10)

36 Norwegian dramatist, poet and theatre director who wrote *A Doll's House* and *The Master Builder* (5)

37 Region of West London, site of King's Road and Sloane Square (7)

38 A simple type of bit for use with a bridle with a single set of reins (7)

40 __ the Merciless; villain in the *Flash Gordon* comic strips (4)

41 Country that hosted the 1968 Summer Olympics, during which John Stephen Akhwari completed a marathon with a dislocated knee (6)

43 Christian sacrament commemorating the Last Supper (9)
47 Derived SI unit of electric charge (7)
50 Another name for the bitter orange, used to make marmalade and to flavour Grand Marnier (7)
52 Each of the several pieces of the Earth's crust which, combined, form the lithosphere (5)
54 Shakespeare character whose last words are: "I kiss'd thee ere I kill'd thee: no way but this; Killing myself, to die upon a kiss." (7)
55 __ *Wine*; song covered by various artists including Eartha Kitt, Nina Simone, Elkie Brooks and Katie Melua (5)
56 The capital of Lithuania (7)
57 County in the Munster province of Ireland; also a breed of dairy cattle with a black coat (5)
58 Confection in the form of a chocolate disc covered in hundreds and thousands (9)
59 Extension of a house, built to provide additional living space (5)

Down

1 UK-born Australian Nobel Prize-winning author who wrote a series of novels including *The Tree of Man*, *Voss* and *Riders in the Chariot* (5)
2 In typography, a term for a misprinted letter in a word (7)
3 City in the south of the Netherlands where, in 1891, the Philips company was founded (9)
4 French term for a bluestocking (3-4)
5 Comedian who wrote the *Little Britain* series with David Walliams (5)
6 Almond-flavoured cream used to fill various desserts and pastries (10)
7 The fourth book of the Bible (7)
8 Lily-like, shade-tolerant plant related to asparagus, highly prized by slugs and snails (5)
9 Old ferryman who transported the spirits of the dead across the rivers Styx and Acheron to Hades (6)
10 English painter and leading exponent of op art who created the works *Fall* and *Movement in Squares* (5)
11 French avant-garde composer who wrote *Gymnopédies* (5)
18 Chemical element, atomic number 19, symbol: K (9)

19 Dish of finely-minced meat or fish cooked with other ingredients in a baked-blind pastry shell (7)
21 Dutch Renaissance humanist and theologian who wrote *Colloquies*, *Apophthegmatum Opus* and *De Libero Arbitrio* (7)
23 Another term for a bishop, especially the Pope (7)
24 The 26th president of the US (9)
25 Central boss of a shield; also the highest point of a mushroom cap (4)
27 Scottish poet who wrote the jeremiad *The City of Dreadful Night* (7)
28 Oval boat propelled with an oar (7)
30 One of the three mythological Greek Gorgons (7)
33 Common name of the US award for Broadway plays (4)
35 Birmingham-based professional football club with a blue-and-claret-coloured home kit (5,5)
39 Of choral music, sung without instrumental accompaniment (1,8)
42 Hormone synthesised in theislets of Langerhans (7)
44 One of the culinary plants used in fines herbes mixtures (7)
45 *The __ Job*; 1969 film with a cliffhanger ending (7)
46 To strike the ball before it hits the ground in tennis (6)
47 Dandelion's spherical seed head (5)
48 Member of a wedding entourage responsible for showing guests to their seats (5)
49 UK prime minister 2007-10 (5)
51 British railway engineer who worked with Stephenson and Brunel (5)
53 One of the home counties (5)

54

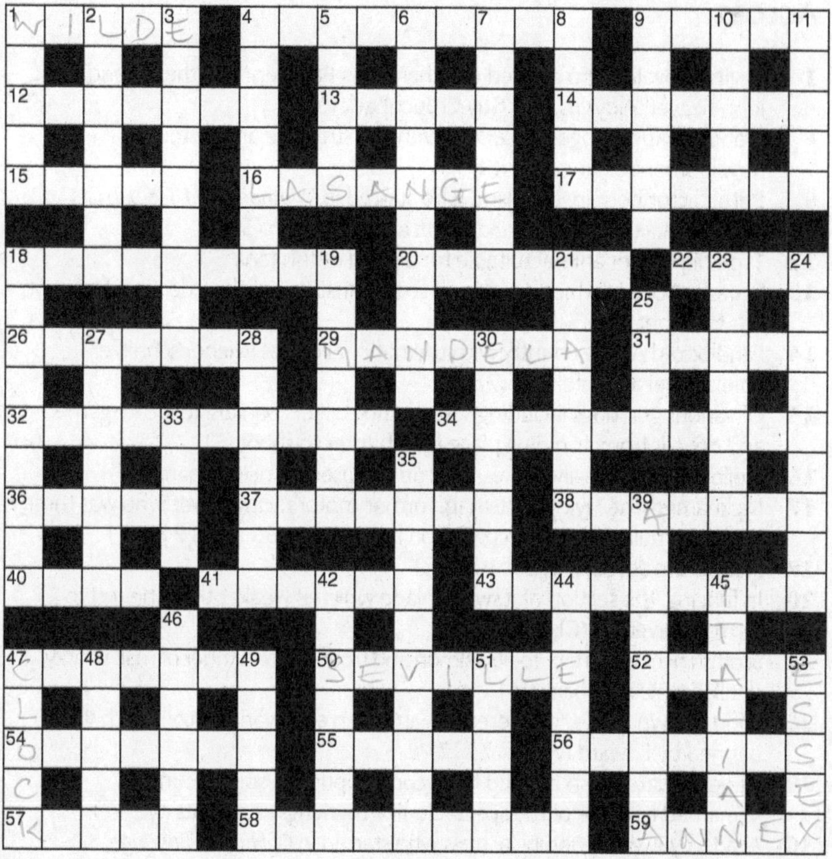

coracle

othello

The Telegraph

55

Across

1   English novelist who created the characters Paul Pennyfeather, Brenda Last, John Beaver, Aloysius, and Guy Crouchback (5)
4   Branch of knowledge concerned with the structure and historical development of languages (9)
9   British actor born in Swaziland who starred in *Withnail and I*, *How to Get Ahead in Advertising*, *Jack and Sarah* and *Wah-Wah* (5)
12   Type of plant or animal suitable for a pond or fish tank (7)
13   Squash stroke in which a ball is played against one of the side walls before it hits the front wall (5)
14   Landlocked Alpine country with the national dishes Wiener schnitzel, apfelstrudel and tafelspitz (7)
15   Of various gun dogs including setters and cocker spaniels, to locate game and drive it from its hiding place for a hunter to shoot (5)
16   Mellow-sounding valved brass instrument used in military bands (7)
17   Nicknamed The Flying Scotsman, former motor racing driver who was three times Formula One world champion between 1965 and 1973 (7)
18   Study of the development of words (9)
20   In fencing, the section of a sword blade which is weaker than the rest in terms of leverage (6)
22   Scottish river important for its salmon and trout and a number of malt whisky distilleries along its banks (4)
26   Sport known as the "gentleman's game"; an early variation of which was banned by Edward IV in 1477 (7)
29   Large predatory fish banned from consumption in some countries; so-named because of the spectacle-like markings around its eyes (7)
30   Academy Award-winning actress who starred in *Of Human Bondage*, *Dangerous*, *All About Eve* and *What Ever Happened to Baby Jane?* (5)
31   Obsolete keyed brass instrument that was superseded by the tuba (10)
33   Method of musical composition devised by Arnold Schoenberg based on the use of all the notes of the chromatic scale (6-4)
36   The Latin word for shadow (5)
37   Traditional gemstone gift for a 55th wedding anniversary (7)
39   Country that hosted the 1972 World Chess Championship, nicknamed the "match of the century" (7)
41   The founder of Christian Science (4)

42 Book of the Old Testament containing 150 sacred songs (6)
43 Soldier and statesman who was created the first Duke of Wellington and served as the UK prime mister from 1828-30 (9)
47 Daughter of a lighthouse keeper who rescued 13 people from the wreck of the SS Forfarshire in extreme weather conditions with her father and a single rowing boat (7)
50 Wild African animal related to pigs (7)
52 Batman's crime-fighting partner, also known as the Boy Wonder (5)
54 Academy Award-winning Italian film director who wrote *La Strada* and *La Dolce Vita* (7)
55 19th-century French historian and philosopher who wrote the controversial work *Vie de Jésus (Life of Jesus)* (5)
56 Transparent textile predominantly used for evening and bridal wear (7)
57 Town in Surrey where The Derby has been held annually since 1780 (5)
58 Simple piece of equipment used by an artist to steady their brush hand (9)
59 Carp-like fish of muddy waters (5)

Down

1 Quayside area for mooring, loading and unloading ships (5)
2 South American country with the capital city Montevideo (7)
3 English director and producer whose films include *Rebecca*, *Notorious*, *Rear Window* and *The Birds* (9)
4 Spanish artist whose 1932 painting *Nude, Green Leaves and Bust* sold at Christie's in New York for $106.5 million in 2010 (7)
5 Destination for incoming email (2-3)
6 Located in the West Wing of the White House, the official work base of the president of the US (4,6)
7 Recurring every eight years (9)
8 Nobel Prize-winning Irish poet and dramatist who wrote *The Countess Cathleen* and *The Winding Stair* (5)
9 Ring of rubber, metal or paper used to seal the junction between two spaces in an engine (6)
10 Largest artery of the human body (5)
11 2010 film based on Nigel Slater (5)
18 Section of a racecourse exclusively for members and winners (9)
19 Agricultural output of a crop (5)

21 Rock on the eastern bank of the Rhine which, according to legend, was the home of a siren who lured sailors and fishermen to their death (7)

23 Dessert consisting of a thick meringue base with a fruit and fresh whipped-cream topping (7)

24 1965 song by The Beatles (9)

25 The __; stage name of U2 guitarist David Howell Evans (4)

27 Biblical brother of Ahitub (7)

28 Hero who slew the Minotaur with the help of Ariadne and her ball of thread (7)

32 Shellfish served in chowder (4)

34 In printing, the last line or few words of a paragraph appearing at the top of a page, considered undesirable (5)

35 Posterior thigh muscles or tendons behind the knees, strengthened with exercises including squats (10)

38 Explorer who accompanied Roald Amundsen on his second effort to fly over the North Pole in an airship (9)

40 Plant traditionally used as a remedy for complaints of the ocelli (9)

44 Former name of the registration documents of a motor vehicle (7)

45 Country with the cedar tree as its national emblem (7)

46 Sister of Moses and Aaron (6)

47 Novelist who wrote *Moll Flanders* (5)

48 English motoring and aviation pioneer who founded a company with Henry Royce in 1906 (5)

49 Either of two brothers who compiled an anthology of fairy tales including *Hansel and Gretel* and *Rapunzel* (5)

51 The capital of Vietnam (5)

53 Town linked with Port Talbot (5)

55

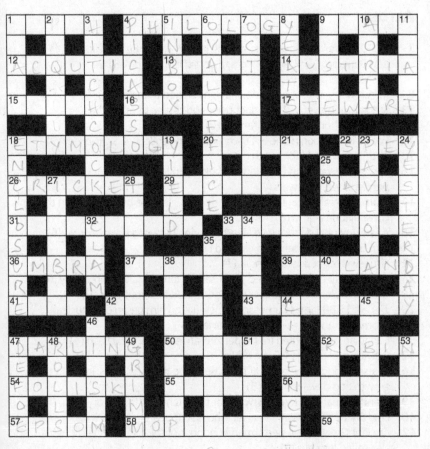

etomol   Runga Jackie
    umbra   Stewart
                    Kandle
Bono   Philology   Spey
        Croquet
Finland   France
Iceland   Lebanon

56

Across

1   2011 Steven Spielberg epic starring Jeremy Irvine, Emily Watson and Benedict Cumberbatch, based on a children's novel by Michael Morpurgo (3,5)

6   In geometry, the longest side of a right-angled triangle (10)

13   Stone fruit pulverised with anchovies and capers to make the Provençal hors d'œuvre tapenade (5)

14   Poet with the pen name H. D. who wrote the collection *Sea Garden* (9)

15   The Spanish word for beach (5)

16   Springtime woodland plant in the buttercup family with scarlet, crimson, purple or white flowers (7)

17   From the Arabic literally meaning "flying eagle", the brightest star in the constellation Aquila (6)

18   A fast downhill ski race involving zigzagging between poles or trees (6)

19   Sign of the zodiac between Leo and Libra (5)

21   Figure with eight sides and angles (7)

24   Fine, loosely-twisted worsted yarn used for tapestry and embroidery (6)

28   Chemical element, atomic number 60, used to colour glass (9)

29   *The __*; 1989 James Cameron science-fiction film based on a nuclear submarine and an alien aquatic species (5)

30   Canadian pianist noted for his performances of works by Bach (5)

32   2001 novel by Ian McEwan (9)

34   Pea-sized endocrine gland at the base of the hypothalamus, important for growth and development (9)

39   Brand of heat-resistant glassware for the kitchen or laboratory (5)

40   Enid Blyton's Toytown character who first appeared in 1949 (5)

42   Ancient Greek hymn performed in honour of the god of wine Dionysus, also called Bacchus (9)

44   One of three former administrative divisions of Yorkshire that were subdivided into wapentakes (6)

46   China, Japan and other Asian countries collectively (3,4)

47   *Rosemary and __*; television mystery series that starred Felicity Kendal and Pam Ferris (5)

49   Atoll in the Pacific Ocean, capital of the Gilbert and Ellice Islands (6)

51   Leather or plastic device used to fasten a Scout's neckerchief (6)

54 Before the introduction of custody centres in 1982, an institution for detaining young offenders (7)
57 Informal term for one's habitually requested drink in a pub (5)
58 Victoria's __; Australian creature in the family Paradisaeidae; the male of which has velvety-black plumage, blue tail feathers and a harsh call (9)
59 Preston-born actor remembered for his role as Mr Humphries in the sitcom *Are You Being Served?* (5)
60 Botanical term for a plant that grows on bare rocks or stones, deriving nourishment from the atmosphere and rain (10)
61 Irish human rights campaigner, revolutionary and nationalist who was hanged for alleged involvement in the Easter Rising (8)

Down

2 Heroine in stories by Lewis Carroll (5)
3 The science and study of sacred literature or lore (9)
4 Steering apparatus hinged to the stern of a ship or boat (6)
5 Portuguese city in the municipality of the same name which is one of the UNESCO World Heritage Sites (5)
6 Set of flags raised as a signal; also section of a flag nearest the mast (5)
7 Property inherited from one's father or male ancestor (9)
8 Unit of weight used in the 46 Across equal to around 38 grams; also a former Chinese monetary unit (4)
9 Landlocked republic with the capital city Kathmandu, one of the poorest countries in the world (5)
10 Bird with a red throat which spends most of its time on the wing (7)
11 Small case of puff pastry with a rich, savoury filling of chicken, mushrooms or prawns (3-2-4)
12 A cat with a ginger-coloured coat with brown streaks; also a conserve made from Seville oranges (9)
20 Versatile variety of red-skinned potato, good for baking, boiling, mashing and roasting (7)
22 Seeds of a plant in the parsley family, used to make garam masala (5)
23 Mythological Greek hero in Homer's *Iliad,* son of Telamon (4)
25 English lexicographer who compiled a thesaurus (5)
26 Singer-songwriter who released *You Don't Bring Me Flowers* with Barbra Streisand in 1978 and *Love on the Rocks* in 1980 (7)

56

27 Liberal statesman who was the second-longest serving UK prime minister of the 20th century after Margaret Thatcher (7)

31 Ethelred the __; King of England who fled to Normandy and briefly lost his throne to the Danish king Sweyn Forkbeard (7)

33 US president who resigned from office due to his involvement in the Watergate scandal (5)

35 Major river which flows from Tibet through India and Pakistan to the Arabian Sea (5)

36 Quick-drying adhesive used by actors to affix wigs and fake beards (9)

37 Mr Edward__; the evil personality of Dr Henry Jekyll in Robert Louis Stevenson's 1886 novella (4)

38 Sport of descending down a rock face or mountain with a rope (9)

41 One of the fastest-flying insects (9)

43 Element between thulium and lutetium on the periodic table (9)

45 King of Persia, 522–486 (6,1)

48 Ancient city on the shore of the Hellespont, scene of the legend of Hero and Leander (6)

50 Actress in *One Million Years B.C.* (5)

52 Diving waterbird which is unable to walk on dry land (5)

53 One of the first electronic computers, nicknamed a "giant brain" (5)

55 *The Life of __ of Athens*; play by William Shakespeare (5)

56 Device for hurling a clay pigeon (4)

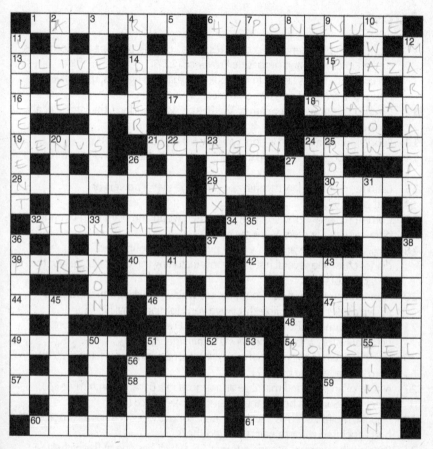

57

Across

1 French dish of aubergines, courgettes, garlic, onions, peppers and tomatoes stewed in olive oil and herbes de Provence (11)

7 According to James Lipton in his book *An Exaltation of Larks*, the collective noun for a group of crossword puzzlers (9)

12 Covering around 46 per cent of the Earth's water surface, the largest of all the oceanic divisions (7)

13 Subdivision of a Roman legion, typically 60 or 120 men (7)

14 Synthetic polymer invented in 1935 by organic chemist Wallace Hume Carothers (5)

15 Latin term used in law meaning beyond one's legal powers or authority (5,5)

16 Common name of the creeping evergreen woodland plant with lavender blue-coloured flowers, *Vinca major* (10)

18 English writer and gardener whose posthumously-published diaries chronicle several historic events including the Great Plague and the Great Fire of London (6)

20 German composer of the Romantic era who wrote the comic opera *Der Rosenkavalier* with the librettist Hugo von Hofmannsthal (7)

21 The pen name of the Nobel Prize-winning French novelist who wrote the fictional history *L'Ile des pingouins* (*Penguin Island*) (6)

26 Hairstyle in which the head is shaved except for a central spiked strip stretching from the nape to the brow (7)

27 Notice of an intended marriage announced in a parish church three successive Sundays before the ceremony takes place (5)

29 Aquatic mollusc such as a scallop, mussel or oyster, which has a compressed body enclosed within a pair of hinged shells (7)

31 Rare-earth chemical, atomic number 66, which has one of the highest magnetic strengths of the elements (10)

33 1963 novel by Kurt Vonnegut (4,6)

35 ___ Chapel; section of the official residence of the Pope, decorated with frescoes by Michelangelo and Botticelli (7)

36 Centre of the nervous system which stops growing by around 25 years of age in humans (5)

37 A person who does not believe in the existence of a god (7)

38 In football, the instance of kicking the ball between an opponent's legs (6)

40 The Glorious __; in the UK, the day of the year on which the grouse-shooting season commences (7)

43 The second in a series of science-fiction horror films by James Cameron starring Sigourney Weaver (6)

48 The long green stringy edible pod of the vine *Phaseolus coccineus* (6,4)

50 Name of one of the buck rabbits in Richard Adams's 1972 novel *Watership Down* (10)

53 Person who does not eat or use any animal products including eggs and milk (5)

54 The US "Motor City" (7)

55 __ violet; common name of the flowering perennial house plant with heart-shaped velvety leaves, *Saintpaulia* (7)

56 The host of a late-night television talk show in the US since 1982 (9)

57 The national tree of Japan (11)

Down

1 1981 hit single by Blondie (7)

2 Latin word literally meaning "it is silent", used in musical direction (5)

3 Artist and interior designer associated with Art Nouveau who developed the richly iridescent favrile glass (7)

4 Old term for a hedgehog (6)

5 English composer and conductor who wrote *The Rio Grande* and was the musical director of Sadler's Wells between 1930 and 1947 (7)

6 Tallest active volcano in Europe (4)

7 Northern constellation named after the husband of Cassiopeia and father of Andromeda (7)

8 One of the 50 Nereids, mother of Achilles (6)

9 Situated on the right bank of the Red River, the capital of Vietnam (5)

10 Heavily waterproofed canvas or cotton cloth used to make wet-weather gear for sailors and fishermen (7)

11 English priest and metaphysical poet who served as the Dean of St Paul's Cathedral from 1621-31 (5)

17 *The* __; series which starred Roger Moore as Simon Templar (5)

19 City that was the site of the Temple of Artemis, one of the Seven Wonders of the Ancient World (7)

22 Croquet ball that has passed all the hoops and is ready to be pegged out (5)

The Telegraph

57

23 Any one of the 118 chemical substances presented on a table originally developed by Dmitri Mendeleev (7)
24 Flavour similar to liquorice (7)
25 Relating to the deepest regions of the ocean, 3000-6000 metres down (7)
26 High-speed track cycling event for teams of typically two riders in continuous relay (7)
27 Publisher's description of a book (5)
28 Country with a national football team nicknamed La Roja (5)
30 Protester against unemployment who destroyed labour-saving machinery in English factories in the 19th century (7)
32 One of the longest rivers in Europe (5)
34 Information tag attached to a tree or plant (5)
39 News-magazine television series currently hosted by Julie Etchingham (7)
41 Author of *The Age of Innocence* (7)
42 The author of *Anna Karenina* (7)
44 Imperial standard of Constantine the Great with the chi-rho monogram (7)
45 Nobel Prize-winning dramatist who wrote *The Lion and the Jewel* (7)
46 Latin word meaning " in the same place", used in citing references (6)
47 One eighth of a circle (6)
48 Composer who wrote *Boléro* (5)
49 Acronym of a computer associated with Premium Bonds (1,1,1,1,1)
51 Fast-moving harmless snake (5)
52 Neck ornament of twisted metal (4)

Pacific

Ibid ultra vires Brittan
wharton ragatoullie NYLON
fathoms cherry
Campanelle

Across

10 2011 Academy Award-winning black-and-white movie by Michel Hazanavicius which has won more awards than other French film (3,6)

11 Poet, novelist and short story writer whose work *Solitude* begins: "Laugh, and the world laughs with you; Weep, and you weep alone." (6)

12 Unit of matter that was originally presented as a philosophical concept by Leucippus and his pupil Democritus in the 5th century BC (4)

14 Author and playwright who suffered from manic depression for most of his life but wrote nearly 30 novels including *Brighton Rock* and *The Power and the Glory* (6)

15 Port and commune on the west coast of Corsica (7)

16 The fifth track on Coldplay's debut album *Parachutes* (6)

17 7th Earl of __; title of the peer who disappeared following the murder of his children's nanny in 1974, declared legally dead in 1999 (5)

19 Birthplace in Scotland of Walter Scott, Alexander Graham Bell, Robert Louis Stevenson and Arthur Conan Doyle (9)

21 French composer who wrote *Pavane, Requiem* and *Clair de lune* (5)

24 Open-roofed entrance to an Ancient Roman house; also either of two cavities of the heart from which blood is passed to the ventricles (6)

26 Animal's coat colouring, typically tawny-brown with a stripe pattern (7)

27 Songwriter who discovered Katie Melua and wrote much of the material on her albums *Call Off the Search, Piece by Piece, Pictures* and *The House* (4)

30 Astringent lotion made from the bark and leaves of the shrub *Hamamelis virginiana*, typically used to treat bruises and skin complaints (5,5)

31 Island country without an official capital that was formerly known as the Pleasant Island and is the world's smallest republic (5)

33 Hundred __ Wood; A. A. Milne's fictional land where Winnie-the-Pooh, Piglet, Kanga, Owl and Eeyore live (4)

34 Spanish surrealist painter and sculptor whose works typically depict colourful amoebic shapes on plain backgrounds (4)

35 Variety of red, white and rosé wines made at the Bodegas Faustino vineyards in the Spanish region of the same name (5)

37 The grandson of the founder of the Mongol Empire (6,4)

38 Nickname of Oliver Hardy and George Herman Ruth (4)

39 The third-largest moon of Saturn, discovered by Giovanni Domenico Cassini in 1671; also a mythological Greek Titan, father of Atlas (7)

41 Syd __; stage name of Cyril Mead who formed part of a double act with Eddie Large (6)

43 The common name for the radiocarpal joint (5)

46 Deep and heavy-lidded pot for slow-cooking dishes of the same name or meat such as lamb shanks, oxtail or topside of beef (9)

48 __ orange; codename of one of the "rainbow herbicides" used by the US military during the Vietnam War (5)

51 Author who wrote her first novel under the pen name "By a Lady" (6)

52 Baptismal name of the Dutch Renaissance humanist, theologian and scholar who wrote the 1524 work known in English as *The Freedom of the Will* (7)

54 Georgina "Piggy" __; British eventer who is competing in the 2012 London Olympics (6)

56 *The Painted* __; 1925 novel by W. Somerset Maugham (4)

57 The 14th president of the US (6)

58 The adopted name of the Pharaoh and husband of Nefertiti (9)

Down

1 Chemical element, atomic number 90, named after a thunder god (7)

2 English pharmacologist who shared the 1936 Nobel Prize in Physiology or Medicine for studying acetylcholine (4)

3 Fish-eating mammal with webbed paws, related to weasels and badgers (5)

4 The alleged assassin of JFK (6)

5 Metal similar to magnesium, used in galvanising (4)

6 In law, a phrase used to describe an unavoidable catastrophe caused by natural forces, not preventable by human foresight or intervention (3,2,3)

7 Large daisy commonly seen in meadows, *Leucanthemum vulgare* (5)

8 Valencian dish based on rice, chicken, seafood, vegetables and saffron (6)

9 In bridge, an ace, King, Queen, Jack or 10; also a group of manors owned by a lord (6)

13 2001 Ridley Scott thriller starring Anthony Hopkins as Dr Lecter (8)

18 Word linking globe and Jerusalem (9)

20 Textile woven from two types of yarn, especially cotton with silk or linen (5)

22 Son of the Black Prince who succeeded him as king aged 10 (7,1,1)

23 Architectural style of the Palais Garnier opera house in Paris (5,4)

25 Female singing voice pitched between soprano and contralto (5)

27 In motor racing, item waved at drivers to disqualify them and summon them to the pits (5,4)

28 Natural harbour that was formed from Torquay, Paignton and Brixham (6)

29 Ethiopian runner who won two Olympic marathons, one barefoot (6)

32 Inflorescence characteristic of dill, fennel and parsley plants (5)

36 Mythological Greek consort of Cybele whose death and resurrection were associated with springtime (5)

37 Russian city on the River Volga (8)

40 Disc in blood essential for clotting (8)

42 Lemony __; pen name of the author who wrote *A Series of Unfortunate Events* (7)

44 Carpenter's power tool for creating grooves and mouldings (6)

45 High-backed wooden bench (6)

47 The capital of Zambia (6)

49 Wading bird with a long, straight beak, related to sandpipers and allies (5)

50 Acronym of a regulatory body replaced by Ofgem in 1999 (5)

53 A basic fingerprint pattern (4)

55 Ancient civilisation south-west of modern-day Iran, site of Susa (4)

58

brogue

Lucan

arichoke

zinc

Thorite

Wrist

Tutankamon

eyes

Across

1 A selection of Spanish appetisers which may include olives, cheese, chorizo, aioli and squid (5)
4 The Roman god of wine (7)
8 Globally threatened species of bird, also called a peewit because of its shrill call (7)
12 Tight-fitting one-piece garment worn by gymnasts and dancers (7)
13 An encampment of temporary shelters made with branches and leaves among other things (7)
14 Island nation in the heart of the South Pacific, nicknamed the Friendly Islands (5)
15 Carriage drawn by two pairs of horses driven by one person; also another name for the schoolboy knot (4-2-4)
16 Instrument of the clarinet family, two of which feature in Serenade No. 10 for Thirteen Winds by Mozart (6,4)
18 Branch of philosophy concerned with moral principles (6)
20 English author who was the father of Virginia Woolf and Vanessa Bell (7)
21 Slow-moving cat-sized marsupial which may play dead if threatened by a predator (6)
25 Road in Whitehall, London, official residence of the elected First Lord of the Treasury (7,6)
28 Coniferous shrub with berries used to flavour gin, related to cypress (7)
30 Substance which turns litmus paper red (4)
31 In mathematics, a term for the number one (5)
32 "Stars, hide your fires; Let not light see my __ and deep desires..." *Macbeth, Act I, Scene 4* (5)
33 One of the basic patterns of a fingerprint (4)
37 Bivalve molluscs eaten raw from the shell, served with lemon juice (7)
38 Iridescent nacreous internal layer of clam, nautilus and tusk shells (6-2-5)
39 The second longest river in Europe, starting in the Black Forest and emptying in the Black Sea (6)
41 A type of snare or noose for catching game (7)
44 Muscle in the human body responsible for flexing the elbow and rotating the hand (6)
48 Thick Italian soup containing vegetables, beans, herbs and pasta or rice (10)
49 Image produced by X-rays (10)

52   A short stanza concluding a poem such as a ballade (5)
53   Genus of flowering plants including cowslip, cyclamen, oxlip, pimpernel and water violet (7)
54   Heavy tool used as a lever (7)
55   Physical state of good health through exercise (7)
56   Toxic chemical element, atomic number 48, used as a control in nuclear fission (7)
57   West Indian dance involving bending backwards under a steadily lowering pole (5)

Down

1   Confection of chocolate and ganache dusted in cocoa powder (7)
2   Literally meaning "hairy", an old nickname for a French infantryman (5)
3   2003 drama movie based on a non-fiction book by Laura Hillenbrand (10)
4   Spiritual teacher born Siddhartha Gautama circa 563 BC (6)
5   In the UK government, the Council of Ministers collectively (7)
6   Town on the south coast of England, neighbouring Brighton (4)
7   Long robe of black silk or other material, also called a cassock (7)
8   Swarming migratory insect which can descend on crops and rapidly destroy them (6)
9   Tapestry technique using small diagonal stitches (5,5)
10   A type of rock which is formed by the solidification of magma (7)
11   Small state in India (3)
17   "The more haste, the less ___." (5)
19   English privateer and slave trader who helped build the fleet which defeated the Spanish Armada in 1588 (7)
22   Parade or sports event official; also a bulldog or proctor's assistant at Oxford University (7)
23   Principal character in a literary work; also a muscle which causes movement through contraction (7)
24   Mechanical device in a firearm for discharging the empty case after firing (7)
25   The hardest naturally occurring mineral known (7)
26   An inanimate object, living being or creature regarded as a spiritual symbol of a clan (5)
27   Diacritical sign in the form ~, placed over the letter *n* in Spanish (5)
29   A closely-woven fine cotton fabric used to make bedclothes (7)

34 English county, site of Bakewell, Buxton and the Peak District (10)

35 The identifying colours and lightweight kit worn by a sports team, also worn by supporters (5)

36 Chinese style snack consisting thinly sliced vegetable and bean sprouts encased in a pancake (6,4)

40 The newest territory in Canada, officially confederated on April 1, 1999 (7)

42 Chief of the Ottawa tribe who led an unsuccessful rebellion against the British from 1763-66 (7)

43 The basic monetary unit in Paraguay (7)

45 From the Italian literally meaning "joke", a piece of music forming part of a symphony (7)

46 *The __ of Wrath*; John Steinbeck novel for which he was awarded the 1962 Nobel Prize for Literature (6)

47 Informal term for a radio or television show which features the same characters in every episode (6)

50 A collection of photographs and a book holding such a collection (5)

51 A city in southern Sweden (4)

52 Diminutive supernatural being of European folklore (3)

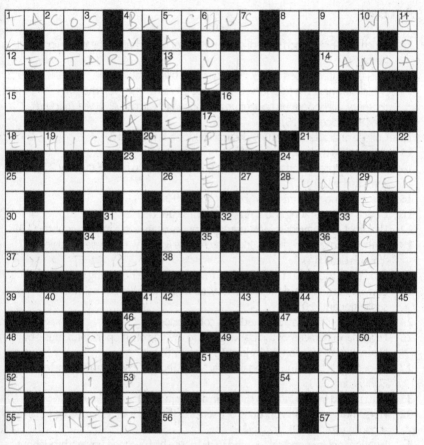

Samoa

Tacos   Raleigh   album

pastvo   Danube   Stephen

derby

Across

1 A rich one-pot French stew of various types of meat, haricot beans, onions and herbs (9)

6 Felt-like material used for covering card and billiard tables (5)

9 "I shall stay here the forehorse to a smock, Creaking my __ on the plain masonry, Till honour be bought up and no sword worn..." *All's Well That Ends Well*, Act II, Scene 1 (5)

12 College or academy to study classical music or fine arts (13)

13 Defenceless male honey bee (5)

14 Number represented as a one followed by 48 zeros in the UK (and by 27 zeros in the US) (9)

15 *The ___;* piano rag written by Scott Joplin in 1902 (11)

16 Device for generating and amplifying microwaves (5)

17 Diplomat of the highest rank, used as a representative in a foreign country (10)

19 Author whose unfinished work *A Death in the Family* was released two years after his death (4)

21 In archery, the section of a bow or arrow carrying the bowstring (4)

23 Low-ranking officer in the Royal Navy, above naval cadet but below sublieutenant (10)

24 Deep-blue silica glass, coloured with cobalt oxide (5)

25 Legendary character of the Dark Ages; also the title of an opera with music by Henry Purcell and libretto by John Dryden (4,6)

27 All-seeing dictator and fictional character in George Orwell's novel *Nineteen Eighty-Four* (3,7)

31 Item passed from runner to runner in a relay race (5)

32 Horse-riding exercise consisting of a series of three to four S-shaped figures in a schooling arena (10)

34 Network of pipes and cables used to distribute high-voltage power throughout a region (4)

36 Species of elliptical flatfish (4)

37 Record-breaking champion chess player of the early 20th century, nicknamed the "Human Chess Machine" (10)

39 Codeword of the Nato phonetic alphabet between November and Papa (5)

42 British Prime Minister whose name is identified with the appeasement of Hitler (11)

43 A collection of poems, songs, writings or paintings (9)

45 *Spitting* __; television series featuring caricatured puppets of various politicians and royalty (5)

46 A person who arranges and composes sequences of dance steps and moves (13)

47 An established fundamental principle or belief, especially one relating to politics or religion (5)

48 Ancient city and UNESCO World Heritage Site in a Portuguese municipality with the same name (5)

49 The ancient Greek known as the "Father of History" (9)

Down

1 Tropical tree associated with Willie Harcourt-Cooze (5)

2 The hymn *Holy, holy, holy,* adapted from *Isaiah* 6:3 (7)

3 Feudal superior; also the operational name of the invasion of Normandy by Allied forces during the Second World War (8)

4 Plant of the buttercup family with delicate blue or white flowers, lace-like leaves and bracts yielding a hazy appearance (4-2-1-4)

5 The largest moon of Saturn which is the only known moon to have a dense nitrogen atmosphere (5)

6 Protective overall worn for heavy manual work (6,4)

7 Tendency to stay still, described in the first of Newton's three laws of motion (7)

8 The soft feathers of a species of northern hemisphere sea duck, used to stuff upholstery and quilts (9)

9 An advertising or political party catchphrase, originally a clan war cry (6)

10 A scientist who studies physical and biological properties of the seas (13)

11 Sucrose-rich plant in the Chenopodiaceae family (5,4)

16 The capital of Belarus, largely destroyed during the Second World War (5)

18 Musical notation indicating a piece must be repeated (3)

20 The largest city in Norway (4)

22 A group of stars formed in a recognisable pattern, usually named after a mythological figure (13)

26 The Italian river flowing through Florence and Pisa (4)

28 Nocturnally-hunting endangered and aggressive carnivore native to India (6,5)

29 __ Cup; golf trophy awarded biennially since 1927, last captained by Paul Azinger and Nick Faldo (5)

60

30 World Heritage Site in the Swiss canton of Ticino, famous for its three castles (10)

31 Survival and wilderness skills associated with author and presenter Ray Mears (9)

32 A fruity highball cocktail containing vodka, cranberry and grapefruit juice (3,6)

33 Unit of weight equal to 2240lb or 1016kg (3)

35 German protectorate in West Africa divided into two in 1922; one part joined with Ghana in 1957 (8)

38 Capital of the French department of Corse-du-Sud in Corsica; the birthplace of Napoleon (7)

40 Decorative handicraft similar to knitting but formed using a hook rather than needles (7)

41 An administrative region or division of Russia and the former Soviet Union (6)

43 Resembling an ox's head, the first letter of the Hebrew alphabet (5)

44 One of three First World War battles in Belgium in which the Germans used considerable amounts of mustard gas as a weapon (5)

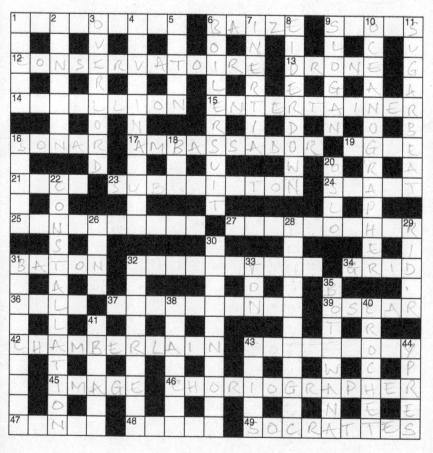

SOLUTIONS

1

ACROSS: 1 Jacques, **5** Bingo, **8** Rubicon, **12** Ghost, **13** Pavarotti, **14** Indri, **15** Lancashire, **16** Asparagine, **18** Renoir, **20** Ragtime, **22** Primus, **26** Beryl, **27** Ladette, **29** Decagon, **31** Shortbread, **32** Canis Minor, **35** Oakland, **37** Harissa, **38** Aloha, **39** Nettle, **41** Pavlova, **43** Zouave, **47** Demography, **49** Infrasonic, **52** Squat, **53** Lithology, **54** Euler, **55** Sparrow, **56** Lynch, **57** Extinct.
DOWN: **1** Jugular, **2** Crown, **3** Ultraviolet, **4** Sappho, **5** Bavaria, **6** Nero, **7** Oates, **8** Rhinal, **9** Bric-a-Brac, **10** Cadmium, **11** Noise, **17** State, **19** Norfolk, **21** Maenads, **23** Sangria, **24** Alfredo, **25** Admiral, **26** Bassoon, **28** Drachma, **30** Gondola, **33** Meadowsweet, **34** Krill, **36** Alligator, **40** Tempura, **42** Van Gogh, **44** Excerpt, **45** Harlow, **46** Argyle, **47** Discs, **48** Hotel, **50** Nylon, **51** Boon.

2

ACROSS: 1 Wodehouse, **6** Quire, **9** Piper, **12** Izmir, **13** Triceps, **14** Thistle, **15** Epstein, **16** Tsarina, **17** Shako, **18** Noyes, **19** Vermicelli, **22** Gang, **25** Leghorn, **28** Lily pad, **30** Coven, **31** Nova Scotia, **33** Patisserie, **36** Baton, **37** Othello, **38** Embassy, **40** Joel, **41** Hygrometer, **44** Habit, **47** Masse, **49** Secondo, **51** Taverna, **53** Uranium, **54** Tristan, **55** Owens, **56** Alder, **57** Stake, **58** Chlorosis.
DOWN: **1** White, **2** Dempsey, **3** Hortensio, **4** Ustinov, **5** Eliot, **6** Quesadilla, **7** Inspire, **8** Extra, **9** Priest, **10** Pitta, **11** Reed organ, **18** Nolan, **20** Raleigh, **21** Luddite, **23** Adverbs, **24** Acts, **26** Gavotte, **27** Neology, **29** Pea coat, **32** Sine, **34** Egypt, **35** Clementine, **36** Bujumbura, **39** Behaviour, **42** Ricotta, **43** Retinol, **45** Burgess, **46** Denier, **48** Sward, **49** Semis, **50** Optic, **52** Apsis.

3

ACROSS: 1 Hughes, **4** Aberdeen, **9** Rebec, **13** Sword, **14** Apostle, **15** Regatta, **16** Entertainer, **17** Ice hockey, **18** Aeschylus, **20** Eclair, **21** Bond, **24** Lebanon, **26** Aileron, **28** Bates, **29** Riboflavin, **31** Bombardier, **35** Molar, **36** Conduit, **37** Crochet, **39** Nine, **40** Handel, **42** Raspberry, **45** Meteorite, **47** Nostradamus, **50** Tequila, **51** Fetlock, **52** Minim, **53** Reeve, **54** Insanity, **55** Ankara.
DOWN: **1** Hesse, **2** Glottis, **3** Endorphin, **5** Brown, **6** Ritornello, **7** Ezekiel, **8** Norwegian, **9** Region, **10** Batik, **11** Charybdis, **12** Casablanca, **18** Adler, **19** Sea lion, **22** Ostrich, **23** T-bar, **25** Babylon, **27** Rooster, **30** Ford, **32** Backstroke, **33** Ratty, **34** Burlington, **35** Manometer, **36** Charivari, **38** Ombudsman, **41** Dreyfus, **43** Romania, **44** Police, **46** Toque, **48** Scott, **49** Samba.

4

ACROSS: 11 The Kings Speech, **12** Apiary, **13** Wood pigeon, **14** Breve, **15** Tang, **16** Times Square, **19** Girandole, **23** Metric, **25** Paladin, **26** Chadic, **27** Valhalla, **29** Begonia, **31** Orzo, **32** Volt, **34** Diabolo, **35** Cytology, **37** Pippin, **38** Centime, **40** Canape, **42** Churchill, **44** Aposiopesis, **47** Jack, **50** Stile, **51** Revelation, **54** Bolero, **55** Papua New Guinea.

DOWN: 1 Chlorine, **2** NKVD, **3** Gneiss, **4** Isle, **5** Spandrel, **6** Derby, **7** Chretien, **8** Galena, **9** Pint, **10** Wren, **17** Earth, **18** Uppsala, **20** Draco, **21** Leipzig, **22** Adagio, **24** Celadon, **26** Clastic, **28** Anouilh, **29** Browne, **30** Nucleus, **33** Tapir, **36** Lance, **38** Calliope, **39** Imperial, **41** Prisoner, **43** Huston, **45** Oology, **46** Tempo, **48** Aeon, **49** Keel, **52** View, **53** Tail.

5

ACROSS: 11 Rankin, **12** Black Swan, **13** Roan, **14** Metacarpus, **15** Thermostat, **16** Ready-to-wear, **19** Casserole, **23** Clinic, **25** Suffolk, **26** Poland, **27** Lovelace, **29** Veloute, **31** Yolk, **32** Berm, **34** Cadency, **35** Bullseye, **37** Tanner, **38** Piccolo, **40** You Bet, **42** Contralto, **44** Mockingbird, **47** Canterbury, **50** Eastertide, **53** Foot, **54** Great Bear, **55** Lorica.

DOWN: 1 Harebell, **2** Skua, **3** Infant, **4** Tbsp, **5** Falstaff, **6** Skate, **7** Zwieback, **8** Animus, **9** Iris, **10** Taka, **17** Dance, **18** West End, **20** Rally, **21** Langley, **22** Volley, **24** Chaucer, **26** Presley, **28** Oregano, **29** Venice, **30** Unblock, **33** Monet, **36** Squab, **38** Pot-au-feu, **39** Odometer, **41** Eurydice, **43** Auriga, **45** Needle, **46** Wyatt, **48** Avon, **49** Tito, **51** Sard, **52** Tory.

6

ACROSS: 11 Carmen, **12** Platoon, **13** Plover, **14** Ammonite, **15** Johnson, **16** King, **17** Grant, **19** Scarecrow, **22** Stock, **26** Clarinet, **27** Shift, **28** Austen, **30** Onomastics, **33** Depot, **34** Rain, **35** Cube, **36** Raven, **38** Passionate, **39** Tragic, **40** Tyrol, **41** Baguette, **43** Knock, **45** Dodecagon, **46** Mitre, **49** Mews, **51** Lithium, **54** Kiribati, **56** Cerium, **57** Parsley, **58** Purple.

DOWN: 1 Balmoral, **2** Umbo, **3** Snail, **4** Uppercut, **5** Hajj, **6** Rothschild, **7** Ants, **8** Spine, **9** Locket, **10** Vein, **18** Nuremberg, **20** Roses, **21** Octopus, **23** Cheviot, **24** Innsbruck, **25** Cartridge, **29** Serengeti, **31** Neutron, **32** In vitro, **37** Nerve fibre, **38** Polka, **41** Brooklyn, **42** Throttle, **44** Casein, **47** Flume, **48** Crape, **50** Eden, **52** Tope, **53** Mill, **55** Bard.

The Telegraph

7

ACROSS: 1 Fiennes, **5** National Trust, **12** Adams, **13** Vers Libre, **14** Cohen, **15** Red Deer, **16** Afraid, **17** Sierra, **18** Capo, **20** Caraway, **22** Osprey, **27** Donizetti, **28** Score, **29** Black, **30** Napalm, **31** Shrew, **33** Knight, **36** Cupid, **37** Cinch, **39** Harlequin, **40** O'Neill, **42** Knock-on, **44** Lego, **47** Hecuba, **49** Humans, **51** Lincoln, **54** Blair, **55** Ankle bone, **56** Rhine, **57** Alpha Centauri, **58** Siemens.

DOWN: 1 Fratricide, **2** Eland, **3** Nasser, **4** Severn, **5** Norma, **6** Talaria, **7** Obbligato, **8** Area, **9** Tactics, **10** Usher, **11** Tanganyika, **19** Pineapple, **21** Aries, **23** Roadhouse, **24** Izzard, **25** Stomach, **26** Selkirk, **28** Sarah, **29** Blixen, **32** Wahoo, **34** Acrophobia, **35** Encounters, **38** Nantucket, **41** Liberia, **43** Chapeau, **45** Pliers, **46** Entree, **48** Clamp, **50** Shoji, **52** Olive, **53** Kale.

8

ACROSS: 1 Marlborough, **7** Chokedamp, **12** Galleon, **13** Lilac, **14** Stun gun, **15** Elastoplast, **16** Old Bailey, **17** Istanbul, **19** Seneca, **21** Eagle, **24** Marvell, **27** Aitken, **29** Stalag, **32** Budgerigar, **33** The Prophet, **35** Velvet, **36** Fennec, **37** Swindon, **40** Ugric, **42** Factor, **44** Remember, **47** Cathedral, **49** Machiavelli, **52** Intrude, **53** Roget, **54** Sardius, **55** Grisaille, **56** Aeronautics.

DOWN: 1 Magnesium, **2** Reliant, **3** Brent, **4** Run-up, **5** Upload, **6** Holst, **7** Cyclone, **8** Obsidian, **9** Educate, **10** Algol, **11** Pennyweight, **18** Nyerere, **20** Etty, **22** Galahad, **23** Tamale, **25** Riddler, **26** Loin, **28** Ethics, **30** Thorite, **31** Apis, **32** Bivouacking, **34** Inro, **38** Narcissus, **39** Ofarrell, **41** Caesura, **43** Calorie, **45** Bellini, **46** Scoter, **48** Tutti, **49** Magma, **50** Ibsen, **51** Virtu.

9

ACROSS: 1 Stephenson, **6** Six Nations, **13** U-turn, **14** Matinee, **15** Collier, **16** Tethys, **17** Crow, **18** Atonement, **20** Eyrie, **21** Polyhedron, **24** Open, **27** Osborne, **29** Rutland, **31** Peron, **32** Khrushchev, **35** Grandstand, **38** Paean, **39** Crystal, **40** Shiatsu, **42** Zest, **43** Madagascar, **45** Oriel, **48** Inspector, **51** Pods, **53** Shaded, **55** Aconite, **56** Polenta, **57** Roast, **58** Oxeye Daisy, **59** Bridle Path.

DOWN: 1 Shuttlecock, **2** Equator, **3** Honey Bear, **4** Numb, **5** Otter, **7** Iceland, **8** Nacho, **9** Teller, **10** Ogive, **11** Serotonin, **12** Snow White, **19** Epee, **22** Larceny, **23** Ogden, **25** Parfait, **26** Opus, **28** Burgess, **30** Acrylic, **33** Sine, **34** Cocoa, **36** Double Dutch, **37** Straw Poll, **38** Pizzicato, **40** Sard, **41** Iron Horse, **44** Atropos, **46** Indiana, **47** Belize, **49** Scone, **50** Theta, **52** Dinar, **54** Hand.

10

ACROSS: 11 Barium, **12** Ulysses, **13** Octave, **14** Coventry, **15** Archery, **16** Kilo, **17** Birds, **19** Charlotte, **21** Crane, **24** Coleslaw, **26** Thomson, **27** Volt, **29** Prosciutto, **31** Youth, **33** Nash, **34** Dana, **35** Tesla, **37** Tabula Rasa, **38** Shoe, **39** Fashion, **41** Regicide, **43** Troop, **46** Dashboard, **48** Weber, **51** Tutu, **52** Perseus, **54** Asterisk, **56** Hearst, **57** Cricket, **58** Tobago.
DOWN: 1 Palomino, **2** Rice, **3** Smith, **4** Gunyah, **5** Lyra, **6** Psychology, **7** Asbestos, **8** Tokyo, **9** Stoker, **10** Evelyn, **18** Deep Space, **20** Retro, **22** Plaintiff, **23** Anthology, **25** Watts, **27** Ventricle, **28** Lists, **30** Roach, **32** Umber, **36** Arithmetic, **37** Tango, **40** Shamrock, **42** Dressage, **44** Reuben, **45** Oeuvre, **47** Rialto, **49** Spitz, **50** State, **53** Saki, **55** Ruby.

11

ACROSS: 1 Scallop, **5** Daphne, **8** Scream, **12** Frost, **13** Ethiopia, **14** Romans, **16** Roulette, **17** Legato, **18** Clove, **19** Chino, **21** Pharmacology, **27** Pound, **28** Burgundy, **29** Anoa, **33** Kiss of life, **34** Rugby fives, **36** Spin, **37** Richards, **38** Horus, **41** Achilles' heel, **42** Penne, **46** Peace, **48** Custer, **50** Denebola, **53** O'Brien, **54** Coca Cola, **55** Gofer, **56** Newman, **57** Aeneid, **58** Durrell.
DOWN: 1 Safari, **2** Aeolus, **3** Latte, **4** Preston, **5** Dahl, **6** Promethium, **7** Naira, **9** Chow chow, **10** Erato, **11** Mystery, **15** Wogan, **20** Hudson, **22** Red Guard, **23** Omnivore, **24** Spikes, **25** Gunsmith, **26** Griffith, **28** Bell, **30** Assisi, **31** Ibis, **32** Afghan, **35** Cheesecake, **39** Aloe vera, **40** Peach, **41** Alphorn, **43** Emerald, **44** Toffee, **45** Carrel, **47** Arrow, **49** Stole, **51** Elgar, **52** Gold.

12

ACROSS: 10 Simnel, **12** Maypole, **13** Easter, **14** Demeter, **15** Dodgson, **16** Ashe, **17** Poppy, **19** Hamstring, **21** Barry, **24** Betelgeuse, **26** Dutch metal, **29** Eggs, **31** Meade, **32** Yonne, **33** Lamb, **34** Lent, **35** Magic, **38** Tarka, **40** Pane, **41** Dendrology, **42** Urbi et orbi, **44** Aspel, **47** Pentecost, **48** a deux, **51** Gris, **52** Trudgen, **54** Coulomb, **56** Antrim, **57** Pearson, **58** Nebula.
DOWN: 1 Wind rose, **2** Pluto, **3** Omer, **4** Byrd, **5** Good Friday, **6** Kensington, **7** Verne, **8** Asmara, **9** Benhur, **11** Nim, **18** Press stud, **20** Aruba, **22** Agamemnon, **23** Shoemaker, **25** Ewe, **27** Ellipsoid, **28** Amman, **30** Grebe, **36** Goosebumps, **37** Cryptogram, **38** Tau, **39** Rebus, **43** Bluebell, **45** Spring, **46** Eostre, **49** Stamp, **50** Bunny, **53** Nest, **54** Cana, **55** Orb.

13

ACROSS 1 Neptune, **5** Siberia, **9** Ralph, **12** Wanda, **13** Metronome, **14** Nadir, **15** Etonian, **16** Yorker, **17** Celery, **18** Leek, **20** Whippet, **22** Kung fu, **27** Nicaragua, **28** Ester, **29** Chord, **30** Oligarchy, **31** Lindbergh, **36** Cabot, **37** Lodge, **39** Newcastle, **40** Warhol, **42** Haddock, **43** Peso, **46** Israel, **48** Corral, **50** Risotto, **53** Zebra, **54** Off-the-peg, **55** Aioli, **56** Rondo, **57** Olympus, **58** Trident.
DOWN: 1 New Zealand, **2** Pinto, **3** Urania, **4** Edmund, **5** Satay, **6** Biographer, **7** Roosevelt, **8** Acer, **9** Rondeau, **10** Ladle, **11** Hurdy-gurdy, **19** Excalibur, **21** Heath, **23** Georgette, **24** Bright, **25** Egg roll, **26** Bradawl, **29** Caesar, **32** Ionic, **33** Schweitzer, **34** Readership, **35** Penologist, **38** Dragonfly, **41** Oregano, **44** Wright, **45** Osmani, **47** Robin, **49** Lupus, **51** T-bone, **52** Solo.

14

ACROSS 1 Faber, **4** Quadrille, **9** Tulip, **12** Moliere, **13** Indus, **14** Desktop, **15** Ruritania, **16** Dog's mercury, **17** Bocce, **18** Providence, **19** Zeno, **21** Iowa, **23** Manila hemp, **27** Drake, **29** Diocletian, **31** Gibson girl, **34** Sugar, **35** Chinese red, **36** Snip, **38** Mobs, **40** Douglas fir, **44** Heinz, **47** Bay of Bengal, **48** Set square, **51** Erosion, **52** Leech, **53** Rhenium, **54** Extra, **55** Desert rat, **56** Spelt.
DOWN: 1 Femur, **2** Baldric, **3** Roentgen, **4** Quern, **5** Agitato, **6** Red admiral, **7** Lasagne, **8** Endemic, **9** Tishri, **10** Lettuce, **11** Puppy Love, **17** Baird, **18** Plastic, **20** Odin, **22** Wrong, **24** Imari, **25** Elite, **26** Pasteur, **28** Alien, **30** Lyre, **32** Lopez, **33** Derailleur, **34** Semibreve, **37** Chequers, **39** Boycott, **41** Oceanid, **42** Goggles, **43** Fischer, **45** Imagine, **46** Africa, **49** Tarot, **50** Emmet.

15

ACROSS: 1 Mealor, **4** Redcap, **8** Wipeout, **13** Nymph, **14** Palladium, **15** Lydia, **16** Tendril, **17** Stolon, **18** Avenue, **19** Elbe, **21** Octagon, **23** Puffin, **28** Speak easy, **29** Mayer, **30** Torso, **31** Delphinus, **32** Twitching, **38** Maple, **40** Epsom, **42** Reservoir, **43** Norway, **44** Brioche, **45** Pere, **48** Engels, **50** Zephyr, **52** Mirages, **55** Scott, **56** Anchorman, **57** Pearl, **58** Supreme, **59** Rhebok, **60** Nereid.
DOWN: 1 Monotheism, **2** Amman, **3** Others, **5** Ellis, **6** Coat of arms, **7** Philology, **8** Wump, **9** Pole vault, **10** Ogden, **11** Trade union, **12** Spill, **20** Beekeeper, **22** Coypu, **24** Farandole, **25** Skip, **26** Mariner, **27** British, **33** Worth, **34** Harp, **35** Amanuensis, **36** Smoothbore, **37** Greek salad, **39** Epaulette, **41** Streetcar, **46** Ament, **47** Frappe, **49** Group, **51** Romeo, **53** Grace, **54** Fame.

16

ACROSS: 1 Ballesteros, **7** Drum major, **11** Larch, **12** Utamaro, **13** Senecio, **14** Agnostic, **15** Welsh rarebit, **16** Agama, **18** Boom, **20** e-tailer, **25** Busby, **26** Francium, **27** Scup, **31** Coronation, **32** Hippodrome, **34** Sage, **35** Kilogram, **36** Sushi, **39** Fellini, **40** Auer, **41** Krone, **45** Rosetta Stone, **48** Overture, **51** Ukraine, **52** Piccolo, **53** Deuce, **54** Auschwitz, **55** Saudi Arabia.
DOWN: 1 Ballad, **2** Lorenz, **3** Ethos, **4** Thulium, **5** Ream, **6** Stagecoach, **7** Doors, **8** Mondrian, **9** Jacob, **10** Rooster, **13** Surrey, **17** Guyana, **19** Meuniere, **21** Lacrosse, **22** Abacus, **23** Astragal, **24** Japonica, **26** Fate, **28** Precis, **29** Spam, **30** Edison, **33** Copernicus, **37** Dietrich, **38** Pilate, **39** Fortuna, **42** Ravioli, **43** Suburb, **44** Seneca, **46** Sorts, **47** Topaz, **49** Ryder, **50** Tofu.

17

ACROSS: 1 Logue, **4** Sovereign, **9** Aesop, **12** Miocene, **13** Chump, **14** Topsail, **15** Gittern, **16** Discography, **17** Oratorio, **20** Octogenarian, **24** Edwards, **26** Arnica, **28** Regina, **30** Denis, **31** Carbonara, **32** Triad, **33** Misery, **35** Estate, **36** Rollmop, **39** Carbohydrate, **41** Anderson, **44** Nucleic acid, **47** Kingdom, **50** Oxonian, **51** Award, **52** Picasso, **53** Heron, **54** Hydrofoil, **55** Lenin.
DOWN: 1 Limestone, **2** Georgia, **3** Event, **4** Stere, **5** Vicuna, **6** Round, **7** Impasto, **8** Nitrogen, **9** Aspartame, **10** Sharp, **11** Pollyanna, **18** Orris, **19** Insect, **21** Consonant, **22** Iridium, **23** Harris, **25** Windsor, **27** Chanel, **29** Warren, **32** Tulle, **33** Macintosh, **34** Rhodesian, **37** Pantaloon, **38** Hyacinth, **40** Richard, **42** Simpson, **43** Skidoo, **45** Choir, **46** Draco, **48** Nepal, **49** Decal.

18

ACROSS: 1 Strauss, **5** Nigeria, **8** Lilac, **11** Orion, **12** Chowder, **14** Grammar, **15** Trent, **16** Oriel, **17** Lithology, **18** Castro, **19** Twenty-one, **22** Pane, **26** Corelli, **28** Crumpet, **30** Kafka, **32** Riboflavin, **34** Battlement, **36** Nerve, **37** Orpheus, **38** Orinoco, **40** Apse, **41** Vientiane, **43** Betony, **47** Toscanini, **50** Talon, **52** Oxlip, **54** Erasmus, **55** Apolune, **56** Keats, **57** Nadal, **58** Nucleus, **59** Odyssey.
DOWN: 1 Scout, **2** Raiders, **3** Unnatural, **4** Sector, **5** Naomi, **6** Gadolinium, **7** Argot, **8** Llanos, **9** Limbo, **10** Carlyle, **13** Riley, **18** Cochran, **20** Wickiup, **21** Notation, **23** Alfredo, **24** Rigatoni, **25** Skye, **27** Roberts, **29** Pearson, **31** Anthony, **33** Fret, **35** Heliotrope, **39** Ice hockey, **40** Actaeon, **42** Naira, **44** Orleans, **45** Mammal, **46** Angelo, **48** Skald, **49** Ibsen, **51** Louis, **53** Pusey.

19

ACROSS: 1 Einstein, **5** Sacramento, **12** Nepal, **13** Sextuplet, **14** Gable, **15** Catcher, **16** Nylon, **17** Clinton, **18** Wader, **20** Paramount, **24** Heine, **26** Roosevelt, **28** Adam's needle, **29** Twins, **30** Thor, **31** Rhea, **33** Tacet, **36** Little Women, **38** Arboretum, **40** Avens, **41** Rochester, **42** Virgo, **43** Farrell, **46** Dubai, **49** Satchel, **51** Okapi, **52** Gun cotton, **53** Mason, **54** Stagecoach, **55** Steinway.
DOWN: 2 Input, **3** Sulphur, **4** Nixon, **5** Skull, **6** Calendula, **7** Aztec, **8** English setter, **9** Tibet, **10** Knackwurst, **11** Meuniere, **13** Strophe, **19** Doolittle, **21** Ratio, **22** Mead, **23** Tesla, **25** Indicator, **27** Easy listening, **30** Tower, **32** Heart, **34** Tom Collins, **35** Knee, **36** Leapfrog, **37** Macedonia, **39** Bergson, **42** Vitamin, **44** Roast, **45** Logic, **47** Bloch, **48** Ictus, **50** Hosta.

20

ACROSS: 1 Stubbs, **4** Nightjar, **9** Charm, **13** Libya, **14** Dragonfly, **15** Topaz, **16** Maltese, **17** Crewel, **18** Nevada, **19** Neon, **21** Embassy, **23** Venice, **28** Extension, **29** Ninja, **30** Twill, **31** Donizetti, **32** Toothache, **37** Hooke, **38** Tribe, **40** Gladiator, **41** Scythe, **43** Evening, **44** Gwyn, **47** Rackle, **49** Ararat, **51** Dreyfus, **54** Royce, **55** Acetylene, **56** Samba, **57** Satin, **58** Fusilier, **59** Alfred.
DOWN: 1 Salamander, **2** Umbel, **3** Blazer, **5** Isaac, **6** Hootenanny, **7** Jefferson, **8** Rays, **9** Cat's eye, **10** Alpha, **11** Mozzarella, **12** ad rem, **20** Osteology, **22** Monet, **24** Irish stew, **25** Endive, **26** Biretta, **27** Eastman, **30** Thalia, **33** Organ, **34** Phosprorus, **35** Pennyroyal, **36** Grandstand, **39** Inverness, **42** Holbein, **45** Adder, **46** Bessel, **48** Crypt, **50** Theme, **52** Femur, **53** Calf.

21

ACROSS: 1 Stanley, **5** Thompson, **9** Talc, **13** Giant, **14** Rambler, **15** Platoon, **16** Treble, **17** Frog, **18** Gremolata, **20** Anatomy, **21** Botanist, **22** Bohr, **24** Insulin, **26** Rhombus, **29** Gibbs, **31** Subkingdom, **33** Penicillin, **36** Chest, **37** Norfolk, **38** Rigging, **40** Sack, **42** Twitcher, **45** Parapet, **48** Acoustics, **49** Cote, **51** Oberon, **53** Detroit, **54** Ariadne, **55** Llama, **56** Adam, **57** Heraldry, **58** Thistle.
DOWN: 1 Sagittarius, **2** Alameda, **3** Little owl, **4** Yard, **5** Timor, **6** Obligation, **7** Paragon, **8** Orpheus, **10** Avocado, **11** Centaurus, **12** Bacon, **19** Cyanogen, **21** Barbour, **23** Ugli, **25** Sable, **27** Breaker, **28** Stirrups, **30** Balti, **32** Iota, **34** Nightingale, **35** Rothschild, **36** Cassandra, **39** Garibaldi, **41** Croatia, **43** Whittle, **44** Tostada, **46** Parfait, **47** Ascot, **50** Toddy, **52** Vent.

22

ACROSS: 11 Famous Five, **12** Khyber Pass, **13** Pierce, **14** Number Ten, **15** Rose, **16** Bobby, **18** Frankfurt, **21** Gauge, **25** Geranium, **27** Netball, **28** Mole, **29** Culbertson, **31** Nixon, **33** Rill, **34** Wiki, **35** Lunge, **37** Pentathlon, **38** Kong, **39** Antigua, **41** Narrator, **43** Anode, **45** Starboard, **47** Kendo, **50** Ajax, **52** Zinfandel, **55** Hubble, **57** Khmer Rouge, **58** Basset horn.
DOWN: 1 Baritone, **2** Boar, **3** Aspen, **4** Winner, **5** Beam, **6** Skye, **7** Hysteria, **8** Terne, **9** Sparta, **10** Isis, **17** Brambling, **19** Ninon, **20** Futon, **22** Galileo, **23** Gibraltar, **24** Glengarry, **26** Mason, **28** March Hare, **30** Unicorn, **32** Xenon, **36** Elgar, **37** Prado, **40** Titanium, **42** Old Glory, **44** Dexter, **46** Relish, **48** Azure, **49** Wheel, **51** John, **53** Ares, **54** Debs, **56** Baht.

23

ACROSS: 11 Porter, **12** Bugle, **13** Roly-poly, **14** Respighi, **15** Scottie, **16** Iota, **17** Field, **19** Universal, **21** Stook, **24** Smuggler, **26** Guppy, **27** Au fait, **30** Hart, **32** Chain, **33** Young, **35** Indy, **36** Ogee, **37** Bombe, **39** Picot, **40** Apse, **41** Terror, **42** Peril, **43** Emulsion, **45** Skate, **48** Dietetics, **50** Kelly, **53** Bale, **54** Colombo, **56** Autobahn, **58** Jew's harp, **59** Clyde, **60** Plasma.
DOWN: 1 Nobelium, **2** Step, **3** Bragg, **4** O'Brien, **5** Eggs, **6** Demography, **7** Brittany, **8** Fleet, **9** Sprint, **10** Clotho, **18** Light-year, **20** Vegan, **22** Blackbird, **23** Mangetout, **25** Realm, **28** Fricassee, **29** Indus, **31** Angle, **34** Uncle, **38** Eurythmics, **39** Pilot, **42** Phillips, **44** Oklahoma, **46** Kraken, **47** Theism, **49** Craven, **51** Ocean, **52** Stupa, **55** Onyx, **57** Bear

24

ACROSS: 1 Morocco, **5** Nemesis, **9** Balsa, **12** Naira, **13** Titania, **14** Islands, **15** Albatross, **16** Grizzly bear, **17** Hawse, **18** Tourmaline, **20** Abel, **23** Vice, **25** Fairground, **29** Parka, **30** Numerology, **32** Trifoliate, **35** Forge, **36** Nutcracker, **37** King, **39** Oryx, **40** Compositor, **43** Tudor, **46** Suffragette, **49** Publicist, **51** O'Connor, **52** Leister, **53** Molto, **54** Derby, **55** Anaemia, **56** Sororal.
DOWN: 1 Mensa, **2** Rainbow, **3** Chartres, **4** Outpost, **5** Notes, **6** Montgomery, **7** Spaniel, **8** Spitz, **9** Boleyn, **10** Lance, **11** Australia, **17** Haven, **19** Upright, **21** Biryani, **22** Opal, **24** Comfrey, **26** Allen, **27** Utrecht, **28** Defoe, **31** Reef, **33** Edgar, **34** Proscenium, **35** Fool's gold, **38** Strimmer, **41** Patella, **42** Roberts, **44** Daimler, **45** Granny, **47** Flour, **48** Garda, **49** Pitta, **50** Troll.

25

ACROSS: 1 Walpole, **5** Phoenix, **9** Flush, **12** Ounce, **13** Shutter, **14** Bourbon, **15** Goldeneye, **16** Charcuterie, **17** Gigot, **18** Disclosure, **20** Cali, **23** Iron, **25** Mastermind, **29** Worth, **30** Daisy wheel, **32** Philosophy, **35** Trick, **36** Collarbone, **37** Asia, **39** Earl, **40** Referendum, **43** Atlas, **46** White spirit, **49** Bumblebee, **51** Nairobi, **52** Calypso, **53** Later, **54** Ormer, **55** Emerald, **56** Hogarth.
DOWN: 1 Wrong, **2** Long Leg, **3** Omelette, **4** East End, **5** Plume, **6** Optical Art, **7** Normans, **8** Xebec, **9** Fruits, **10** Umber, **11** Hindemith, **17** Guild, **19** Sitwell, **21** Atropos, **22** Owls, **24** Olivier, **26** Ad hoc, **27** Ichabod, **28** Dylan, **31** Yoke, **33** Yeats, **34** Lacertilia, **35** Tae kwon do, **38** Rawlplug, **41** Earache, **42** Mammoth, **44** Lobster, **45** Renoir, **7** Ilium, **48** Pride, **49** Biped, **50** Earth.

26

ACROSS: 1 Bolt, **3** Sweetpea, **8** Diamond, **13** Shakespeare, **14** Kilometre, **15** Everest, **16** Gates, **17** Tankard, **18** Lisbon, **20** Clarify, **22** Bodkin, **26** Taiga, **27** Diarchy, **29** Painted, **31** Magna Carta, **33** Wellington, **36** Orchard, **37** Chiffon, **38** Rally, **39** Chaise, **41** Hexagon, **43** Eureka, **47** Opossum, **49** Epode, **50** Insects, **52** Heyerdahl, **53** Antiquarian, **54** Treadle, **55** Roadster, **56** Tail.
DOWN: 1 Boswell, **2** Lease, **4** Wapiti, **5** Evangel, **6** Puerto Rico, **7** Ankus, **8** Daleth, **9** Amman, **10** Ostmark, **11** Dresden, **12** Denebola, **19** Sting, **21** Flyleaf, **23** Orion, **24** Edwards, **25** Apolune, **26** Tempo, **28** Article, **30** Dinky, **32** Adams, **34** Tilde, **35** Pina Colada, **38** Rousseau, **39** Crochet, **40** Acolyte, **42** Orestes, **44** Arsenal, **45** Impale, **46** Bisque, **48** Sarod, **49** Euler, **51** China.

27

ACROSS: 1 Victory, **5** Lucas, **8** Festoon, **12** Comet, **13** Retriever, **14** Doors, **15** Yarrow, **16** Nickel, **17** Ukulele, **19** Santa Fe, **20** Gunmetal, **21** Myth, **23** Isfahan, **25** Aquatic, **27** Abbot, **29** Epiglottis, **31** Parachutes, **35** Royal, **36** Olympia, **37** Coconut, **39** Bach, **41** Off-piste, **43** Cellini, **46** New Moon, **47** Alonso, **49** Facing, **51** Orlon, **52** Avalanche, **53** Haiku, **54** Diptych, **55** Hayes, **56** Oenomel.
DOWN: 1 Vichyssoise, **2** Cameron, **3** Osteopath, **4** Yurt, **5** Lathi, **6** Chicken Run, **7** Seville, **8** Formulaic, **9** Sodium, **10** Orogeny, **11** Nissen hut, **18** Jennet, **20** Gravity, **22** Mach, **24** Fairy, **26** Teacake, **28** Baton, **30** Lulu, **32** Alcock, **33** Sitting Bull, **34** Episcopacy, **35** Robin Hood, **36** Offenbach, **38** Callaghan, **40** Cowslip, **42** Pharaoh, **44** Iridium, **45** Bounty, **48** Sachs, **50** Nemo.

28

ACROSS: 1 Nesbit, **4** Bellini, **8** Crouch, **13** Ratty, **14** Robinson, **15** Tendon, **17** Agrology, **18** Africa, **19** Largo, **20** Cleat, **22** Flag, **24** Logbook, **28** Grant, **29** Oratorio, **30** Parr, **35** Awakenings, **36** Antarctica, **38** Area, **39** Jalousie, **40** Liszt, **43** Rorqual, **45** Dodo, **46** Oscar, **49** Babel, **50** Oakley, **52** Plumbing, **55** Chisel, **56** Gymkhana,**57** Coign, **58** Austen, **59** Skirret, **60** Carina.

DOWN: 1 Norway, **2** Saturn, **3** Idyll, **5** Elba, **6** Longfellow, **7** Naomi, **9** Rheology, **10** Undergo, **11** Hancock, **12** Braggadocio, **16** Sally, **21** Luther, **23** Guinness, **25** Iguana, **26** Canape, **27** Vanguard, **31** Ahimsa, **32** Rialto, **33** Dar Es Salaam, **34** Scylla, **37** Woodpecker, **41** Bull's-eye, **42** Blood, **43** Rebecca, **44** Robbins, **47** Bikini, **48** Uganda, **51** Kayak, **53** Mocha, **54** Sage.

29

ACROSS: 1 Atalanta, **5** Circus, **9** Kappa, **13** Beano, **14** Croatia, **15** Norfolk, **16** Tom Sawyer, **17** Reichstag, **18** Blair, **19** Nobel prize, **21** Ziti, **24** Anna, **26** Lexicology, **30** Cress, **31** Cummerbund, **33** No-man's-land, **36** Libra, **37** Waterhouse, **38** Idol, **40** Moat, **41** Hieroglyph, **45** Laban, **48** Chieftain, **49** Nantucket, **51** Gardner, **52** Thinker, **53** Ionia, **54** Rummy, **55** O'Brien, **56** Exchange.

DOWN: 1 Abbot, **2** Anaemia, **3** Avogadro, **4** Tachyon, **6** Inter alios, **7** Clavier, **8** Sanchez, **9** Karate, **10** Prong, **11** Alkaloids, **12** Torr, **18** Blanc, **20** Beignet, **22** Ireland, **23** Acts, **25** Namibia, **27** Elbow, **28** Otology, **29** Yeats, **32** Edam, **34** Dylan, **35** Brigantine, **36** Limburger, **39** Flourish, **42** Inferno, **43** Reactor, **44** Hendrix, **46** Bakunin, **47** Sidney, **48** CD-rom, **49** Nike, **50** Thane.

30

ACROSS: 1 Chamberlain, **7** Kissinger, **12** Coulomb, **13** Ravioli, **14** Paris, **15** Award, **16** Nicosia, **17** Oceanid, **18** Panama, **20** Ottoman, **22** Faerie, **25** Otter, **26** Patriot, **28** Britten, **31** Eros, **32** Grout, **33** Knoll, **34** Faro, **38** Baklava, **39** Artemis, **40** Yahoo, **41** Sphinx, **43** Sirloin, **45** Legacy, **48** Saffron, **49** Sinatra, **50** Scale, **53** Icing, **54** Eardrum, **55** Bangles, **56** Armstrong, **57** Despatch box.

DOWN: 1 Cocoa, **2** Aruba, **3** Bloody Mary, **4** Rubens, **5** Apricot, **6** Nova Scotia, **7** Krona, **8** Saigon, **9** Impresario, **10** Gardner, **11** Rushdie, **18** Proverb, **19** Network, **21** Antonym, **23** Sporran, **24** Obelisk, **27** Tsunami, **29** Trachea, **30** Neology, **35** Wainwright, **36** Stalingrad, **37** Hypersonic, **41** Sestina, **42** Hafnium, **44** Isthmus, **46** Angelo, **47** Balboa, **49** Shrug, **51** Ad-lib, **52** Essex.

31

ACROSS: 11 Halley, **12** Rondo, **13** Asteroid, **14** Freetown, **15** Wyndham, **16** Drey, **17** Assam, **19** Kimberley, **21** Snipe, **25** Antigone, **27** Ombre, **28** Pomona, **30** Watt, **32** Clock, **33** Noble, **35** Cook, **36** Diet, **37** Schwa, **39** Aleph, **40** Aunt, **41** Manege, **42** Kirov, **43** Mantissa, **45** Verdi, **47** Lampblack, **49** Ascot, **52** Weir, **54** Chamois, **56** Charcoal, **58** Vindaloo, **59** Ivory, **60** Urania.
DOWN: 1 Harrison, **2** Sloe, **3** Byron, **4** Brunei, **5** Snow, **6** Round robin, **7** Cashmere, **8** Stamp, **9** Dryden, **10** Fife, **18** Aristotle, **20** Brook, **22** Pontoon, **23** Worcester, **24** Upper hand, **26** Enoch, **29** Mechanics, **31** Alidade, **34** Bream, **38** Acrophobia, **39** Anvil, **42** Krakatoa, **44** Slovakia, **46** Dorado, **48** Coccyx, **50** Scull, **51** Hague, **53** Emir, **55** Shot, **57** Cram.

32

ACROSS: 1 Polonium, **5** Talmud, **9** Cupel, **13** Dracula, **14** Cartier, **15** Sinew, **16** Myocardium, **17** Gladiators, **19** Tahini, **21** Azurite, **22** Oswald, **27** Romania, **29** Rastafarian, **32** Cartwright, **33** Goldilocks, **35** Scotch broth, **36** Royalty, **38** Soweto, **40** Avocado, **43** Coleus, **47** Bellingham, **49** Electorate, **52** Swami, **53** Roulade, **54** Mankind, **55** Leech, **56** Cutter, **57** Gin rummy.
DOWN: 1 Pedometer, **2** Llano, **3** Neumann, **4** Uganda, **6** Aura, **7** Maillot, **8** Dirndl, **9** Costa, **10** Pandora, **11** Lewis, **12** Schulz, **18** Brass, **20** Humerus, **23** Shirley, **24** Degas, **25** Tapioca, **26** Waldorf, **28** Newport, **29** Rehab, **30** Azoth, **31** Nacelle, **32** Cetus, **34** Joyce, **37** Yesterday, **39** Wallace, **41** Viaduct, **42** Dolmen, **44** O'Connor, **45** Agaric, **46** Scampi, **47** Basil, **48** Irish, **50** Apium, **51** Dame.

33

ACROSS: 1 Brooke, **5** Waugh, **8** Jungle, **13** Pluto, **14** Edinburgh, **15** Trump, **16** Element, **17** Takes, **18** Sellers, **19** Nisan, **21** Aerospace, **24** Sabre, **26** Penguin, **29** Flash, **31** Embargo, **33** Square mile, **34** Prosciutto, **36** Marines, **37** Sheet, **38** Nectary, **39** Riley, **41** Semaphore, **44** Eyrie, **47** Domingo, **50** Nails, **52** Globule, **54** Egypt, **55** Hurricane, **56** Klein, **57** Greene, **58** Homer, **59** Osmium.
DOWN: 2 Reuters, **3** Ozone, **4** Electra, **5** Whist, **6** Uzbekistan, **7** Harissa, **8** Johns, **9** Nettles, **10** Loupe, **11** Spleen, **12** Epistemology, **20** Neutron, **22** Raffles, **23** Emerson, **25** Biretta, **26** Post meridiem, **27** Neutral, **28** Nemesis, **30** Horatio, **32** Brioche, **35** Delphinium, **40** Yangtze, **42** Monarch, **43** El Greco, **45** Rouleau, **46** Exeunt, **48** Mayor, **49** Ochre, **51** Starr, **53** Oakum.

34

ACROSS: 1 Walker, **4** Cowdrey, **8** Massif, **14** Ionesco, **15** Ecuador, **16** Tenor, **17** Meitnerium, **18** Greek salad, **20** Nepeta, **22** Edward V, **24** Pretty, **27** Kipling, **28** Cairo, **29** Hodgkin, **32** Note, **33** Straw, **34** Kelly, **35** Crib, **39** Siemens, **40** Clare, **41** Crystal, **42** Muffin, **44** Ortolan, **46** Bronte, **50** Xylography, **52** Arithmetic, **55** Lycra, **56** Dragons, **57** Natural, **58** Apache, **59** Chagall, **60** Fraser.

DOWN: 1 Whitman, **2** Lanai, **3** Eisenstein, **5** Oresund, **6** Drum, **7** Elder, **9** Autostrada, **10** Singlet, **11** Faraday, **12** Lowry, **13** Aries, **19** Satie, **21** Pipette, **23** Diocese, **25** Egotism, **26** Shylock, **27** Kings, **28** Chaucer, **30** Keratin, **31** Nobel, **36** Heliograph, **37** Radon, **38** Hygrometer, **42** Maxilla, **43** Felucca, **45** Aerosol, **47** Escolar, **48** Caddy, **49** Stone, **51** Heath, **53** Tarts, **54** Gong.

35

ACROSS: 11 Mozart, **12** Alexander, **13** Pawn, **14** D-Day, **15** Rembrandt, **16** Sloane, **17** Turner, **20** Ruritania, **23** Dhow, **24** Oslo, **26** Polar bear, **28** Energy, **30** Pleonasm, **32** Everest, **34** Gill, **36** Anoa, **37** Lucerne, **38** Yeomanry, **39** Howard, **42** Ephesians, **44** Dahl, **45** Ross, **47** Maharishi, **49** Newark, **51** Animal, **52** Scapa Flow, **55** Rome, **57** Alto, **58** Nuremberg, **59** Erebus.

DOWN 1 Rood, **2** Banyan, **3** Star, **4** Balmoral, **5** Pear, **6** Walnut, **7** Adit, **8** Brisbane, **9** Upload, **10** Swan song, **18** Upsilon, **19** Raphael, **21** Rare earth, **22** Nursery, **25** Odonata, **27** Elevenses, **29** England, **31** Macbeth, **33** Thomson, **35** Lurcher, **40** O'Connell, **41** Dumpling, **43** Axiology, **46** Samson, **48** Realms, **50** Warren, **52** Sard, **53** Ares, **54** Wren, **56** Maul.

36

ACROSS: 1 Burnett, **5** Parry, **8** Francis, **12** Silicon, **13** Collage, **14** Creel, **15** Royal Flush, **16** Psychiatry, **18** Octet, **20** Coronet, **22** Neuron, **27** Tunic, **28** Camelot, **30** Shellac, **32** Agra, **33** Grant, **34** Anvil, **35** Ymir, **39** Gnocchi, **40** Guarani, **41** Cream, **42** Rob Roy, **44** Warwick, **46** Twite, **50** Flashpoint, **52** Aboukir Bay, **55** Kebab, **56** Scheele, **57** Cezanne, **58** Riemann, **59** Marat, **60** Narayan.

DOWN: 1 Bistre, **2** Rally, **3** Excellency, **4** Tangle, **5** Picasso, **6** Roll, **7** Yeats, **8** French, **9** Archimedes, **10** Chester, **11** Sally, **17** Boyle, **19** Con brio, **21** Estonia, **23** Nichrome, **24** Stranger, **25** Scorpio, **26** Aspirin, **29** Managua, **31** Lambert, **36** Acrophobia, **37** Maewo, **38** Schweitzer, **43** Bramble, **45** Cobbett, **47** Robson, **48** Vulcan, **49** Wyvern, **50** Fakir, **51** Nahum, **53** Benny, **54** Lehr.

37

ACROSS: 1 White, **4** Wilkinson, **9** Faust, **14** Florence, **15** Nonet, **16** Ridley, **17** Dean, **18** Comte, **19** Agora, **20** Nash, **21** Adrian, **22** Boycott, **24** Tahiti, **27** Minotaur, **29** Scherzo, **31** Rank, **32** Asparagine, **35** Linseed oil, **36** Floc, **37** Chorizo, **38** Incident, **41** United, **42** Jasmine, **44** Little, **46** Oboe, **49** Accra, **51** Tapir, **53** Yang, **54** Monaco, **55** Debug, **56** Pentagon, **57** Smash, **58** Swiss roll, **59** Ebony.
DOWN: 2 Halberd, **3** Tarantino, **5** I-beam, **6** Kennedy, **7** Ninja, **8** Outpost, **10** Auden, **11** Saens, **12** Anaconda, **13** Breastbone, **22** Burrito, **23** Othello, **25** Herod, **26** Tension, **28** Insulin, **29** Species, **30** Rankine, **33** Ascot, **34** Archdeacon, **39** Chlorine, **40** Dithyramb, **42** Jackdaw, **43** Integer, **45** Lincoln, **47** Broom, **48** Evans, **50** Abbas, **52** Pupil.

38

ACROSS: 1 Morris, **5** Matilda, **9** Medlar, **12** Birdsong, **13** Auxin, **14** Xavier, **15** Torc, **16** Flash, **17** Salem, **18** Soho, **19** Joshua, **20** Chariot, **22** Turret, **25** Jacobean, **27** Andrews, **29** Iota, **30** Cottage pie, **33** Atmosphere, **34** Hope, **35** Austria, **36** Espalier, **39** Cestus, **40** Jenkins, **42** Thatch, **44** Roux, **47** Orczy, **49** Cymru, **51** Bail, **52** Turnip, **53** Smuts, **54** Ethology, **55** Joiner, **56** Nigeria, **57** Oxygen.
DOWN: 2 Orinoco, **3** Radicchio, **4** Snowflake, **5** Magma, **6** Trachea, **7** Lexis, **8** Annulet, **9** Myxomatosis, **10** Davis, **11** Aleph, **20** Canopus, **21** Indiana, **23** Reith, **24** Euterpe, **26** Apocope, **27** Aveyron, **28** Eumaeus, **31** Trent, **32** Grasshopper, **37** Petruchio, **38** Lead Belly, **40** Jackson, **41** Incisor, **43** Cringle, **45** Oruro, **46** Xenon, **48** Young, **50** Maera.

39

ACROSS: 1 Potter, **4** Fairfax, **8** Cloche, **14** Lethe, **15** Auspice, **16** Amnesty, **17** Alnwick, **18** Diorama, **19** Ovolo, **20** Buchu, **21** The General, **23** Esso, **25** Iris, **27** Cassiopeia, **30** Awdry, **32** Summertime, **34** Wizard Of Oz, **37** Siren, **38** Montego Bay, **39** Webb, **41** Lady, **43** Bridgehead, **46** Umbra, **49** Tibia, **50** Don Juan, **52** Haggard, **54** Igraine, **55** George I, **56** Tully, **57** Eeyore, **58** Oloroso, **59** Enzyme.
DOWN: 1 Polka, **2** Titanic, **3** Emeritus, **5** Assad, **6** Rhinoceros, **7** Acetate, **9** London, **10** Customs, **11** Etymology, **12** Packet, **13** Taramasalata, **20** Bliss, **22** Eastman, **24** Baud, **26** Izmir, **28** Ante Meridiem, **29** Episode, **31** Defoe, **33** Edna, **35** Zebra, **36** De Beauvoir, **37** Solitaire, **40** Tungsten, **42** Dubarry, **44** Donegal, **45** Dahlia, **47** Bradley, **48** Napier, **51** Negus, **53** Doyle.

40

ACROSS: 1 Sidney, **4** Thulium, **8** Fawkes, **14** Bologna, **15** Aspects, **16** Busby, **17** Embargo, **18** Iceberg, **19** Rural, **20** Castle, **22** Fechner, **24** Attlee, **28** Ancon, **30** Biscuit, **32** Seismic, **35** Myocardium, **36** Entomology, **38** Rubella, **39** Ferrari, **40** Onion, **41** Beauty, **43** Dempsey, **45** Pyrope, **49** Nacho, **51** Macbeth, **53** Ammeter, **56** Hyena, **57** Strauss, **58** Proximo, **59** Mayday, **60** Tempest, **61** Tethys.
DOWN: 1 Sable, **2** Delibes, **3** Elgar, **5** Hyalite, **6** Leprechaun, **7** Uncle, **9** Amber, **10** Kestrel, **11** Sky blue, **12** Cabot, **13** Osage, **20** Cranmer, **21** Landaulet, **23** Estonia, **25** Tribology, **26** Abidjan, **27** Osmosis, **29** Coomb, **31** Souffle, **33** Maori, **34** Cayenne, **37** Triple jump, **41** Bentham, **42** Archery, **44** Ephesus, **46** Ostrich, **47** Amish, **48** Campo, **50** Omaha, **52** Curie, **54** Moore, **55** Roots.

41

ACROSS: 11 Oliver, **12** Matisse, **13** Router, **14** Moon, **15** Acorn, **16** Aiken, **17** Cyan, **18** Edward, **20** Herbert, **22** Hamlet, **23** Font, **25** Noddy, **27** Pesto, **29** Neon, **31** Deneb, **32** Aviatrix, **34** Settle, **37** Aleppo, **38** Noumenon, **39** Drake, **41** Byrd, **43** E-zine, **44** Sonny, **45** Anne, **46** Stamps, **48** Mesclun, **50** Rhodes, **52** Disc, **53** Cinch, **55** Ouzel, **56** Joel, **57** Powell, **58** Decibel, **59** Ganges.
DOWN: 1 Almond, **2** Avon, **3** Great Dane, **4** Smooth, **5** Stingray, **6** Asia, **7** Becket, **8** French toast, **9** Dutchman, **10** Hecate, **19** Antwerp, **21** Ex parte, **24** Overlay, **26** Da Vinci, **28** Saxhorn, **30** Oilskin, **33** Amulets, **35** Tornado, **36** Honeysuckle, **40** Hydrology, **42** Damocles, **44** Salcombe, **47** Tricot, **48** Monody, **49** Nozzle, **51** Eleven, **54** Hock, **56** Jung.

42

ACROSS: 1 Collins, **5** Forum, **8** Thurber, **12** Barth, **13** Iguanodon, **14** Inlet, **15** East Anglia, **16** Psephology, **18** Jubilee, **21** Mouse, **23** Mandrel, **25** Mural, **27** Turkey red, **29** Loren, **31** Atomic pile, **32** Psilocybin, **34** Akkad, **35** Amazonant, **36** Shirr, **37** Autonym, **40** Dagon, **42** Novisad, **44** The Postman, **47** Sweetheart, **52** Amigo, **53** Mint sauce, **54** Eider, **55** Procyon, **56** Lorry, **57** Spassky.
DOWN: 1 Cable, **2** Loris, **3** Ishmael, **4** Swing, **5** Fauvism, **6** Rune, **7** Midas, **8** Ton-up, **9** Unicorn, **10** Balfour, **11** Ratty, **17** Queen, **18** Jambalaya, **19** Burdock, **20** Ectoplasm, **22** Eurasia, **23** Middleton, **24** Leningrad, **26** Laird, **28** Rolland, **29** Lucas, **30** Robbins, **33** Rouge, **38** Trevino, **39** Noology, **41** Newbury, **43** Vihuela, **44** Tramp, **45** Timon, **46** Annal, **48** Egeus, **49** Andes, **50** Terry, **51** Tsar.

The Telegraph

43

ACROSS: 11 Monroe, **12** Primula, **13** Cravat, **14** Vignette, **15** Upsilon, **16** Apex, **17** Psalm, **19** Objet d'art, **21** Manse, **25** Knitwear, **26** Alley, **27** Lepton, **29** Polo, **31** Eliot, **32** Apple, **34** Rare, **35** Otto, **36** Utica, **38** Synge, **39** Funk, **40** Jekyll, **41** Baker, **42** Ideology, **44** Pluto, **46** Guinevere, **47** Hogan, **50** Gwyn, **52** Paladin, **53** Thallium, **55** Pigeon, **56** Wrecker, **57** Sparta.
DOWN: 1 Robinson, **2** Wren, **3** Perth, **4** Apse, **5** Lieutenant, **6** Quesadilla, **7** Earl Grey, **8** Scone, **9** Panama, **10** Face, **18** Lithology, **20** Bernini, **22** Sporran, **23** Venezuela, **24** Blue Peter, **28** Portfolio, **30** Oatmeal, **33** Pannier, **37** Atkins diet, **38** Stravinsky, **41** Blue laws, **43** Gratuity, **45** Tandem, **48** Spine, **49** Waist, **51** Whip, **53** Tare, **54** Loam.

44

ACROSS: 11 Laurie, **12** Union, **13** Ex libris, **14** Peterson, **15** Hexagon, **16** Rose, **17** Edison, **19** Rushmore, **22** Knave, **25** Francium, **27** Oldie, **28** Edward, **30** Wheatstone, **33** Assai, **35** Alee, **36** Biro, **37** Leeds, **39** Photometry, **40** Scream, **41** Chain, **42** Tarboosh, **45** Stone, **47** Flagship, **49** A level, **51** Watt, **53** Enfield, **56** Cassette, **58** Molecule, **59** Serge, **60** Dial-up.
DOWN: 1 Lavender, **2** Brae, **3** Helsinki, **4** Turner, **5** Fish, **6** Knox, **7** Kedgeree, **8** Flynn, **9** Oberon, **10** Ribs, **18** Singapore, **20** Spode, **21** Medea, **23** Vermeer, **24** De Niro, **26** Moore, **29** Whalebone, **31** Haircut, **32** Salami, **34** Stoat, **38** Slang, **39** Punch, **41** Cold Feet, **43** Rhapsody, **44** Spectrum, **46** Nutmeg, **48** Picket, **50** Venus, **52** Amos, **54** Easy, **55** Dart, **57** Edam.

45

ACROSS: 1 Goldsmith, **6** Tchaikovsky, **12** Rangers, **13** Baronet, **14** Eilat, **15** Halfpenny, **16** Atom smasher, **17** Mayer, **18** Palliative, **21** Frei, **23** Lure, **25** Stonemason, **27** Realm, **29** Highlander, **31** The Tempest, **34** Milan, **35** Annihilate, **36** Barn, **38** Nike, **40** Neapolitan, **42** Igloo, **45** Benedictine, **47** Pendennis, **50** Arete, **51** Steroid, **52** Anaheim, **53** Cryobiology, **54** Agamemnon.
DOWN: 1 Garth, **2** Langley, **3** Sleepers, **4** Ibsen, **5** Hobby, **6** Terra firma, **7** Handout, **8** Ictus, **9** One Day, **10** Sulphur, **11** Ytterbium, **17** Mulch, **18** Potentate, **19** Linnean, **20** Vingt-et-un, **22** Tram, **24** Rigel, **26** Scheldt, **28** Akela, **30** Lung, **32** Tanto, **33** Chalcedony, **34** Mont Blanc, **37** Airedale, **39** Kennedy, **41** Primero, **43** Lantern, **44** Adverb, **46** Cisco, **47** Padua, **48** Nyala, **49** Simon.

46

ACROSS: 11 Hobbit, **12** Fortuna, **13** Hammer, **14** Lordship, **15** Windsor, **16** Indy, **17** Warm-up, **19** Samoa, **21** Woolsack, **23** Dynamite, **25** Still, **26** Edmund, **28** Clod, **30** Thetis, **32** Hierarchy, **34** Schnitzel, **36** Truman, **38** Luau, **40** Museum, **41** Alone, **42** Porpoise, **44** Keeshond, **46** Steam, **47** Harrow, **49** Lake, **51** Retinol, **54** Roly-poly, **56** Boleyn, **57** Bangkok, **58** Tirana.
DOWN: 1 Coronary, **2** Ib idem, **3** Utah, **4** Off-piste, **5** Crow, **6** Guinea pig, **7** Cars, **8** Charioteer, **9** emails, **10** Meld, **18** Point, **20** Muslin, **21** William, **22** Cynthia, **24** Al dente, **27** Morello, **29** Lecture, **31** Emerald, **33** Greene, **35** Tambourine, **37** North, **39** Consonant, **42** Pembroke, **43** Scotland, **45** Shekel, **48** Rupert, **50** AWOL, **52** Toby, **53** Luke, **55** Loti.

47

ACROSS: 1 Hogmanay, **5** Africa, **9** Orpah, **13** Gatha, **14** Isagoge, **15** Mah-jong, **16** New Forest, **17** Thackeray, **19** Dryad, **20** New Zealand, **22** Snap, **24** Nile, **26** Monte Carlo, **28** Rebus, **30** Rowlandson, **32** Nottingham, **35** Boyce, **36** Radiometer, **37** Klee, **39** Ulna, **41** Ballantyne, **43** Anjou, **46** Roundhead, **47** Vermilion, **49** Abyssal, **51** Iron Man, **52** Telex, **53** Envoy, **54** Big Ben, **55** Ascanius.
DOWN: 1 Hogan, **2** Getaway, **3** Anaconda, **4** Alice-in-Wonderland, **6** Front bench, **7** Icefall, **8** Arm, **9** Others, **10** Procyon, **11** High Hopes, **12** Kant, **18** King of the herrings, **19** Dinar, **21** Watford, **23** Wren, **25** Lowry, **27** Rookery, **29** Bohol, **31** Aves, **33** Mweru, **34** Lorna Doone, **35** Blue whale, **38** Damietta, **40** Nureyev, **42** Leeming, **44** Jaia lai, **45** Pudsey, **47** Vamp, **48** Naxos, **50** Lob.

48

ACROSS: 1 Sewell, **4** Cardiff, **8** Septum, **14** Atlanta, **15** Class, **16** Rooster, **17** Croissant, **18** Ad hoc, **19** Orion, **20** Electron, **22** Emerald Isle, **27** Siamang, **29** Clutch, **31** Tsetse, **33** Bacon, **34** Narcissus, **35** White, **36** Snooze, **38** O'Brien, **39** Rollmop, **42** Synchromesh, **44** Blizzard, **48** Bosch, **50** Straw, **52** Sugar Plum, **54** Risotto, **55** Coral, **56** Sleight, **57** Saigon, **58** Mondays, **59** Renoir.
DOWN: 1 Snatchers, **2** Walpole, **3** Lungs, **5** Alcott, **6** Diana, **7** Fischer, **9** Economics, **10** Tutsi, **11** Marina, **12** Fata Morgana, **13** Dracula, **21** Twain, **23** Mauritius, **24** Lithium, **25** Scarab, **26** Gene, **28** Anchovy, **30** Casino, **32** Astrologist, **33** Best, **35** Waltz, **37** Zucchetto, **40** Pedometer, **41** Preston, **43** Morocco, **45** Allegro, **46** Iberis, **47** Ashley, **49** Sushi, **51** World, **53** Reeve.

The Telegraph

49

ACROSS: 1 The Borrowers, **7** Jackaroo, **13** Loire, **14** Flipper, **15** Unicorn, **16** Union Jack, **17** Edith, **18** Heart, **19** Innocent, **21** King, **23** Buffalo, **26** Mugwump, **29** Review, **31** Caruso, **33** Coast, **34** Paparazzi, **35** Honey, **36** Roosts, **38** Lyceum, **39** Celesta, **42** Otalgia, **43** Sash, **44** Earthnut, **48** Raker, **50** Drift, **52** Ascending, **54** Promote, **55** Lily pad, **56** Krona, **57** Yokohama, **58** Open sandwich.
DOWN: 1 Tellurium, **2** Edition, **3** Odeon, **4** Refrain, **5** Whisky, **6** Rupee, **8** Abu Dhabi, **9** Kniphofia, **10** Rioja, **11** Ornithology, **12** Irving, **20** Court, **22** Inverness, **24** Aquinas, **25** Trophy, **27** Granola, **28** Pope, **30** Enzyme, **32** Zinc, **33** Cartography, **35** Holst, **37** Tiger moth, **40** Autograph, **41** Daydream, **43** Stifle, **45** Arcadia, **46** Nairobi, **47** Sampan, **49** Kiosk, **51** Tulip, **53** Naked.

50

ACROSS: 1 McGonagall, **6** Beckinsale, **13** Genus, **14** Ivanhoe, **15** Thulium, **16** Epstein, **17** Ukraine, **18** Onion, **19** Issachar, **21** Rosa, **22** Utopia, **26** Memphis, **29** Octant, **31** Typhon, **33** Triangulum, **34** Clydesdale, **37** Salute, **39** Legato, **40** Nigella, **43** Starch, **44** Dupe, **45** Amaretto, **50** Robin, **52** Rebecca, **53** Alumnae, **55** Chorizo, **56** Shih-tzu, **57** Bosie, **58** School Days, **59** Sauerkraut.
DOWN: 1 Magnesium, **2** Genesis, **3** Nashe, **4** Goiania, **5** League, **7** Evelina, **8** Kotzebue, **9** Neurology, **10** Aditi, **11** Ermine, **12** Charlotte, **20** Cohen, **23** Ishmael, **24** Volume, **25** Anne, **27** Maillot, **28** Scud, **30** Nelson, **32** Aden, **33** Test, **35** Sugar, **36** Carpaccio, **38** Tarantino, **41** Atonement, **42** Sherwood, **44** Debussy, **46** Measure, **47** Tunisia, **48** Crocus, **49** Mantua, **51** Booth, **54** Uzbek.

51

ACROSS: 1 Fauntleroy, **6** Portcullis, **13** Inuit, **14** Ex parte, **15** Animals, **16** Acetate, **17** Electra, **18** Egham, **19** Steatite, **21** Alms, **22** Insect, **26** Echelon, **29** Sonata, **31** Blixen, **33** Misericord, **34** Billet doux, **37** Storms, **39** Irving, **40** Rhombus, **43** Sydney, **44** Muir, **45** Stingray, **50** Yates, **52** Corelli, **53** Rossini, **55** San Juan, **56** Boswell, **57** Aioli, **58** Promethium, **59** Heisenberg.
DOWN: 1 Fricassee, **2** Ukulele, **3** Tetra, **4** Everest, **5** Osprey, **7** Orestes, **8** Tia Maria, **9** Universal, **10** Loach, **11** Sesame, **12** Greenland, **20** Tiler, **23** Coxcomb, **24** Usurer, **25** Onyx, **27** History, **28** Neck, **30** Triage, **32** Blur, **33** Miso, **35** Thorn, **36** Civil List, **38** Mint sauce, **41** Skydiving, **42** Hyacinth, **44** Marabou, **46** Turtles, **47** Rhizome, **48** Hyssop, **49** Bireme, **51** Tondo, **54** Spain.

52

ACROSS: 11 Newman, **12** Tapioca, **13** Aquila, **14** Shanghai, **15** Lombard, **16** Joey, **17** Peregrine falcon, **21** Abbey, **23** Ice cream, **25** Yttrium, **26** Sole, **27** Psilocybin, **29** Yalta, **31** X-ray, **33** Lamb, **34** Evans, **36** Proserpina, **37** Omer, **39** Sagitta, **41** Asphodel, **43** Slype, **45** Independence Day, **48** Levi, **49** Scallop, **51** Buchanan, **53** Cruise, **54** Innings, **55** Engels.
DOWN: 1 Lechwe, **2** Oman, **3** One-horse, **4** Etui, **5** Opal, **6** Cosmolatry, **7** Macaroni, **8** Haydn, **9** Punjab, **10** Bluebell, **18** Excalibur, **19** Namibia, **20** Flynn, **22** Impale, **24** Costa, **26** Saxophone, **28** Cleese, **30** Leotard, **32** Annie, **35** Sutherland, **36** Plane, **38** Mulberry, **40** Gunga Din, **42** Pinochet, **44** Philip, **46** Arable, **47** Asher, **50** Pink, **51** Bose, **52** Alga.

53

ACROSS: 1 Peacock, **5** Berry, **8** Theorem, **12** Usual, **13** Yankees, **14** Oceanid, **15** Blue Peter, **16** Tribe, **17** Guess, **18** Ioannina, **20** Treasure Hunt, **23** Erasure, **26** Stein, **28** Pancake, **30** Hesperides, **31** Greek salad, **34** Dempsey, **36** Tiara, **37** Spanner, **39** Elgin Marbles, **43** Somerset, **47** Agora, **48** Blake, **49** Oriflamme, **51** Seymour, **52** Basmati, **53** Corgi, **54** Diocese, **55** Guild, **56** Realism.
DOWN: 1 Plumb line, **2** Arugula, **3** Oxlip, **4** Krypton, **5** Binary, **6** Reel-to-reel, **7** Yeshiva, **8** Thoreau, **9** Evergreen, **10** Rondeau, **11** Midas, **19** Neume, **21** Tweed, **22** Aspect, **24** Assam, **25** Emily, **27** Norman, **28** Poets, **29** Allen, **30** Hedge, **32** Skate, **33** Paderewski, **35** Singapore, **38** Ruthenium, **40** Gromyko, **41** Auberge, **42** Beanbag, **44** Olivier, **45** Samurai, **46** Poland, **47** Assad, **50** Lucca.

54

ACROSS: 1 Wilde, **4** Bullfinch, **9** Ceres, **12** Ictinus, **13** Charm, **14** Scarlet, **15** Earth, **16** Lasagne, **17** Acolyte, **18** Pole vault, **20** Pisces, **22** Spur, **26** Titanic, **29** Mandela, **31** Munro, **32** Shortbread, **34** Trampoline, **36** Ibsen, **37** Chelsea, **38** Snaffle, **40** Ming, **41** Mexico, **43** Eucharist, **47** Coulomb, **50** Seville, **52** Plate, **54** Othello, **55** Lilac, **56** Vilnius, **57** Kerry, **58** Nonpareil, **59** Annex.
DOWN: 1 White, **2** Literal, **3** Eindhoven, **4** Bas-bleu, **5** Lucas, **6** Frangipane, **7** Numbers, **8** Hosta, **9** Charon, **10** Riley, **11** Satie, **18** Potassium, **19** Timbale, **21** Erasmus, **23** Pontiff, **24** Roosevelt, **25** Umbo, **27** Thomson, **28** Coracle, **30** Euryale, **33** Tony, **35** Aston Villa, **39** A Cappella, **42** Insulin, **44** Chervil, **45** Italian, **46** Volley, **47** Clock, **48** Usher, **49** Brown, **51** Locke, **53** Essex.

55

ACROSS: 1 Waugh, **4** Philology, **9** Grant, **12** Aquatic, **13** Boast, **14** Austria, **15** Flush, **16** Saxhorn, **17** Stewart, **18** Etymology, **20** Foible, **22** Spey, **26** Cricket, **29** Escolar, **30** Davis, **31** Ophicleide, **33** Twelve-tone, **36** Umbra, **37** Emerald, **39** Iceland, **41** Eddy, **42** Psalms, **43** Wellesley, **47** Darling, **50** Warthog, **52** Robin, **54** Fellini, **55** Renan, **56** Organza, **57** Epsom, **58** Mahlstick, **59** Tench.
DOWN: 1 Wharf, **2** Uruguay, **3** Hitchcock, **4** Picasso, **5** In-box, **6** Oval Office, **7** Octennial, **8** Yeats, **9** Gasket, **10** Aorta, **11** Toast, **18** Enclosure, **19** Yield, **21** Lorelei, **23** Pavlova, **24** Yesterday, **25** Edge, **27** Ichabod, **28** Theseus, **32** Clam, **34** Widow, **35** Hamstrings, **38** Ellsworth, **40** Eyebright, **44** Logbook, **45** Lebanon, **46** Miriam, **47** Defoe, **48** Rolls, **49** Grimm, **51** Hanoi, **53** Neath.

56

ACROSS: 1 War Horse, **6** Hypotenuse, **13** Olive, **14** Doolittle, **15** Playa, **16** Anemone, **17** Altair, **18** Slalom, **19** Virgo, **21** Octagon, **24** Crewel, **28** Neodymium, **29** Abyss, **30** Gould, **32** Atonement, **34** Pituitary, **39** Pyrex, **40** Noddy, **42** Dithyramb, **44** Riding, **46** Far East, **47** Thyme, **49** Tarawa, **51** Woggle, **54** Borstal, **57** Usual, **58** Riflebird, **59** Inman, **60** Lithophyte, **61** Casement.
DOWN: 2 Alice, **3** Hierology, **4** Rudder, **5** Evora, **6** Hoist, **7** Patrimony, **8** Tael, **9** Nepal, **10** Swallow, **11** Vol-au-vent, **12** Marmalade, **20** Rooster, **22** Cumin, **23** Ajax, **25** Roget, **26** Diamond, **27** Asquith, **31** Unready, **33** Nixon, **35** Indus, **36** Spiritgum, **37** Hyde, **38** Abseiling, **41** Dragonfly, **43** Ytterbium, **45** Dariusi, **48** Abydos, **50** Welch, **52** Grebe, **53** Eniac, **55** Timon, **56** Trap.

57

ACROSS: 1 Ratatouille, **7** Catchword, **12** Pacific, **13** Maniple, **14** Nylon, **15** Ultra Vires, **16** Periwinkle, **18** Evelyn, **20** Strauss, **21** France, **26** Mohican, **27** Banns, **29** Bivalve, **31** Dysprosium, **33** Cat's Cradle, **35** Sistine, **36** Brain, **37** Atheist, **38** Nutmeg, **40** Twelfth, **43** Aliens, **48** Runner bean, **50** Blackberry, **53** Vegan, **54** Detroit, **55** African, **56** Letterman, **57** Cryptomeria.
DOWN: 1 Rapture, **2** Tacet, **3** Tiffany, **4** Urchin, **5** Lambert, **6** Etna, **7** Cepheus, **8** Thetis, **9** Hanoi, **10** Oilskin, **11** Donne, **17** Saint, **19** Ephesus, **22** Rover, **23** Element, **24** Aniseed, **25** Abyssal, **26** Madison, **27** Blurb, **28** Spain, **30** Luddite, **32** Rhine, **34** Tally, **39** Tonight, **41** Wharton, **42** Tolstoy, **44** Labarum, **45** Soyinka, **46** Ibidem, **47** Octant, **48** Ravel, **49** ERNIE, **51** Racer, **52** Torc.

58

ACROSS: 10 The Artist, **11** Wilcox, **12** Atom, **14** Greene, **15** Ajaccio, **16** Yellow, **17** Lucan, **19** Edinburgh, **21** Faure, **24** Atrium, **26** Brindle, **27** Batt, **30** Witch hazel, **31** Nauru, **33** Acre, **34** Miro, **35** Rioja, **37** Kublai Khan, **38** Babe, **39** Iapetus, **41** Little, **43** Wrist, **46** Casserole, **48** Agent, **51** Austen, **52** Erasmus, **54** French, **56** Veil, **57** Pierce, **58** Akhenaten.
DOWN: 1 Thorium, **2** Dale, **3** Otter, **4** Oswald, **5** Zinc, **6** Act of god, **7** Oxeye, **8** Paella, **9** Honour, **13** Hannibal, **18** Artichoke, **20** Union, **22** Richard II, **23** Beaux Arts, **25** Mezzo, **27** Black flag, **28** Torbay, **29** Bikila, **32** Umbel, **36** Attis, **37** Kostroma, **40** Platelet, **42** Snicket, **44** Router, **45** Settle, **47** Lusaka, **49** Snipe, **50** Offer, **53** Arch, **55** Elam.

59

ACROSS: 1 Tapas, **4** Bacchus, **8** Lapwing, **12** Unitard, **13** Bivouac, **14** Tonga, **15** Four-in-hand, **16** Basset horn, **18** Ethics, **20** Stephen, **21** Possum, **25** Downing Street, **28** Juniper, **30** Acid, **31** Unity, **32** Black, **33** Arch, **37** Oysters, **38** Mother-of-pearl, **39** Danube, **41** Springe, **44** Biceps, **48** Minestrone, **49** Radiograph, **52** Envoi, **53** Primula, **54** Crowbar, **55** Fitness, **56** Cadmium, **57** Limbo.
DOWN: 1 Truffle, **2** Poilu, **3** Seabiscuit, **4** Buddha, **5** Cabinet, **6** Hove, **7** Soutane, **8** Locust, **9** Petit point, **10** Igneous, **11** Goa, **17** Speed, **19** Hawkins, **22** Marshal, **23** Agonist, **24** Ejector, **25** Diamond, **26** Totem, **27** Tilde, **29** Percale, **34** Derbyshire, **35** Strip, **36** Spring roll, **40** Nunavut, **42** Pontiac, **43** Guarani, **45** Scherzo, **46** Grapes, **47** Sitcom, **50** Album, **51** Lund, **52** Elf.

60

ACROSS: 1 Cassoulet, **6** Baize, **9** Shoes, **12** Conservatoire, **13** Drone, **14** Octillion, **15** Entertainer, **16** Maser, **17** Ambassador, **19** Agee, **21** Nock, **23** Midshipman, **24** Smalt, **25** King Arthur, **27** Big Brother, **31** Baton, **32** Serpentine, **34** Grid, **36** Sole, **37** Capablanca, **39** Oscar, **42** Chamberlain, **43** Anthology, **45** Image, **46** Choreographer, **47** Tenet, **48** Evora, **49** Herodotus.
DOWN: 1 Cacao, **2** Sanctus, **3** Overlord, **4** Love-in-a-mist, **5** Titan, **6** Boiler Suit, **7** Inertia, **8** Eiderdown, **9** Slogan, **10** Oceanographer, **11** Sugar beet, **16** Minsk, **18** Bis, **20** Oslo, **22** Constellation, **26** Arno, **28** Bengal tiger, **29** Ryder, **30** Bellinzona, **31** Bushcraft, **32** Sea breeze, **33** Ton, **35** Togoland, **38** Ajaccio, **40** Crochet, **41** Oblast, **43** Aleph, **44** Ypres.

Also available from Hamlyn:

Telegraph All New Toughie Crosswords
£5.99

Volume 1: 978-0-600-62502-5
Volume 2: 978-0-600-62495-0

Telegraph All New Cryptic Crosswords
£5.99

Volume 1: 978-0-600-62468-4
Volume 2: 978-0-600-62500-1
Volume 3: 978-0-600-62499-8

Telegraph All New Big Book of Cryptic Crosswords
£6.99

Volume 1: 978-0-600-62467-7

(publishing in September 2012)

To order these or other Telegraph Books:

Call: 0844 871 1514
Visit: books.telegraph.co.uk
Post: Send cheques made payable to
Telegraph Books to the following address

Orders Dept
PO Box 582
Norwich
NR7 0GB

All UK orders will be subject to a 99p postage and packing charge (call for overseas rates).
Products are supplied by and your contract is with Bertrams Group Ltd not Telegraph Media Group Limited.

For more puzzles go to
www.puzzles.telegraph.co.uk